PRAISE FOR
THEY KNOW EVERYTHING ABOUT YOU

"Scheer acquits himself as a passionate advocate for privacy rights; you'd want him by your side at a protest."
—*Los Angeles Times*

"Scheer powerfully connects the dots of our chilling Orwellian present, one in which privacy is considered a luxury, rather than a right."
—*Publishers Weekly*

"A vital piece of work that demands attention."
—*Kirkus Reviews*

"Robert Scheer reminds us that privacy is everything—the protector of our liberty, the guarantor of our personal autonomy, the fountainhead of our democracy—and yet it's disappearing faster than an electronic blip moving at warp speed from your computer to the NSA. With clarity and precision, Scheer dissects the military-intelligence complex, showing it to be neither very secure nor very intelligent, but, rather, dangerous to us all."
—ROBERT B. REICH, Chancellor's Professor of Public Policy, University of California at Berkeley

"*They Know Everything About You* is a brilliant book. Robert Scheer, who covered my 1971 trial after I released the Pentagon Papers, has been following privacy and surveillance issues for decades. He is a key voice and his book—cogent, timely, and fascinating—is an indispensable text for our time."
—DANIEL ELLSBERG, author of *Secrets: A Memoir of Vietnam and the Pentagon Papers*

"Robert Scheer has undertaken a penetrating examination of Americans' disappearing privacy and issued a clarion call in these pages, lest we unwittingly click-away our freedom."

> —JOHN W. DEAN, bestselling author and
> former Nixon White House counsel

"Scheer is one of the most important journalists in America. He is not only brilliant, possessed by a fierce and uncompromising integrity, but is a lyrical and often moving writer. All of these talents are on full display in his latest book about the rise of the security and surveillance state and the terrifying dystopia that will be visited upon us all unless our right to privacy is returned to us."

> —CHRIS HEDGES, author of *Wages of Rebellion*

"This is what journalism looks like, provided by one of the greatest reporters of our times. Scheer has written a powerful indictment of the present-day corporate-government surveillance regime that has effectively eliminated the right to privacy. Like a master surgeon, he dissects the self-serving rationales for the wholesale illegal spying on Americans and shows them to be nonsense."

> —ROBERT W. MCCHESNEY, author of
> *Blowing the Roof Off the Twenty-First Century*

THEY KNOW
EVERYTHING
ABOUT YOU

Also by Robert Scheer

The Great American Stickup: How Reagan Republicans and Clinton Democrats Enriched Wall Street While Mugging Main Street

The Pornography of Power: How Defense Hawks Hijacked 9/11 and Weakened America

Playing President: My Close Encounters with Nixon, Carter, Bush I, Reagan, and Clinton—and How They Did Not Prepare Me for George W. Bush

The Five Biggest Lies Bush Told Us About Iraq (with co-authors Christopher Scheer and Lakshmi Chaudhry)

Thinking Tuna Fish, Talking Death: Essays on the Pornography of Power

With Enough Shovels: Reagan, Bush, and Nuclear War

America After Nixon: The Age of the Multinationals

How the United States Got Involved in Vietnam

Cuba: An American Tragedy (with co-author Maurice Zeitlin)

Edited by Robert Scheer

The Cosmetic Surgery Revolution

Eldridge Cleaver: Post-Prison Writings and Speeches by the Author of "Soul on Ice"

The Diary of Che Guevara

THEY KNOW
EVERYTHING
ABOUT YOU

*How Data-Collecting Corporations
and Snooping Government Agencies
Are Destroying Democracy*

ROBERT SCHEER
with
Sara Beladi

NATION
BOOKS
New York

To my sons:

*Christopher, a terrific writer whose polishing of my prose
makes me look good and is decent enough not to rub it in;*

Joshua, who once again did the heavy lifting research; and

Peter, whose editing of Truthdig frees me to write books.

Published by Nation Books, A Member of the Perseus Books Group
116 East 16th Street, 8th Floor
New York, NY 10003
Nation Books is a co-publishing venture of the Nation Institute and
the Perseus Books Group.

Books published by Nation Books are available at special discounts for bulk purchases in the United States by corporations, institutions, and other organizations. For more information, please contact the Special Markets Department at the Perseus Books Group, 2300 Chestnut Street, Suite 200, Philadelphia, PA 19103, or call (800) 255-1514, or e-mail special.markets@perseusbooks.com.

Book design by Linda Mark

Library of Congress Cataloging-in-Publication Data
Scheer, Robert.
    They know everything about you : how data-collecting corporations and snooping government agencies are destroying democracy / Robert Scheer with Sara Beladi and Joshua Scheer.
        pages cm
    Includes bibliographical references and index.
    ISBN 978-1-56858-452-2 (hardcover)—ISBN 978-1-56858-453-9 (electronic)—ISBN 978-1-56858-518-5 (paperback) 1. Privacy, Right of—United States. 2. Democracy—United States. 3. Data protection—United States. 4. Electronic surveillance—United States. 5. Intelligence service—United States. 6. National security—United States. I. Beladi, Sara. II. Scheer, Joshua. III. Title.
    JC596.2.U5S24 2015
    323.44'80973—dc23
    2014034638

10 9 8 7 6 5 4 3 2 1

Contents

Preface

FOR DEMOCRACY, PRIVACY IS THE BALL GAME. WITHOUT the assurance of a zone of inviolate space, both physical and mental, that a citizen can inhabit without fear of observation by others, there is no guarantee of the essential sovereignty of the individual promised in the First and Fourth Amendments to the US Constitution. That should be clear, as it is to most people who have been oppressed by the tyranny of authoritarian regimes. Indeed, as Aldous Huxley and George Orwell brilliantly established in their classic writing on this subject, the totality of societal observation over the individual is the defining antithesis of freedom, even when that observation is gained through hidden and subtle persuasion.

That much used to be obvious, particularly after the starkly revealing experiences in the last century with overtly totalitarian regimes; Germany under both fascism and communism offers the most startling example. In both instances, the advanced educational level of the population provided no significant barrier to the population's surrender of freedom and its accommodation of total surveillance of individual activity.

Unfortunately, with the sudden dominance of the Internet— which has come upon us worldwide and with more crushing, and yes, liberating consequences—we have been overwhelmed with the illusion that surveillance and freedom are compatible. That is because the culture of the Internet, driven by its core economic model, has succeeded in equating privacy with anonymity. In reality, that is not the case. Privacy is a matter of individual choice as to what to reveal about one's behavior to others, whereas anonymity, in the modern commercialized celebrity-driven world, is assumed to represent a harsh societal dismissal of individual worth.

The profit model of targeted advertising has sustained the Internet since its original development as a Cold War–era military project of the Pentagon's science and technology research wing DARPA (Defense Advanced Research Projects Agency) meant to ensure military communications in the event of an all-out nuclear war with the Soviet Union. That compelling business application of the Internet, the ability of advertisers to anticipate and manipulate consumer consumption, is what has financed the phenomenal growth of the wired world at a pace of change that dwarfs all such transformations in communications that came before. Broadcast television held that distinction previously, with its ability to deliver content to millions of viewers—but it was only a glimpse into our desires that, by the standards of the Internet, was quite limited.

Previous to the Internet, the number of prospective buyers delivered by any conventional mass medium were inefficiently undifferentiated. Experts, with their surveys and ratings, could only speculate as to the demographics of potential customers attracted by a billboard, radio, or TV commercial. These methods were even more imperfect in the all-important estimate of the end goal: how an advertisement resulted in an actual sale that would prove the ad's efficacy. The advertising bonanza of the Internet that fuels this communications revolution is based on a far more precise entry point into the mind of the consumer.

Even now in the early phase of mapping our minds, this access to our thoughts already exceeds the powers of the most invasive Big Brother government that Orwell imagined. At the command of Internet-driven signals, people everywhere in the world have been willing to abandon the concerns and safeguards of privacy, developed painstakingly throughout human history, for the convenience of plucking that perfect item off a virtual shelf and paying for it without looking up from their devices. The public's willingness to voluntarily—nay, enthusiastically—sacrifice privacy is fueled by a very modern fear of being ignored in a culture where the most observed are the most valued.

Just consider Yelp and Facebook, two exemplary manifestations of Internet culture and commerce. With the former, for the convenience of finding the best local diner, we surrender the most important piece of information a secret police force ever wanted to have on the population it was surveilling—one's physical location. The temptation to answer the frequently asked question "Can we use your location?" has proved compelling. Yet from the start, along with other refined methods, tracking one's journey—actual as well as virtual—is routinely realized, achieving what oppressive governments could never even have fantasized about attaining.

Combine that constant intrusion into your physical movement with the interior movement of your mind, as is revealed (again, routinely and with little controversy) by more than a billion Facebook users—photos of friends that can be biometrically scanned and compared with other data on them, chats and every other confession of thoughts, doubts, and fears documented for others, including, of course, your government to read and exploit. Then, further expand that database to include all of the apps and avenues of data collection, merged with the massively powerful data-mining capabilities of digital surveillance—which not only encompasses activity on desktops and phones but can also include our every movement in the home and in the outside world.

Welcome to the brave new world—a wired panopticon that even Huxley couldn't have imagined.

But why should we care, you ask, if the government has all this information, as Edward Snowden so courageously revealed? One oft-used argument for keeping the private- and public-sector surveillance state intact was famously forwarded by Google CEO Eric Schmidt: "If you have something that you don't want anyone to know, maybe you shouldn't be doing it in the first place," he said to a live audience in 2009.[1]

But consider the original import of that sentiment. It assumes a stance on the part of the citizen that on its face spells the end of any hope of a just and effective representative democracy. The peril to democracy highlighted by both Huxley and Orwell was one of self-censorship as the norm in a totalitarian culture, one that denies the possibility of the unobserved moment. In the eyes of the original American revolutionaries who gave us the constitutional restraints on the power of the state, the unobserved moment was essential to their bold new experiment. The concept of the Fourth Amendment was born in English common law, asserting that even the poorest peasant should enjoy the sovereignty of the home as a refuge from the power of the king, even a good king.

During the past decade, the power of corporations exploiting the data we wittingly or in ignorance provide to the data miners—even in those rare instances when it is fully transparent—has been acceptable to most because it was viewed inherently as a voluntary adjunct to consumerism. Privacy was traded for the convenience of shopping. The trade-off generally seemed harmless as long as it remained in the commercial sector. There was the presumption that the relationship with a particular search engine or social networking site could be ended whenever the intrusive reach bothered a consumer.

However, that all-too-convenient assumption was rudely shattered with the leaks from Snowden. They revealed the previously unknown government agency vacuuming up and analyzing data privately collected by corporations like Google, Facebook, and Yahoo. This was alarming not just to US consumers of those services but, more broadly, to the denizens of a World Wide Web, who are the basis for Internet growth and profit.

Suddenly, we learned of the significance of what in this book we refer to as the military-intelligence complex, which grew out of the military-industrial complex against which President Dwight D. Eisenhower warned the nation in his 1961 Farewell Address. Modern warfare and the profits associated with military preparedness now depend far less on the old industrial basis of weaponry focused on ships, airplanes, and ground forces than on the smart weapons of cyber war and unmanned drones. In this age of computer-directed warfare, government intelligence agencies such as the NSA and the CIA have thrust the private companies of Silicon Valley to the forefront of a war-making industry, which bears signs of having swiftly morphed into a war against the citizenry. These seemingly progressive corporations, at the behest of these intelligence agencies, have become intricately involved with the American war machine—far more so than the conventional bureaucrats of the Pentagon who have traditionally directed the show.

That alliance of Washington intelligence agencies and Silicon Valley techies was, as this book details, deliberately constructed as a project of DARPA and the CIA, when it was helmed by George Tenet from 1997 to 2004. It was a marriage of convenience between the spy agencies that needed the freewheeling brilliance of the Silicon Valley engineers and the tech companies that opportunistically wanted concessions by the government on regulation and taxes, as well as the hefty contracts it offered.

The attacks of 9/11 brought a massive increase in government spending on computer-assisted spy operations, leading to an alliance between private and public agencies that became as intimate as it was profitable. The assumption of the new surveillance state is that we the citizens are all potential enemies of the government. This reverses the US Constitution's assumption that it is the leaders of our government who should be viewed with a deep suspicion—an assumption based on the notion that power corrupts and that absolute power corrupts absolutely. We the citizens are the ultimate guardians of our liberty, and our right to be informed, by the press and by whistleblowers when our governors deceive us, is sacred to the enterprise of a representative republic.

The main price paid by turning the war on terror into a war on the public's right to know, a bipartisan crusade, is that it destroys the foundation of democracy—an informed public. The George W. Bush administration initiated this dangerous trend, and Barack Obama has expanded on that horrid legacy by cracking down on the press, and prosecuting whistleblowers under the Espionage Act more than all previous US presidents combined. The result is that our privacy and hence our freedom has been plundered with abandon. Our most private moments are now captured in exquisite detail by a newly emboldened surveillance state—resulting in a shutout of democracy.

But the game's not over, yet.

one

The TED Moment:
His Head on a Robot

T
HE SUDDEN APPEARANCE OF THE DISEMBODIED HEAD
of Edward Snowden thrilled the tech industry royalty
gathered at the thirtieth-anniversary TED conference. A
closely cropped image of his face was displayed on a small screen
affixed atop a mobile "telepresence" robot, but it wasn't the technological wizardry that wowed the sold-out crowd of 1,200; they
didn't know when they paid $7,500 each for casual seating in the
tricked-out waterfront venue that they would hear from an alleged
spy who had embarrassed the most powerful nation on Earth.

On this day, March 18, 2014, Snowden's actual body remained
safely ensconced in Moscow, because if he had actually shown up
in Vancouver in corporeal form, he would more than likely have

faced immediate extradition across the border to confront charges of espionage leveled by the Obama administration for his release of classified documents uncovering an array of secret global surveillance programs run by American and allied spy agencies in apparent collaboration with giant tech and telecom corporations. Yet the electricity his visage generated was palpable and clearly delighted his interviewer, TED conference curator and digital pioneer Chris Anderson.

The former journalist, whose nonprofit Sapling Foundation bought TED in 2001, had to feel relieved to see Snowden's face after spending months working to pull off the virtual appearance of the world's most famous (or infamous, depending on your perspective) whistleblower. Anderson had turned to a personal contact in the American Civil Liberties Union for help, and Snowden was trained in using the robot, which allowed him to see, hear, and project his image and voice—even activate a "party mode" that triggers more ambient microphones—while it was based at the ACLU's New York City offices. The first time Snowden controlled it, Anderson told *Mashable*'s Amanda Wills, "he rolled it to the window and looked at the Statue of Liberty."[1]

Now the Oxford-educated Anderson, sporting his signature casual attire—blue plaid long-sleeved shirt, black pants, and no tie—was announcing the topic of the moment. "The rights of citizens, the future of the Internet," he intoned to an audience painfully aware that lurid tales of government surveillance of private data exposed by Snowden and others have threatened consumers' trust in the culture of the Internet and, consequently, the fabulous profitability of the multinational corporations spawned by this suddenly wired world.

"So I would like to welcome to the TED stage the man behind those revelations," Anderson continued, to loud applause. "Ed is in a remote location somewhere in Russia, controlling this bot from his laptop, so he can see what the bot can see. Ed, welcome to the TED stage. What can you see as a matter of fact?"

Snowden responded, his voice projected over the sound system: "Ha, I can see everyone. This is amazing." The crowd—only half of whom raised hands when asked by Anderson earlier whether they considered Snowden "fundamentally heroic"—laughed. Afterward, as the Snowden-controlled robot moved about the hall, there were frequent stops for selfies with the "Snowbot."

"You never know who you might bump into at TED," tweeted Anderson, accompanying an image of Google co-founder Sergey Brin posing with his arm around the gadget.

Amid the hoopla, it was easy to forget that Snowden was in a very different position from that of his fellow techies. They were free to come and go as they pleased, regaling people with stories of their virtual encounter with perhaps the world's most hunted individual. Snowden himself had no choice but to remain in hiding, his safety dependent on the whim of Russian leader Vladimir Putin who, at that time, was under great pressure to turn over the American while also dealing with Western powers' outrage over his incursion into the Crimea.

Nor was Snowden, having defected from the National Security establishment, in line to benefit from lucrative contracts with the same governments he had exposed—contracts that instead would go to many in the seemingly supportive crowd. That was certainly true of Google's Brin who, while appearing quite tickled to get up close and personal with the Snowbot, knew that his own ties to the NSA and other intelligence entities were being called into question. The top executives of Google, Microsoft, Apple, Yahoo, and Facebook, in interviews, social media posts, and joint statements, had expressed outrage about the NSA's raiding their customer data, but they almost certainly knew the relationship was far cozier than their outrage would suggest.[2]

Two days later, Anderson was interviewing another TED guest, Richard Ledgett, deputy director of the NSA, via video feed. Anderson had invited the NSA to the conference before Snowden's appearance was confirmed, but the agency had refused to participate—until Snowden and his bot appeared, apparently astonishing the NSA.

"We didn't realize he was going to show up there. So kudos to you guys for arranging a nice surprise like that," Ledgett dryly admitted to Anderson.

Despite the friendly banter, there was nothing nice about Ledgett's portrayal of Snowden. "Characterizing him as a whistleblower actually hurts legitimate whistleblowing activities," he argued. Yet he admitted, without providing details, that "[w]e need to be more transparent," just not with "the bad guys."[3] He also acknowledged that the NSA had given American tech companies a black eye.

So what was this NSA honcho's central defense of the epic privacy-busting collaboration Snowden had exposed? Essentially: "Everybody does it."

"Companies are in as tough [a] position as are we. We compel companies to provide information, just like every nation in the world does," Ledgett said. "Every industrialized nation has a lawful intercept program compelling companies to provide information, and companies comply with those programs as they do in Russia, the UK, China, India, or France, in any country you choose to name. The fact that these revelations have been broadly characterized as, 'You can't trust Company A because your privacy is suspect with them,' is only accurate in that it's accurate with every other company in the world dealing with those countries in the world."

Basically, he said, US tech firms are being pilloried globally for helping the spies because those companies happen to be dominant in the marketplace. "It's been marketed by countries, including some ally countries, that 'You can't trust the US but you can trust our [non–US-based] telecoms because we're safe.' They're using that to counter the very large technology edge US companies have in the cloud."

A day later, Google co-founder Larry Page was interviewed by Charlie Rose and tried to remove any blame from his and his colleagues' shoulders.

"For me, it's tremendously disappointing that the government sort of secretly did all these things and didn't tell us," said Page. "I don't think we can have a democracy if we're having to protect you and our users from the government for stuff that we never had a conversation about."[4]

The government was not smart in the way it went about acquiring the data from Google and other companies, Page argued. "The government actually did itself a tremendous disservice by doing all that in secret," he said. "I think we need to have a debate about it or we can't have a functioning democracy. It's not possible."

But just how secret was the government action? Could Google and the other tech conglomerates really claim, with a straight face, to be surprised?

The question of who knew what and when exploded to the surface only six weeks later when the name of Brin, who had appeared so chummy with the Snowbot, would appear in media reports about an interesting letter sent from General Keith Alexander, the director of the NSA, to Google CEO Eric Schmidt.

The letter, declassified under a Freedom of Information Act request by Jason Leopold of *Al Jazeera America,* was dated June 28, 2012. It was an invitation to Schmidt to participate in a top-secret collaboration between the Defense Department, Homeland Security, and the NSA, along with eighteen CEOs of US companies.

The collaboration was described in the letter as "an effort called the Enduring Security Framework (ESF) to coordinate government/industry actions on important (generally classified) security issues."[5] The letter invited Schmidt to attend because Google founder "Sergei [sic] Brin has attended previous sessions but cannot make this meeting for scheduling purposes." Schmidt regretted that he wouldn't be in town for the briefing, either.

In an earlier email from the NSA's Alexander to Brin dated December 23, 2011, the spy chief wrote to the Google founder: "Thank you for your team's participation in the Enduring Security Framework (ESF). I see ESF's work as critical to the nation's progress against the threat in cyberspace and really appreciate Vint Cerf [chief Internet evangelist for Google, widely known as one of the "fathers of the Internet"], Eric Grosse [vice president of security and privacy engineering at Google] and Adrian Ludwig's [lead engineer for Android security] contribution to these efforts during the past year."

Clearly, the high-level participants and their counterparts from the other seventeen companies that took part in the "Enduring Security Framework" project, which General Alexander said had been ongoing since 2009, must have had at least a rudimentary inkling into the NSA and other intelligence agencies' intrusion into the data networks of their companies.

Commenting on the importance of the declassified emails from Alexander to the Google execs, Nate Cardozo, a staff attorney for the digital civil liberties organization Electronic Frontier Foundation, noted the contradiction implicit in the NSA fox posing as a guard for the security of Google's network henhouse.

"The NSA has no business helping Google secure its facilities from the Chinese and at the same time hacking in through the back doors and tapping the fiber connections between Google base centers," said Cardozo. "The fact that it's the same agency doing both of those things is in obvious contradiction and ridiculous."[6]

Certainly Brin, who seems to have been the key NSA contact, must have had some indication that the connection with the government might be compromising Google's obligation to protect the privacy of its customers worldwide. The declassified emails indicate that his connection with the NSA was quite extensive.

"You recently received an invitation to the ESF Executive Steering Group meeting, which will be held on January 19, 2012," said one. "The meeting is an opportunity to recognize our 2011 accomplishments and set direction for the year to come. We will be discussing ESF's goals and specific targets for 2012. We will also discuss some of the threats we see and what we are doing to mitigate those threats. I look forward to seeing you and to your participation in the discussions. Your insights, as a key member of the Defense Industrial Base, are valuable to ensure that ESF's efforts have a measurable impact."[7]

This was blunt: the NSA regarded Google and the others as tools to be used at the convenience of the US military. According to the Department of Homeland Security, "The Defense Industrial Base Sector is the worldwide industrial complex that enables research and development, as well as design, production, delivery, and maintenance of military weapons systems, subsystems, and components or parts, to meet U.S. military requirements. . . . Defense Industrial Base companies include domestic and foreign entities, with production assets located in many countries. The sector provides products and services that are essential to mobilize, deploy, and sustain military operations."[8]

How revealing to learn that Brin, to whom NSA director Alexander is referring in his email, is labeled a "key member" of this

base of the US "military-industrial" establishment about which
President Dwight D. Eisenhower famously warned the nation in
his farewell address on January 17, 1961:[9]

> Akin to, and largely responsible for the sweeping changes in our
> industrial-military posture, has been the technological revolution
> during recent decades. In this revolution, research has become
> central; it also becomes more formalized, complex, and costly. A
> steadily increasing share is conducted for, by, or at the direction
> of the federal government. Today, the solitary inventor, tinkering
> in his shop, has been overshadowed by task forces of scientists in
> laboratories and testing fields. In the same fashion, the free uni-
> versity, historically the fountainhead of free ideas and scientific
> discovery, has experienced a revolution in the conduct of research.
> Partly because of the huge costs involved, a government contract
> becomes virtually a substitute for intellectual curiosity. For every
> old blackboard there are now hundreds of new electronic comput-
> ers. The prospect of domination of the nation's scholars by federal
> employment, project allocations, and the power of money is ever
> present and is gravely to be regarded. Yet, in holding scientific re-
> search and discovery in respect, as we should, we must be alert
> to the equal and opposite danger that public policy could itself
> become the captive of a scientific technological elite.[10]

Yet one gets the sense from the various interviews and statements by Brin and other Google leaders that they are never quite
sure just what their participation in the military-industrial complex entails. Are they the head, the tail, or a completely separate
beast?

In fact, these companies had soared to the top of the stock market and public consciousness by brilliantly piggybacking on the

military-funded programs that spawned the computer revolution. The Internet itself began as a military-funded program when Eisenhower was president and military tech contracts were flowing to Bay Area universities, creating the infrastructure of Silicon Valley. Were the new tech moguls, many of them quite young, so naive as to believe they were truly independent from the juggernaut Ike had so passionately described?

ᴬᵛ ᴬᵛ ᴬᵛ

THE CONCEIT OF THE SILICON VALLEY ELITES, AS EVEN A casual perusal of their pre-Snowden public pronouncements makes clear, was the assumption that governments, here and abroad, are largely creaky anachronisms, entities that are at best out of touch and at worst meddlesome. Hence the libertarian bent of the Web's entrepreneurial elite. There is also no small dose of smugness in this stance common among the new rich claiming to be self-made; better to ignore the money that taxpayers poured into schools like Michigan and Stanford, where Brin was educated, to fund myriad research-and-development breakthroughs that enabled the wiring of the world.

During the decade of the tech boom, in fact, when newly minted start-ups made billions overnight, it was quite easy to believe that whatever the government had done to facilitate this enterprise, it now should be thought of charitably as a kindly but forgetful uncle best left nattering on the sidelines of serious business enterprise.

This was a posture quite easy to accept if you were Brin, glancing at the email from General Alexander and then moving on to more pressing and profitable business at hand. Much less easy a scant eighteen months later, however, when the bomb of Snowden's disclosures exploded onto the scene and Google's entire business model—based as it was on the trust of its customers—was danger-ously threatened, as were those of so many other cooperating tech corporations.

Those disclosures raised the prospect that the industry had been hustled, that maybe all of that close cooperation on making the Internet more secure had in fact exposed Google and friends to a backdoor assault and in their naïveté they, the code sharpies, didn't even know it.

Alternatively, they may have known the broad outline—that the NSA was not merely deflecting cyber attacks against companies like Google but initiating its own—while being blissfully ignorant of the awkward details, such as the tracking of personal phone calls of the prime ministers of friendly nations Germany and Bra-zil. Snowden's 2013 leaks revealed how this was done through a cyber attack against Google's own data fiber-optic cables. Pub-licly, the companies held that they were legally helpless, insist-ing they turned over a treasure trove of their customers' personal data only when compelled by the proceedings of the ultra-secret Foreign Intelligence Surveillance Act (FISA) court supervising NSA's various data-gathering activities.

In a move to mitigate the PR crisis precipitated by the revela-tions, Google, along with Yahoo and Facebook, in September 2013 filed an amended petition with the FISA court requesting per-mission to publicly detail the types of national security requests they receive under the act. "We filed the suit today because we are not authorized at present to break out the number of requests, if any, that we receive for user data under specific national secu-rity statutes," wrote Yahoo legal counsel Ron Bell in a blog post. "The U.S. government prohibits companies from disclosing this information."[11] Four months later, the Justice Department eased the gag order that prevented technology and telecommunications companies, like Yahoo and Google, from making the number and nature of these requests public.

In February 2013, Google Law Enforcement and Information Security legal director Richard Salgado, in a blog post announcing the company's first annual disclosure of FISA data requests, lamented the government's ongoing chokehold on the supposedly transparency-oriented company. "We believe the public deserves to know the full extent to which governments request user information from Google," he wrote. Publishing these numbers is a step in the right direction. . . . But we still believe more transparency is needed so everyone can better understand how surveillance laws work and decide whether or not they serve the public interest. . . . [W]e need Congress to go another step further and pass legislation that will enable us to say more."[12]

The image of Google as an innocent victim of NSA overreach was convenient to a company intent on assuring its customers that their privacy was protected. However, the reality is that Google is a mind-boggling financial success precisely because it breaches privacy more effectively than any enterprise before it in history. The NSA is piggybacking on Google rather than the other way around.

No one knows this better than Brin, whose entire professional life has been bound up with what is politely called data mining, the practice of analyzing large stores of information to uncover patterns and relationships in data. Data mining has been this Russian immigrant's focus ever since his days as a doctoral student at Stanford in 1995, when the Internet was in its infancy. Brin was searching for a PhD dissertation topic and his interest turned to the subject of data mining. He was mentored by a young professor he had befriended, Rajeev Motwani, and joined a research group Motwani had founded called MIDAS, the acronym of "Mining Data At Stanford." Brin's original project involved using algorithms that connected the viewing habits and other practices of people rating films they had found through Brin's search engine. Such techniques would become the basis for Google's dominance of the Web's advertising market.

Data mining is, of course, also the main focus of the National Security Agency. Following Snowden's revelations, key questions emerged: How was the agency obtaining individuals' private communications and data? Should customers have a reasonable expectation that their searches, conversations, and download histories would not be turned over to the government? Was it not a fair assumption that, when you were searching for a nearby restaurant and your phone asked you for permission to use your location, this data would not be "mined" by the NSA to connect you with your dining companions?

At the TED conference on March 18, the tension between the marketing activities at the heart of Internet profit and the relentless probing of government spies was the proverbial elephant in the room. Contradicting the carefully and effectively constructed illusion of free debate in a civil setting was the reality that whistleblower Snowden had effectively been forced to live as a fugitive abroad; and yet his crime was only that of revealing a truth of enormous embarrassment to the government that now targeted him. It was also embarrassing to Google and other Internet executives in the TED audience whose cooperation with the NSA had been disclosed.

Imagine Galileo and his command appearance before the cardinals in Rome. Only in this version, the gathered church fathers of the digital age, despite enormous wealth and other accruements of their dizzying success and enormous political influence, still managed to think of themselves as heretics rebelling against a stifling traditional order.

After all, the information age these tech gurus had helped develop carried with it the potential to end all that came before; they represented unbounded knowledge free to revolutionize established spheres of thought. Wealthy and powerful as they may be, they still were the real revolutionaries—as Google chair Schmidt and Google Ideas director Jared Cohen indicated in their book *The New Digital Age: Reshaping the Future of People, Nations and Business,* published two months before the first Snowden revelations appeared in the news. They were the enablers of a new world order.

"We believe that modern technology platforms, such as Google, Facebook, Amazon and Apple, are even more powerful than most people realize, and our future world will be profoundly altered by their adoption and successfulness in societies everywhere. These platforms constitute a true paradigm shift," opined Schmidt and Cohen.[13]

But Snowden's revelations had exposed the dark side of the basic business model of the Internet, dependent as it is on the massive data collection of its customers' habits.

TED released the Snowden interview under the heading "Here's How We Take Back the Internet," but for many in the room, including the Google hotshots, that must have struck a disturbing note, for the Internet was something they hadn't known they had lost. Certainly in the book Schmidt wrote with Cohen, published before the Snowden revelations, while there was recognition that the Internet could be blocked or exploited by bad actors throughout the world, it was never suggested that our own government might be one of them, or that the tech companies would be—already were, in fact—key players in the scheme.

If the government had demanded such information regarding emails and phone conversations openly and directly, that act would likely have been viewed as a totalitarian intrusion and met with stiff opposition. But when the companies that collected that information turned it over to government agencies without informing their customers, they clearly had betrayed a trust that was the basis of their business model. It is one thing to have a private company mine your data for better leads on shopping or viewing but quite another for your government to be doing that snooping for reasons of "national security."

In sum, the initial response of the tech corporations to the Snowden revelations was a mixture of claims of ignorance and, when that came to be seen as disingenuous, defensive announcements that they only grudgingly surrendered the material under the duress of secret court orders. That gloss would become a matter of public contention between the companies and the government, a topic we will deal with in subsequent chapters. But what many of the folks in the room at the TED conference knew is that the dispute over why the information was turned over would be less important to their business model than the fact that the information was in no way protected as a matter of privacy. Nor did it help them when the Obama administration went on the offensive to make the "Everyone is doing it" argument—and claimed that the private sector was being even more invasive of citizens' privacy than the government.

⁂ ⁂ ⁂

THE MODERN SURVEILLANCE STATE BEGAN NOT WITH THE overreaching spy agencies of government such as the NSA but, rather, with companies led by Google that provide the aggregate data for government agencies to mine. The mining of our personal data, an art of exploitation the company has come to epitomize, is what the end of privacy is all about. But until the NSA was exposed by the treasure trove of documents leaked by Edward Snowden, few among us realized the extent to which the tech giants were providing the essential building blocks for the creation of the modern surveillance state.

Suddenly, it was revealed that nothing about the sanctity of individual space, that basic requirement of the open society, was inviolate. Instead, the very essence of the democratic experience— the notion of individual freedom, which assumes the full integrity of an individual citizen's effort to privately define one's interaction in the company of others—was now deeply threatened.

But this assault on individual privacy had been justified by the private sector's insistence that it was extending consumer choice and by the government's contention that it was providing citizens with security against terrorist attacks. The perfect image of the marriage of necessity that both the private and government sectors could claim was that of a bomb exploding in a shopping mall.

The power of the security state came to be fortified by the ultimate extension of consumer sovereignty, the one expression of human freedom most critical to the functioning of the modern economy. It was a prospect foretold by philosophers as varied as Karl Marx and John Stuart Mill, at work in the first centuries of modern capitalism, who warned that consumption of goods and services might become the dominant definition of the human experience. They argued that this extremely narrow but compellingly addictive component of modern life would crowd out other pursuits—enlightenment or compassion, for example—and that the notion of consumer sovereignty would, like the most dangerous weed in the garden of human expression, kill all competing manifestations of the human experience.

The dire consequence of this contagion was on clear display in a June 2013 brief that Google filed in federal court in San Jose for a class action lawsuit alleging the company "read and mined the content of email messages for target advertising and to build user profiles." In its motion to dismiss, Google claimed that "[j]ust as a sender of a letter to a business colleague cannot be surprised that the recipient's assistant opens the letter, people who use Web-based email today cannot be surprised if their emails are processed by the recipient [email] provider in the course of delivery." Citing a 1979 court ruling (*Smith v. Maryland*) in a legal filing, the search giant contended that, "[i]ndeed, 'a person has no legitimate expectation of privacy in information he voluntarily turns over to third parties.'"[14]

Coincidentally, this was the same month Snowden, a mid-level techie working with high-level security clearances for NSA defense contractor Booz Allen Hamilton, went public with the first wave of his leaked data, revealing to the world in dramatic fashion that our government had taken the same cavalier attitude toward its citizens as Google had in perusing its customers' data. This would quickly come to haunt Google when the Obama administration, in an effort to deflect criticism of its spying programs, issued a report by White House counsel John Podesta pointing the finger at Google and other private companies that had made data mining the profit driver of their business.

"[T]he most significant findings in the [Podesta] report focus on the recognition that data can be used in subtle ways to create forms of discrimination—and to make judgments, sometimes in error, about who is likely to show up at work, pay their mortgage on time or require expensive treatment," explained the *New York Times*. "The report states that the same technology that is often so useful in predicting places that would be struck by floods or diagnosing hard-to-find illnesses in infants also has 'the potential to eclipse longstanding civil rights protections in how personal information is used in housing, credit, employment, health, education and the marketplace.'"[15]

The industry, represented in its response by Michael Beckerman of the Internet Association, whose membership includes Google, Facebook, Twitter, and Amazon, responded that the White House should "turn its attention to the most pressing privacy priorities facing American consumers" by amending prevailing law, the Electronic Communications Privacy Act, with the goal to "reform the government's surveillance law and practices."[16]

The Podesta report's attack on the industry, blame-shifting and self-serving as it was, nonetheless hit the mark. Data mining had been a key component of Google's nascent DNA, for example, three years before it was even registered as a company in 1998, in its primordial form as BackRub, a PhD collaboration of Brin with fellow Stanford graduate student Larry Page.[17] In the beginning, according to most accounts, Brin and Page were driven less by mercenary business motives and more by academic curiosity, yet regardless of motive, the clear purpose of the project was to mine the data of increasing numbers of people interested in using the Internet to do searches.

In June 2000, Google struck a deal with Yahoo to handle all of that company's search traffic, which gave it access to a much larger base of users and their data. That led to angel investors and the launch of Google AdWords, a pay-per-click advertising service, in October 2000. The billions began to roll in. Hence, the connection between spying on consumer habits and mining that information defined the company from its inception; by the time of the Snowden revelations, the ubiquitous intrusion of corporate data collection and mining on the most intimate of personal levels had become an unquestioned and defining aspect of American life.

If the government had been behind this enormous extension of the power of surveillance, many people would have found it threatening, but few did when the proprietors of this private-sector surveillance society intruded not in the clear pursuit of coercion but rather as an extension of consumer sovereignty—the assertion in economic theory that consumer preferences determine the production of goods and services. Because this intrusion was not identified with an assault on other notions of freedom, like the sovereignty of political, cultural, or religious activity, it was viewed as inherently nonthreatening.

In other words, as long as Google's data mining (or Facebook, Yahoo, or AOL's) could be viewed as a guide to shopping, it seemed largely harmless. Who cared that all that data about where you ate and with whom, what books and movies you perused, and email conversations with doctors, lovers, and lawyers was being vacuumed up by Google? Google was a relatively safe universe where dangers stemmed from the manipulations or invasions not of the company but of stalkers, hackers, or just nosy family members peering into our embarrassing search history.

Google searches in the pre-Snowden era might have seemed reckless at times, but in the main they were perceived by most as fueling a dizzying array of choice in a world dominated by 24/7 markets in an endless digital cloud, a convenience or even a thrill that overshadowed the risks. After all, wasn't Google, with its friendly and progressive ever-changing search page logos and unofficial "Don't be evil" mantra, a trustworthy steward of the World Wide Web, that stupendous invention that had promised to unify the global community and transcend our divisions?

When Snowden decided to risk his life to bring us a view of the inner workings of the beast, it blew a huge hole in this casual mass denial, revealing to even the least skeptical that privately mined data was quite accessible to those with a potentially far greater power to violate our rights and freedom.

Until the Snowden leaks, with few exceptions, the tech companies accommodated this ever-expanding government demand for access to customer data. But when that accommodation was made public by his actions, the intimate connection with the US government was viewed as a threat to the companies' means of doing business. Suddenly, the protection of individual freedom had found a profit motive. Exposed was the basic contradiction inherent in being an American multinational corporation: free to operate throughout an increasingly global market and yet beholden to the dictates of individual nation-states, most clearly the one that hosts your main headquarters.

To understand how threatened these companies felt, how they feared they might lose market share, consider how quickly they overcame their historic suspicions of each other and, in December 2013, posted on a common website very strongly worded criticisms of the government's recently exposed surveillance methods.

"The balance in many countries has tipped too far in favor of the state and away from the rights of the individual—rights that are enshrined in our Constitution," read the statement released jointly by AOL, Apple, Facebook, Google, LinkedIn, Microsoft, Twitter, and Yahoo. "This undermines the freedoms we all cherish. It's time for a change."[18]

The digital heavyweights also promised to be better guardians of their customers' privacy. "For our part, we are focused on keeping users' data secure—deploying the latest encryption technology to prevent unauthorized surveillance on our networks and by pushing back on government requests to ensure that they are legal and reasonable in scope," the statement continued. "We urge the U.S. to take the lead and make reforms that ensure that government surveillance efforts are clearly restricted by law, proportionate to the risks, transparent, and subject to independent oversight."

Here was a united front for reform, and each company was also represented by a brief quote from a top executive. Larry Page, then CEO of Google, cited that company's investment in encryption and transparency surrounding the government's request for information—an effort, he noted, that "is undermined by the apparent wholesale collection of data, in secret and without independent oversight, by many governments around the world." He urged the US government to "lead the way" in reform.

Microsoft general counsel and executive vice president Brad Smith was brief but voiced a common concern: "People won't use technology they don't trust. Governments have put this trust at risk, and governments need to help restore it."

The corporate leaders asked world governments to endorse and enact a set of five principles "consistent with established global norms of free expression and privacy and with the goals of ensuring that government law enforcement and intelligence efforts are rule-bound, narrowly tailored, transparent, and subject to oversight."

The principles entail limiting governments' authority to collect users' information and banning bulk data collection of Internet communication; expanding oversight and accountability of intelligence agencies' actions, including more transparency; allowing companies to publish the number and nature of government demands for user information; respecting the free flow of information by not inhibiting access by companies or individuals to lawfully available information stored outside the country; and governing requests for data across jurisdictions.

Those statements made clear that leading multinational tech firms based in the United States stood in opposition to the national security assumptions that had driven the NSA to hack their systems. However, it was unclear how hard or long they would fight for changes, or if this would ultimately amount to little more than posturing for public relations purposes.

ₐᵥ ₐᵥ ₐᵥ

As long as private companies are indeed providing and profiting from services to their customers in a transparently honest way, that is the sort of voluntary private-sector association promised in the Declaration of Independence as an extension of an individual's right to life, liberty, and the pursuit of happiness free of government intervention. But it is another matter altogether when those private corporations are following the government's dictates in surreptitiously monitoring the lawful activities of its citizens.

Key to this monitoring is access to the engineering details of the devices used by consumers as well as the networks that connect their communications. The NSA stated that it is actively involved with the leading tech organizations in preventing cyber attacks. This arrangement, however, also may put it in the position to be the attacker. Shouldn't that concern citizens and leaders of other countries who might begin to challenge the claims of US-based companies that they are free of their own government's coercion?

For example, with much of the world relying on mobile phones supplied by US-based companies, and given the power of those devices to be used to photograph, record, supply location information, and otherwise spy on the most intimate details of private associations, isn't it a bit alarming to read the following email from Keith Alexander to Google executives detailing the close cooperation between the NSA and one of the leading tech companies?

"About six months ago, we began focusing on the security of mobility devices. A group (primarily Google, Apple, and Microsoft) recently came to agreement on a set of core security principles. When we reach this point in our projects, we schedule a classified briefing for the CEOs of key companies to provide them a brief on the specific threats we believe can be mitigated and to seek their commitment for their organization to move ahead," Alexander wrote. "Google's participation in refinement, engineering and deployment of the solutions will be essential."[19]

Does this not suggest that if the NSA intends to go beyond preventing attacks on electronic communications and indeed, as the Snowden documents have made indelibly obvious, to clear the path for attacks of its own, so it can easily scoop up almost all private data in the pursuit of an ever-shifting, omnipresent terrorist threat?

It is not inherently problematic or subversive, as NSA spokespersons and indeed President Obama have suggested, to raise the alarm that our government is carelessly subverting the intent of the Constitution and Bill of Rights. In fact, the very reason the constitutional founders gifted the nation with a written document setting firm limits on government overreach is that they anticipated precisely this act and were offering the citizenry, with our checks and balances and protection of individual freedom, avenues to redress the grievances brought on by overbearing government intrusion.

For those government officials and spooks who were exposed as having invaded the inner workings of cyberspace in ever more audacious ways, they apparently did not see this as a sinister act, however, especially once the 9/11 attacks gave them what amounted to carte blanche to ignore the niceties of constitutional protections now deemed as quaint.

In stark rebuke of the utopian fantasies of the post–Cold War Internet Age, this single shocking act of terrorism, an old-fashioned product of the most primitive of human impulses, was abetted in its execution by technology as limited as a box cutter and as sophisticated as jet travel and global information sharing systems that facilitated dire global conspiracies.

The concept of a cyberworld threatened by cyberterrorism was consolidated instantly, with this brave new world of the Internet seemingly having sown the seeds of its own destruction. Like mushrooms after a rain, support for using "any means necessary" to protect our allegedly fragile way of life blossomed overnight. Torture, preemptive war, discrimination and profiling based on race, religion or creed, the suspension or sidestepping of our civil liberties: everything was on the table as tools to maintain control. In this environment, the NSA and the rest of the intelligence community were liberated from even the limited shackles previously placed on their use of electronic snooping on private networks.

After 9/11, the balance had shifted in the direction of justifying a massive expansion of government power and the undermining of the rights of the individual to resist. In the process, the checks and balances upon which we had relied to guard our freedoms were rendered useless and the priorities shifted from viewing the preservation of individual liberty as the guarantor of freedom to the justification of unbridled government power exercised in the name of preserving national security.

To be sure, in the wake of 9/11 civil rights advocates had been gravely concerned, questioning the alleged necessity of sacrificing privacy for the success of programs ostensibly intended to ensure the nation's safety. However, since details about the top-secret surveillance programs were not factored in, the discussion was largely meaningless and theoretical. It was only after the Snowden revelations and a spate of other leaks surfaced that a national debate of some energy of purpose was provoked.

After the vast trove of details concerning the staggering extent of the loss of private space was revealed, it became possible to investigate the effectiveness of various profoundly questionable and exorbitantly expensive surveillance practices in thwarting terrorist attacks. As discussed in the next chapter, the record on that—informed by a number of investigations conducted from within the executive and legislative branches, along with reinvigorated investigative reporting by the media—indicates that the vast expansion of the surveillance state cannot be justified by the standard of genuine national security.

two

Cyber Sound Bites

I T IS AN ALL TOO ACCURATE CLICHÉ THAT TRUTH IS THE first casualty of war. At no other time is the case for collective security so intense and the claims of logic so easily ignored. The so-called War on Terror, which has been used to justify the government's assault on privacy since 9/11, is a perfect example of how quickly we surrender the restraints on power basic to democracy when attacked by an enemy of alarming consequence, real or imagined.

We had been alerted to that threat to individual freedom by two legendary wartime generals-turned-president, George Washington and Dwight D. Eisenhower, both of whom chose the occasion of their farewell addresses to warn against what Washington termed "the impostures of pretended patriotism."[1] Washington presided over the nation in its most vulnerable phase, but it is argued by some that those were simpler times and the challenges of the modern enemy more demanding. It remained for Eisenhower, informed by governing in a period of nuclear bombs and Cold War hysteria, to warn of the threat to representative democracy posed by the modern "military-industrial complex."

Unfortunately, these impassioned cautions about dangerous appeals to exaggerated images of an enemy threat, so convenient to demagogues and profiteers, have largely fallen on deaf ears—and perhaps never so much as in the aftermath of the coordinated attack on the World Trade Center and the Pentagon. A nation that had only recently begun to adjust to an era of relative peace following seven decades of hot and cold war lost all sense of proportion in response to that terrorist attack, one that, while tragic and horrifying, in no sense posed an existential threat of the sort other nations had experienced. In fact, it paled in comparison to the ones faced by President Washington and the other founders of this nation when they enshrined in our Constitution the ideal of a government restrained by the rights of the people.

Basic to those rights was the Fourth Amendment's guarantee of private space to collect one's thoughts and papers free from the intimidating surveillance of government—a right ensured, as it had evolved in opposition to the power of the King of England, by the blanket prohibition on warrantless searches. It was quite deliberately added to the Constitution by the leaders of the new republic to guard against the inevitable tendency of power to corrupt even well-intentioned leaders like themselves.

The founders insisted on that and other protections of individual liberty at a time when the security of the new nation was very much in question, besieged as it was by enemies abroad and at home. Personal liberty was clearly viewed not as an indulgence to be enjoyed only in the most secure of times but as a necessity for an informed public to self-govern effectively in difficult circumstances. This was an obvious point that President George W. Bush (with the alarming compliance of all three branches of government) ignored in his rush to abandon the rule of law in response to the attacks of September 11.

Although faced with a primitively armed "terrorist" enemy, Bush quickly—and, from the perspective of the defense industry, heroically—reversed his stated policy of winding down Cold War–level military spending, initially with a one-third cut to the defense budget. Those expenditures came to be retroactively justified by the invasion of Iraq, a nation that had nothing to do with 9/11. And by redefining "antiterrorism," a long-standing police issue for all societies, as a new cold war against a shadowy global enemy, Bush succeeded in making hysteria a national policy—the first installment of which was the Patriot Act, which treated the Bill of Rights like it was yesterday's fish wrap.

At the same time, his administration pointedly ignored significant antiterrorist programs that were more selective in ferreting out terrorist activity while also being more sensitive to privacy and civil rights concerns. The most startling example was the Thin-Thread surveillance program, discontinued three weeks before 9/11 and replaced by the Bush administration with a much more privacy-invasive one, then on the drawing board, that ultimately proved an abject failure.

ThinThread was a signals collection and analysis program designed to intercept foreign electronic communications—email and cell phone calls, basically—that might involve threats to the United States or its allies. Its primary purpose was to deal with the data overload that was preventing the NSA from separating the wheat from the chaff; the agency was drowning in information it couldn't meaningfully process.

Developed in 1998 on a scant budget of $3.2 million, this low-cost program was the brainchild of a small team of NSA employees and contractors led by William Binney, a brilliant analyst and crypto-mathematician who joined the NSA during the Vietnam War. In 2000, after a field test demonstrated that ThinThread swept up communications not only of foreign targets but also those of Americans, and thus violated federal law that required a warrant for collecting signals intelligence of American citizens, Binney and his colleagues installed privacy controls that would encrypt American communications until a warrant was issued. Thomas Andrews Drake, a former NSA senior executive charged with the task of "searching NSA for the most promising assets that could be put into the fight immediately and improve the quality of intelligence," strongly believed that the revamped ThinThread was one of these assets.[2]

Still, the NSA cited its legal team's concern that the program's latent capacity to intercept American communications rendered it too privacy-invasive, and it was killed less than a month ahead of the biggest terror attack ever on American soil.

In October 2001, the Bush administration instead opted to pursue the much more expensive and invasive Trailblazer surveillance program, which, six years and $1.2 billion later, was abandoned.[3] "Trailblazer was launched with great fanfare in the spring of 2000 by then NSA Director Lt. Gen. Michael V. Hayden as *THE* flagship program to catapult NSA into the 21st Century," wrote Drake in an email. "[The program] became a multi-billion dollar boondoggle of a program that NSA doubled down on after 9/11, with expanded monies from Congress to ostensibly deal with the new terrorist threat of the 21st Century."[4]

Indeed, the amount of federal budget funds it could soak up was measured in the billions at a time when Congress was desperate to be seen throwing money at anything to do with antiterrorism. "Right after 9/11, NSA Signals Intelligence Director Maureen Baginski told the workforce that '9/11 was a gift to NSA' and that NSA 'would get all the money it wanted and then some.' And she didn't say it as gallows humor," recounted Drake.[5]

Even more alarming to Drake and Binney was that the new program would illegally collect and analyze domestic data on a scale that, according to Binney, would "create an Orwellian state."[6]

Binney, Drake, and two other NSA staffers, along with House Intelligence Committee staffer Dianne Roark, filed a complaint in 2002 with the Inspector General of the Defense Department alleging fraud, waste, and abuse. The complaint was quashed. Worse, in a retributive spectacle that rebukes those who say whistleblowers like Snowden should always use the established internal appeals systems in place rather than turning to the media, the members of the ThinThread group later became the object of FBI raids of their homes—and one was ultimately charged with being a spy. (The investigation was nominally aimed at uncovering the source of an unrelated article on government surveillance published in the *New York Times*.)

No charges were filed under the Bush administration, but in 2010 Drake was charged with spying, one of eight such cases in the first five years of the Obama administration—which has charged more Americans under the Espionage Act than all previous administrations combined. Frustrated by the costs and contradictions of Bush's overreaction to 9/11, America had responded positively to Obama, whose cautious approach to foreign entanglements and law-professor respect for due process helped earn him a sweeping victory in the 2008 presidential election. He even won a Nobel Peace Prize, though it was based more on promise than on achievement.

In a presidential campaign speech on August 1, 2007, in Washington, DC, then-Senator Obama argued that the Bush administration "put forward a false choice between the liberties we cherish and the security we demand." He promised that, in his quasi-utopian administration of "hope and change," things would be different.

"I will provide our intelligence and law enforcement agencies with the tools they need to track and take out the terrorists without undermining our Constitution and our freedom," he said. "That means no more illegal wiretapping of American citizens. No more national security letters to spy on citizens who are not suspected of a crime. No more tracking citizens who do nothing more than protest a misguided war. No more ignoring the law when it is inconvenient. That is not who we are. And it is not what is necessary to defeat the terrorists. The FISA court works. The separation of powers works. Our Constitution works. . . . This Administration acts like violating civil liberties is the way to enhance our security. It is not."[7]

However, as a warning of a civil liberties reversal to come, Obama, even then, waffled: "I will also strengthen our intelligence. . . . We need leadership that forces our agencies to share information, and leadership that never—ever—twists the facts to support bad policies," he said, before creating for himself a huge loophole: "But we must also build our capacity to better collect and analyze information."

Indeed, shocking some of his most ardent supporters, the modern surveillance state that had been ushered into existence by Bush was dramatically expanded during the Obama presidency. However, because foreign and domestic intelligence gathering is the most highly classified arena of governmental activity, the public was largely clueless as to its full extent until the Snowden revelations.

In August 2013, Snowden released documents to the *Washington Post* that revealed a massive "black budget"—expenditures not reviewable by the public or even most of Congress—of $52.6 billion for 2013 for the CIA, NSA, and the country's fourteen additional security agencies.[8] The *Post* noted that the CIA and NSA have enjoyed budget increases of a whopping 50 percent each year since 2004, with the total "black budget" for all sixteen agencies nearly doubling since 2001.[9] Overall, the United States has spent more than $500 billion for intelligence since the 9/11 attacks.[10]

Nevertheless, although US spy agencies have created "an intelligence-gathering colossus . . . [they] remain unable to provide critical information to the president on a range of national security threats," according to the *Post*. The "black budget" for fiscal 2013 "maps a bureaucratic and operational landscape that has never been subject to public scrutiny. Although the government has annually released its overall level of intelligence spending since 2007, it has not divulged how it uses the money or how it performs against the goals set by the president and Congress."

The *Post* published key sections of the 178-page summary of the spending plan, which "describes cutting-edge technologies, agent recruiting and ongoing operations." However, after consultation with US officials who identified much of the information as "sensitive," it published only summary tables and charts featured in the documents.

Included in the "black budget" report are details about the CIA and the NSA engaging in "offensive cyber operations," which involve hacking into foreign computer networks "to steal information or sabotage enemy systems," and information about counterintelligence operations against "priority targets"—namely, China, Russia, Iran, Cuba, and Israel.[11]

Let's consider this: the details are so risky to disclose that the *Washington Post* is holding back many of them, and the budget is "black" because national security would be threatened if the American people—the taxpayers who fund the budget—knew what's in it. Yet thousands of private-sector contract workers like Snowden are privy to the information, which seems the riskiest business of all.

The *Post* noted this incongruity: "Long before Snowden's leaks, the US intelligence community worried about 'anomalous behavior' by employees and contractors with access to classified material. The NSA planned to ward off a 'potential insider compromise of sensitive information' by re-investigating at least 4,000 people this year who hold high-level security clearances."[12]

As Washington and Eisenhower had warned, the actuality of danger is not what drives the concentration of government power. Instead, it is the exaggerations of danger accompanied by the assumption that freedom is an indulgence to be experienced only in the most unthreatening of times rather than the key to formulating and carrying out appropriate responses to the worst of times.

↝ ↝ ↝

SAME AS HIS PREDECESSOR, OBAMA ENGAGED IN NO SUCH public examination of the choices the nation faced, even though as a senator and presidential candidate he paid much lip service to the need for just such a rational and transparent evaluation. Only the Snowden firestorm forced him to engage with the public, in a quite limited way. After six months of startling revelations during which Obama and most in the executive branch and the Congress attempted to blame the messenger, on January 17, 2014, the president provided an accounting of the activities of the National

Security Agency in prepared remarks delivered to an approving audience at the Justice Department.

"At the dawn of our Republic, a small, secret surveillance committee, born out of the Sons of Liberty, was established in Boston and the group's members included Paul Revere. At night, they would patrol the streets, reporting back any signs that the British were preparing raids against America's early patriots," he began dramatically.[13]

It was an absurd introduction to a defense of official government surveillance. The government spies surveilling the population back then were the ones working for the king of England. A junior high school student should be able to figure out that the modern figure analogous to Paul Revere and his fellow Sons of Liberty would be a whistleblower like Edward Snowden, who was warning about the exercise of unbridled government power.

The Sons of Liberty, after all, were rebelling against the established, oppressive order rather than enforcing its intrusion into the lives of a free people with inalienable rights. Their revolution was fought not to ensure the right of government to invade one's home with general writs, à la the NSA, but rather to prevent that invasion of private space, as they later enshrined in the Fourth Amendment to their new Constitution.

Obama's defense of not having acted in any serious way to restrain the NSA's spying on Americans further delved into the realm of the ridiculous when he asserted that "the folks at NSA and other intelligence agencies are our neighbors. They're our friends and family."

More Democracy 101: The point of enshrining the Fourth Amendment and the basic checks and balances of the Constitution was not that "the folks" in government are inherently bad people but, rather, that power tends to corrupt, and limits on that power, beginning with transparency, are essential to preventing coercion and abuse.

Later in the speech, Obama conceded that "even the United States proved not to be immune to the abuse of surveillance. In the 1960s, government spied on civil rights leaders and critics of the Vietnam War. And probably in response to those revelations, additional laws were established in the 1970s to ensure that our intelligence capabilities could not be misused against our citizens."

Yet he did not admit that, since 9/11, the intelligence community has been bent on ignoring those very laws established in the wake of hearings by Idaho Senator Frank Church. When the president admits that "I've often reminded myself I would not be where I am today were it not for the courage of dissidents like Dr. King, who were spied upon by their own government," does he fathom the government's overreach today into the private lives of Americans and the consequences of that intrusion?

How did we, Barack Obama included, come to know that the Reverend Martin Luther King, Jr., had not only been spied on but indeed intimidated with FBI-manufactured fraudulent letters aimed at driving him to suicide? It wasn't because the FBI came clean about its nefarious behavior; rather, we learned the harrowing details of how an American hero was harassed and spied on by his government because of events set in motion by a unique group of radical whistleblowers who broke the law to get out the truth.

In 1971, several years after King's death, a small band of eight dissidents broke into a regional FBI office in Media, Pennsylvania, near Philadelphia, and stole all the files stored there. The documents proved that the agency was spying on civilians and engaging in dirty tricks against dissidents aimed at ruining their lives and livelihoods. The burglars mailed the secret files to two liberal Congress members and three national journalists, resulting in a massive scandal that exposed FBI abuses of power and dirty-tricks operations against dissidents around the country in an operation dubbed COINTELPRO (for Counterintelligence Program).

None of the eight were arrested or identified until January 2014, when the statute of limitations expired, and several of the burglars revealed themselves. Two—John Raines, who was a professor of religion at Temple University at the time, and his wife, Bonnie— told *New York Times* reporter Mark Mazzetti of their feelings of kinship for Edward Snowden, whose disclosures they thought of as "a bookend" to their own revelations about government abuse more than forty years ago.[14]

What they had not known at the time of their illegal action was that the NSA had also targeted, among a group of about 1,600 Americans, King and world-champion heavyweight boxer Muhammad Ali, presumably because of their opposition to the Vietnam War and to attempt to satisfy President Lyndon Johnson's obsession to know if their antiwar activities had the support of "hostile foreign powers."[15] (Witness another era's president willing to violate Fourth Amendment guarantees under the pretense of national security.)

According to the National Security Archive, some NSA officials saw this operation targeting nationally known and respected figures as "disreputable if not outright illegal."[16] It is unfortunate that not one of them had the courage to expose the program.

The sad reality is that the whistleblower who honors an oath to uphold the Constitution is the rare exception, and those who conceal serious evil are the norm. Roughly 5.15 million government employees and contractors have high-security clearances, but few are moved to blow the whistle.[17] Their defense is generally that a higher good justifies such despicable means. Under Johnson, this "higher good" was fighting the spread of communism, while more recently the excuse to overlook the excesses of

the surveillance state (such as the use of torture) has been the need
to protect the nation against terrorists. This was the rationale for
the sweeping and hastily assembled Uniting and Strengthening
America by Providing Appropriate Tools Required to Intercept
and Obstruct Terrorism (USA PATRIOT) Act enthusiastically
passed in October 2001 by Congress, even though many members admitted they did not bother to read it.

It is Section 215 of that ill-conceived legislation upon which
Obama, like Bush before him, relied to support the massive collection of telephone records and other so-called big data. The language of Section 215 allows the government to obtain secret court
orders requiring an entity or person to turn over "any tangible
things . . . for an investigation to protect against international terrorism or clandestine intelligence activities."[18] Those surveilled
under Section 215 orders are never notified of the seizure and
search of their "tangible things," which can include anything from
medical records to Internet browsing history.

To justify that data collection program, Obama cited only one
example, and while it sounded compelling to many, including a
compliant mass media, it was a total fraud. In a statement he made
on January 17, 2014, to address Americans' concerns about mass
data collection, he said: "Why is this necessary? The program grew
out of a desire to address a gap identified after 9/11. One of the 9/11
hijackers, Khalid al Mihdhar, made a phone call from San Diego to a
known al-Qaida safe house in Yemen. NSA saw that call, but it could
not see that the call was coming from an individual already in the
United States. The telephone metadata program under Section 215
was designed to map the communications of terrorists so we could
see who they may be in contact with as quickly as possible."[19]

A compelling case, no? Except that only a week later, the Privacy
and Civil Liberties Oversight Board, appointed by the president in

consultation with Congress, issued an exhaustive 234-page "Report on the Telephone Records Program Conducted Under Section 215 of the Patriot Act and on the Operations of the Foreign Intelligence Surveillance Court" that flatly contradicted the president's statement.[20]

The Oversight Board, formed in response to a recommendation of the 9/11 Commission, supposedly had the full cooperation of the intelligence agencies, including classified briefings with officials from the NSA, the FBI, the CIA, and the White House staff. As a result of the Snowden leaks, the Board undertook a full-scale investigation of claims that the bulk telephone surveillance described in those leaks was justified by the experience with the 9/11 attacks.

The investigation concluded that the NSA surveillance program would *not* have thwarted the al Mihdhar example nor any other attack cited by the NSA to justify its activities. In particular reference to the al Mihdhar case cited by President Obama, the Board concluded: "For two reasons, we do not believe the al Mihdhar example supports continuance of the NSA's Section 215 program. First, the failure to identify al Mihdhar's presence in the United States stemmed primarily from a lack of information sharing among federal agencies, not a lack of surveillance capabilities. As documented by the 9/11 Commission and others, this was a failure to connect the dots, not a failure to collect enough dots. Second, in order to have identified the San Diego telephone number from which al Mihdhar made his calls, it was not necessary to collect the nation's calling records."[21]

This conclusion was not a new revelation that should have caught the president, or at least his top national security advisers, unaware. It was, in fact, the conclusion of every serious study that had been made of the 9/11 attacks, as the Oversight Board report pointed out, quoting the joint report of the US Senate and House committees on intelligence.

> As explained in the 9/11 Commission Report, the joint inquiry into the 9/11 attacks by the House and Senate Intelligence committees, and a Department of Justice Inspector General report, the government had ample opportunity before 9/11 to pinpoint Mihdhar's location, track his activities, and prevent his 2001 re-entry into the United States. By early 2000, the CIA was aware of Mihdhar and knew that he had a visa enabling him to travel to the United States. Yet despite having information that Mihdhar and fellow hijacker Nawaf al Hazmi "were traveling to the United States," the CIA "missed repeated opportunities to act based on the information in its possession." The agency did not advise the FBI of what it knew or "add their names to watch lists."[22]

The joint report of the US Senate and House committees on intelligence, quoted by the Oversight Board, was dated December 2002, more than a decade before Obama's erroneous statement justifying bulk telephone data collection. In fact, as the Oversight Board report noted (quoting from a publicly available report of the Justice Department released in November 2004), at the time of the suspect call to Yemen both al Mihdhar and his accomplice were under active observation by the FBI.

"Furthermore, at the time that al Mihdhar and al Hazmi were in San Diego in early 2000, when the calls to Yemen were made, they were living with 'a long-time FBI asset,'" the report stated. "Mihdhar left the United States in June 2000, and he was able to return in 2001 because he still had not been placed on any watch lists."

As the bipartisan 9/11 Commission appointed by President George W. Bush concluded in its report in 2004, "on four occasions in 2001, the CIA, the FBI, or both had apparent opportunities to refocus on the significance of al Hazmi and al Mihdhar and reinvigorate the search for them."[23] Yet they simply failed to do so.

Perhaps what President Obama meant to imply by citing the al Mihdhar case was to suggest that had the NSA's bulk collection been in place prior to 9/11, finding that a call had been placed from San Diego to the al Qaeda safe house in Yemen would have alerted the otherwise inattentive national security establishment. However, as the Oversight Board noted, "obtaining this knowledge did not require a bulk telephone records program." The report elaborated: "The NSA knew the telephone number of the Yemen safe house. If the telephone calls with al Mihdhar were deemed suspicious at the time, the government could have used existing legal authority to request from US telephone companies the records of any calls made to or from that Yemen number. Doing so could have identified the San Diego number on the other end of the calls. Thus we do not believe that a program that collects all telephone records from US telephone companies was necessary to identify al Mihdhar's location in early 2000, nor that such a program is necessary to make similar discoveries in the future."

More astonishing than their careful debunking of the president's cherry-picked justification for the collection of bulk telephone data was that the Oversight Board could not find any situations before the NSA program was implemented where it would have prevented terrorist activity. Nor could any of the intelligence agencies provide an example of a terrorist threat that had been averted once it came online.

"Based on the information provided to the board, we have not identified a single instance involving a threat to the United States in which the telephone records program made a concrete difference in the outcome of a counterterrorism investigation," the report concluded. "Moreover, we are aware of no instance in which the program directly contributed to the discovery of a previously unknown terrorist plot or the disruption of a terrorist attack. And we believe that in only one instance over the past seven years has the program arguably contributed to the identification of an unknown terrorism suspect. In that case, moreover, the suspect was not involved in planning a terrorist attack and there is reason to believe that the FBI may have discovered him without the contribution of the NSA's program."

Of course, FBI discovery in the single case offered by Obama was hardly the issue because, as the report noted, al Mihdhar and his fellow hijacker were renting rooms from a veteran FBI informant. In fact, informing on young Saudis living in the San Diego area was the job assigned to their landlord, retired professor Abdusattar Shaikh.

"They were not hiding," San Diego County sheriff Bill Gore told Amita Sharma, a reporter for KPBS, the public radio station in San Diego, in 2011. "They were going to school, they were listed in the phone book. They had insurance for their car. They had driver's licenses."[24]

Before being elected sheriff, Gore had been the FBI special agent in charge of the San Diego bureau during the years al Mihdhar was renting a room from Shaikh. After the 9/11 attack, the informant described the hijackers as Bedouins with the lifestyle of simple desert folk who ate and slept on the floor of their rented rooms and left to pray regularly at a local Islamic Center. It seemed a simple lifestyle, except that according to former Florida Democratic Senator Bob Graham, co-chair of the Congressional Inquiry into 9/11, a bit of southern California corruption colored their San Diego stay. Senator Graham told Sharma: "Well, they drank. They went to nightclubs, strip clubs and at one point, al Hazmi wanted to marry one of the strippers, but that was finally quashed."

Who paid for these not-so-pious extracurriculars? According to Graham, his congressional committee was never able to fully explore that question because its investigators ran into a stone wall regarding the Saudi connection. He did learn that a Saudi named Omar Al Bayoumi arranged for the two future hijackers to find apartments and meet other Muslims in San Diego. Al Bayoumi had been receiving $465 a month from a Saudi government contractor, but after he became involved with the apprentice hijackers his monthly stipend shot up to $3,700 a month. According to Graham, "That wasn't the end of it. It turned out that that amount of money was not sufficient to support the somewhat elaborate lifestyle of al Hazmi and al Mihdhar."

The PBS affiliate reported, "Graham believed the funding source was Saudi government officials." Graham said his staff members were foiled in their effort to interview Shaikh about the FBI informant's connection with the Saudi government. "He was taken into protective custody immediately after 9/11 and held for the better part of four years, at the end of which he was given a $100,000 payment and discharged of his responsibilities," the senator continued. "He was withheld from us and in my own opinion, it was purposeful so that we could not get access to whatever information he had."[25] Graham told Sharma that he thought the information might link the hijackers to the Saudi government.

There was clearly a lot of information floating around about these hijackers before they launched their terror attack—including the ominous fact that when they took flying lessons, according to the 9/11 Commission Report, they were suspiciously disinterested in instructions about how to land.[26] The problem was not one of access to information about phone calls but, rather, indifference to the antics of two guys who seemed less interested in effectively hiding their tracks and more interested in having a good time—and maybe even getting caught—before they went on their suicide mission. Sheriff Gore noted in the interview that the CIA knew the two men were connected to al Qaeda and had been in the country, yet the agency never informed the local FBI office he headed. Although the hijackers had left San Diego by then, "local agents could have helped find them . . . that's all pretty clear with 20/20 hindsight."

Again, the pattern was consistent: not a lack of dots, but a failure to connect them.

In other words, they know everything about you—but nearly nothing about the terrorists. "They" of course are the bureaucrats of the military-intelligence complex (to be discussed in Chapter 5), led into the dark by an incestuous group of private- and public-sector agencies, which had a drum major in CIA director George Tenet.

In 1998—his second year as CIA director under President Bill Clinton—Tenet's agents in the field alerted him to the danger of an attack on the US from al Qaeda forces based in Afghanistan. But, according to the 9/11 Commission, Tenet failed to inform the FBI and the White House of those warnings.[27] The aforementioned Inspector General report, completed in 2005 and partially declassified, in part by order of Congress, two years later, concluded: "The agency and its officers did not discharge their responsibilities in a satisfactory manner."[28]

The responsibility, of course, primarily fell upon Tenet, who failed to develop a holistic strategic policy to deal with the al Qaeda threat; thus, the report concluded that Tenet "by virtue of his position bears ultimate responsibility for the fact that no such secret plan was ever created."[29] The other huge misstep was that the CIA and FBI "did not always work effectively and cooperatively." So, instead of learning how to communicate with their fellow spy bureaucrats, they set out to eavesdrop on the communications of everyone else.

Michael F. Scheuer—former head of the Bin Laden Issue Station, the unit charged with finding America's most wanted man, and later special adviser to the chief of the bin Laden unit—referred to CIA staff as "lions led by asses," with Tenet being the top ass. In an interview with the BBC in 2007, soon after the Inspector General's report was made public, Scheuer said: "Many of the difficulties that were listed in the report today—the inability to share information, the lack of people to support and run operations against Osama bin Laden—those were problems that were brought to Mr. Tenet's attention as early as 1996 and he never did anything about them."[30] As is to be expected, these egregious lapses in judgment did nothing to retard Tenet's career. On the contrary: he has the distinction of being the second longest-serving director of the CIA.

The irony is painful to consider. The 9/11 attack—which became the overwhelming excuse for shedding the Constitution's restraints on the government's invasion of privacy and our subsequent transformation into a surveillance society—was caused by a failure to communicate and think clearly by the intelligence officials. Those same guys were, then, rewarded with greater powers, not in communication capabilities but in spying on the very citizens they had ill-served.

In point of fact, there was no need then—or at any time thereafter—to construct a massive haystack of all of the online and offline information on everyone in the world. Tenet's fatal mistake that resulted in our government's losing the chance to thwart the 9/11 attacks—feigning deafness to the vital information provided by intelligence experts at his own agency—was one that old-fashioned intelligence gathering could have avoided.

The fact is that this new military-intelligence complex is not only undemocratic at its core but also unnecessary. Our intelligence officials didn't need to build intrusive spying programs like Trailblazer and the Total Information Awareness project (more on this program in Chapter 5); they didn't need to acquire new state-of-the-art data mining software; they certainly didn't need to plunder private-sector data banks.

They just needed to do lunch.

The Oversight Board recommended the elimination of the bulk data collection program, with the two holdovers from the Bush administration offering dissenting views regarding its legality under the Patriot Act's Section 215. However, there was no disagreement that the executive branch had failed to make the case that the program stopped a single terror attempt. Nor has anyone from the executive branch ever offered a refutation of the report's contention that the massive telephone sweeps were not needed, contrary to the president's claims, in ferreting out al Mihdhar or any other known terrorist.

Nevertheless, the NSA continues to use 9/11 as a carte blanche justification for illegally spying on its own people. An internal NSA talking points brief, obtained in October 2013 by *Al Jazeera* through a Freedom of Information Act request, encourages officials to cite the 9/11 attacks.[31] The talking points borrow heavily from President George W. Bush's War-on-Terror rhetoric.

Under the heading "Sound Bites That Resonate," for example, is the suggested statement: "I much prefer to be here today explaining these programs than explaining another 9/11 event that we were not able to prevent."

In fact, as *Al Jazeera* noted in its initial publication of the document, then-NSA director General Keith Alexander used a version of that statement in his testimony at the House of Representatives Permanent Select Committee on Intelligence open hearing on NSA surveillance, the first public hearing on the subject since the programs were exposed by Snowden. "I would much rather be here today debating this point than trying to explain how we failed to prevent another 9/11," he told the congressional committee on June 18, 2013.[32]

Other sound bites, such as "these programs have helped us connect the dots," "these programs have resulted in intelligence that helped contribute to the disruption of over 50 potential terrorist attacks," and, a personal favorite, the "NSA and affiliates are . . . patriots who serve in silence," have become go-to talking points for the NSA and its partners to defend their work to the public—and likely to friends at dinner parties. Others, such as "US companies have put energy, focus, and commitment into consistently protecting the privacy of their customers around the world, while meeting their obligations under the law," seemed to be too inconvenient to fall into common use.

Substitute *communism* for *terror*, and these could easily have been lifted from an internal memo in Johnson's 1960s administration, justifying the ineffective and unnecessary wars in Indochina. However, back then an increasingly agitated public reacted with outrage to their government's deception. The revelation that government leaders have continuously fed lies to the public—not to keep a foreign enemy in the dark but to sustain the false trust of their citizenry—was sealed with the release of the Pentagon Papers by whistleblower Daniel Ellsberg during the Richard

Nixon administration. The response of Nixon, as later were those of George W. Bush and Barack Obama in defending their post-9/11 excesses, was to destroy the messenger.

ᴧᵛ ᴧᵛ ᴧᵛ

THE HOSTILE RESPONSE OF THE OBAMA ADMINISTRATION to the Snowden revelations paralleled the Bush administration's contempt for the kind of reality-based criticism that had been so disturbing to many Democrats just five years earlier. In fact, it was just the sort of denial of fact and logic that, when employed by Bush to defend his excesses in the name of national security, elicited the scorn of then-Senator Obama.

Yet it was somehow easier for the mainstream media, in its weakened state, to accept that intellectual sleight of hand when Obama delivered it. Whereas Bush was tagged with smugness, Democrats have too often excused Obama as a leader struggling over the competing legitimate demands of national security and personal privacy.[33] But while this may have sounded good in theory, the results, in practice, were the same, with neither president compelled to deal with the factual contradictions in their position.

The *New York Times* editorial board uncharacteristically nailed Obama on this in an editorial June 6, 2013, following Snowden's disclosures of the massive phone data collection:

> Within hours of the disclosure that federal authorities routinely collect data on phone calls Americans make, regardless of whether they have any bearing on a counterterrorism investigation, the Obama administration issued the same platitude it has offered every time President Obama has been caught overreaching in the use of his powers: Terrorists are a real menace and you should just

trust us to deal with them because we have internal mechanisms (that we are not going to tell you about) to make sure we do not violate your rights.

Those reassurances have never been persuasive—whether on secret warrants to scoop up a news agency's phone records or secret orders to kill an American suspected of terrorism—especially coming from a president who once promised transparency and accountability.

The administration has now lost all credibility on this issue. Mr. Obama is proving the truism that the executive branch will use any power it is given and very likely abuse it.[34]

The editorial called the Patriot Act "reckless in its assignment of unnecessary and overbroad surveillance powers," and endorsed the indictment of the FBI by Patriot Act author Rep. James Sensenbrenner (R), who charged that, "Seizing phone records of millions of innocent people is excessive and un-American."[35]

In October 2013, Sensenbrenner and Democratic Senator Patrick Leahy of Vermont moved to curtail data collection and use under the Patriot Act with the introduction of the so-called USA FREEDOM Act, the acronym a lengthy and pointed echo of that created for the Patriot Act—United and Strengthening America by Fulfilling Rights and Ending Eavesdropping, Dragnet Collection, and Online Monitoring Act. Sensenbrenner said of the intelligence agencies: "It's time to put their metadata program out of business."[36] By May 2014, however, the bill was being watered down in Congress, seriously weakening some of its key provisions.

The "new privacy standards" unveiled by Obama in his January 17, 2014, response to the criticism over Snowden's revelations were rather insignificant considering that the leadership of the NSA and the other intelligence agencies was left intact. The president's director of national intelligence, James Clapper, remained in his position after blatantly lying, under oath, before the Senate Intelligence Committee on March 12, 2013, in denying the broad reach of the agencies' surveillance programs.

When asked by Democratic Senator Ron Wyden of Oregon if "the NSA collect[s] any type of data at all on millions, or hundreds of millions of Americans?" he dissembled quickly.[37] "No sir," Clapper began, "not wittingly. There are cases where they would inadvertently, perhaps, collect, but not wittingly."[38] Later, in an interview with *NBC News,* Clapper explained that he has a different understanding of the term *collection* than most, and that this definition allowed him to respond to Wyden's question in "the least untruthful manner" possible.[39] He admitted that the explanation he gave on Capitol Hill was "too cute by half."[40]

In fact, Clapper's lie outraged members of Congress, with some demanding that he be fired and even prosecuted for perjury. "It would be somewhat enlightening for James Clapper and Edward Snowden to share a prison cell," libertarian Senator Rand Paul (R-KY) suggested in a January 2014 *Fox News* interview. "The law has to be applied equally."

The president's promise of "a comprehensive review of big data and privacy" was put in the hands of John Podesta, a political operative who held Clinton's hand, so to speak, during the historic impeachment drama of the battle over the stained blue dress. He had only recently been brought into the Obama White House as a special counsel to manage the political fallout from the NSA and other crises. Podesta was charged by the president to determine "how we can continue to promote the free flow of information in ways that are consistent with both privacy and security."

Lee Tien, senior staff attorney at the Electronic Frontier Foundation (EFF), a leading opponent of government surveillance, had worked with John Podesta in the early 1990s, before Podesta joined the Clinton administration. In those days, Podesta was known on the Hill as one-half of the Podesta Group, a lobbying and public affairs firm he founded with his brother Tony. "EFF was involved with [the Podesta brothers] while they were lobbying. For a long time, [the Podesta brothers] were just very well connected lobbying types who had a fairly progressive agenda and a digital agenda," Tien explained in a June 2014 interview at a café near his home in Berkeley, California. "Podesta had always maintained a really strong privacy and civil liberties association."[41]

Podesta alluded to this connection in his keynote address at a workshop co-hosted by the White House Office of Science and Technology Policy and the University of California Berkeley School of Information, "Big Data: Values and Governance," a day-long conference at Berkeley, billed as a part of the Obama administration's ninety-day review of data privacy policy. He pandered to the audience of mostly academics, lawyers, and technorati:

"I was one of the staff authors of the Electronic Communications Privacy Act. I was working for a then young senator, Pat Leahy, in 1984," he said. "For the next two years, Senator Leahy, along with his House colleagues . . . worked to update the law for modern times. A few years after that, I hosted the Washington D.C. organizing meeting for a new group dedicated to a new civil liberties cause. I knew Lee would be here, so I somehow dug out my membership card—member number 33 of the Electronic Frontier Foundation. Lee Tien and the EFF are still fighting to find balance between civil rights, personal freedom, and technological advancement, and, of course, I've become 'The Man.'"

Indeed, Podesta was the perfect beard, and the report he issued served as the ideal cop-out for the government establishment. It was titled "Big Data: Seizing Opportunities, Preserving Values," but what it seized was the opportunity to deflect criticism of the NSA onto the Internet's private-sector corporations. It more honestly should have been headlined "Hey, if you think the government's destruction of privacy is bad, you'd better worry a lot more about companies like Facebook and Google."

Tien believes "the White House thought that it could at least begin to try to restore a little bit of its image by bringing somebody like [Podesta] into the process. . . . [T]he problem is that it fell short of what most folks who were looking for genuine reform wanted." Instead, he said, "It's a way to escape responsibility for a program that the government started and the government instigated. If the government wants to admit that the program is wrong or ineffective, they should end it. They should not push it over to the private sector and allow the private sector either to be the scapegoat and say they're not going to participate or to not be the scapegoat, because they're afraid that by standing up . . . that they'll be labeled un-American or unhelpful."

In the end, Tien said, the whole thing was an "evasive maneuver" by the White House: "Those big data workshops—three over a period of three months with a whole lot of hoopla—did not discuss the use of big data, machine-learning, or data mining techniques in the intelligence and counterterrorism areas at all. They were completely devoted to other things, and that was a massive turn in a strange direction. I think it was obvious to many people that he [Podesta] wasn't focusing on terrorism or national security."

The Podesta report, issued just three months after it was publicly commissioned, contained scant reference to the government spying on Americans. The lead in the *New York Times* story put it forthrightly enough: "The White House, hoping to move the national debate over privacy beyond the National Security Agency's surveillance activities to the practice of companies like Google and

Facebook, released a long-anticipated report on Thursday that recommends developing government limits on how private companies make use of the torrent of information they gather from their customers online."[42]

And in another misdirection move, the authors of the report viciously equated the actions of Snowden and US Army private Chelsea Manning—who in August 2013 was sentenced to thirty-five years in prison for providing WikiLeaks with a trove of secret documents—with two crazed murderers who slaughtered twenty-five innocent people at two military facilities. Under the heading "Insider Threat and Continuous Evaluation," it read: "The 2013 shooting [twelve killed] at the Washington Navy Yard facility by a contract employee who held a secret security clearance despite a record of arrests and troubling behavior has added urgency to ongoing efforts to more frequently evaluate employees who hold special positions of public trust. It was the latest in a string of troubling breaches and acts of violence by insiders who held security clearances, including Chelsea Manning's disclosures to WikiLeaks, the Fort Hood shooting [thirteen killed] by Major Nidal Hasan, and the most serious breach in the history of US intelligence, the release of classified National Security Agency documents by Edward Snowden."[43]

The Podesta report went on to suggest that government employees and contract workers needed more frequent "evaluation" than the current reinvestigation done every five years on those with top-secret clearance. "Pilot programs have demonstrated the efficacy of using automated queries of appropriate official and commercial databases and social media to identify violations or irregular irregularities, known as 'derogatory information,' that may call into question a person's suitability to continue serving in a sensitive position," it stated.

This shameful character assassination of the whistleblowers helped serve the purpose of the report, which was to deflect blame and shift concern over the Obama administration's sacrifice of privacy in the name of national security and focus it elsewhere, the particular target being commercial data mining of the private sector.

⌁ ⌁ ⌁

WHILE BOTH THE GOVERNMENT AND INDUSTRY REPRESENT real centers of concern for privacy advocates, few would deny that the threat from government, particularly in light of the Snowden leaks, was the subject at hand. But Podesta proved once again to be extremely skillful in changing the narrative. Suddenly the culprits were Google, Yahoo, and the other mega-sized Internet companies that had been mining our private data—and not so much the government, which swooped in to secretly commandeer that information.

It was a neat ploy but fallacious on its face. While there is no doubt the commercial exploitation of our most intimate practices to enhance advertising sales is destructive of privacy, it is a qualitatively different assault than secret monitoring by a government agency.

That's not to minimize the importance of the right of consumers to control their personal data, which would include a requirement for understandable opt-in systems that ask for user permission to make online and offline data available to third parties and, most imperative, a requirement for private companies to inform their customers when government authorities request their data, so as to ensure the legality of searches.

But what the government can do with the data obtained from a Google or Facebook is far more immediate and urgent a threat.

Though tech companies' insidious manipulation of our private information certainly poses a profound threat to democracy—encouraging groupthink and mindless consumerism—a tech company doesn't have the power to arrest and imprison people. General Michael Hayden, former director of the NSA and CIA, outlined the difference succinctly in an April 2013 Johns Hopkins Foreign Affairs Symposium debate: "We kill people based on metadata," he stated starkly.[44]

Google merits significant attention because it is the biggest and quite typical in its invasive behavior. It must operate under laws that require a degree of transparency (addressed in later chapters) and can be subject to class action lawsuits if the company engages in fraudulent activity. Clearly, our relationship with government spy agencies is the extreme opposite.

The difference between the potential powers of government agencies when contrasted with even the most powerful of private companies is precisely the reason that our Constitution's safeguards apply to the former explicitly and only indirectly to the latter. Yes, we have antitrust laws to guarantee competition in the private sector and if companies like Google and Apple attain a market share that hinders competition, there are legal procedures to address that threat to a free-market economy. Voters can influence their elected representatives to move against such restraints of trade. Not so with their ability to reign in a surveillance state, whose actions are concealed by the most opaque layers of secrecy, and woe be to him or her who threatens to cast some light on that dark world.

The threat of the private sector's intrusions on privacy suddenly becomes more menacing when it becomes clear that the largest of companies are, to some degree, beholden to the government. The purpose of the Podesta ploy—issuance of a report at the moment when the nation was at last debating the proper limits of government surveillance of the citizenry—was to obscure the fact that these private companies' exploitation of user information became most dangerous only when the government entwined it so tightly with its own operations.

In an interview with the *New York Times,* Podesta said that Obama was surprised that "the same technologies are not only used by the intelligence community, but far more broadly in the public and private spheres because there is so much collection."[45]

Consider the inherent mendacity of that statement. Both the president and his counselor knew full well that personal information shared among friends on a social network site or in email correspondence is offered on the assumption that the providers of that means of communication—say, Facebook or Google—are private rather than governmental entities. What's more, the president knew that American and British intelligence agencies have largely piggybacked on corporate capabilities for years. The NSA, for example, has been using Google cookies, known as PREF-ID cookies, to track individuals, according to internal NSA presentation slides provided by Snowden to the *Washington Post.* Among the most omnipresent and omniscient of tracking cookies—bits of unique text stored by users' web browsers—PREF-ID cookies track users' cross-site searches, primarily for the purpose of generating targeted advertising, at least according to Google. "The NSA is using these cookies to track people, because they're far better than anything the NSA could design on its own," according to Aleecia M. McDonald, director of privacy at Stanford's Center for Internet and Society.

The president's blurring of the distinction between corporate and government tracking is a denial of the unique power of the state and the need for nongovernmental sources of power as the ultimate barrier to totalitarianism. The concept of a marketplace of ideas, as with any celebration of the free market, is based on the need for independent competitors, be they traditional newspaper publishers or Internet entrepreneurs. It is this need for a multiplicity of offerings that can withstand the controlling power of the state. For Podesta—and more important, the president—not to understand the fundamental distinction between private corporations mining our data and that activity pursued by the intelligence apparatus of government is actually quite bizarre, particularly given this particular president's background in constitutional law.

If the Podesta study had instead been a sincere effort to protect the privacy rights of consumers in the marketplace from fraudulent practices, it would have been thoroughly admirable, even though quite beside the point of international concern over the Obama administration's use of that same data.

The data collected by private companies, as recounted in the next chapter, is alarmingly intrusive and pervasive. Because it is based on the gullible cooperation of individuals deluded into thinking this data will not be shared with governments, the data mining by for-profit corporations provides governments everywhere with a frightening mechanism of totalitarian control.

three

Mad Men Wired

S TANDING IN LINE AT FOUR BARREL COFFEE IN THE San Francisco Mission District, a working-class Latino neighborhood turned techie hub, it's nearly impossible not to catch rumblings of the industry at work. Wedged between the pour-over bar where a mustachioed barista steadily, but with great flourish, pours thin streams of water over a neat row of elevated cones, and a group of young men—many with their company affiliations emblazoned on their chests or bags—one hears breathless chatter about the next "future-defining product." Words like *revolutionary* and *disruptive* come up frequently.

The denizens of places like these don't seem to see the irony of their posturing. They may indeed be making tools and information more widely accessible—comparable to how industrialization eroded the "idiocy of rural life," according to Karl Marx in *The Communist Manifesto*—but their tech also accelerates the dislocation and exploitation of the people whom they are supposed to be liberating. After all, the business model that has driven the enormous profitability of Internet companies requires the ruthless exploitation of the aspirations, fantasies, relationships, and other personal information that constitute what we used to think of as the sacred territory of human privacy.

Don't confuse the thing being sold with the thing itself, an advertising guru once told me. Whereas what's being sold on the Internet is an illusion of instant knowledge and informed choice that draws you in, the thing itself is your data to be mined by those who want to sell you stuff you most likely didn't even know you wanted. It's all about dressing up advertising in a technology vastly different than the pre-Internet world, its purpose so thoroughly veiled as to make the "Mad Men" ad men of the 1960s seem like honest brokers in comparison.

Yesterday's highly compensated consultants who devised methods for the psychological manipulation of the masses would have had nothing on today's mostly unknown data brokers, whose ability to spy on us is comparable to that of large government intelligence agencies. Acxiom, the second-largest company involved in what is known as "database marketing," has monitored the records of hundreds of millions of Americans obtained through 1.1 billion browser cookies, 200 million mobile profiles, and an average of 1,500 pieces of data per consumer, according to Acxiom's first-quarter 2014 report. In that report, ambitious CEO Scott Howe noted, "Our digital reach will soon approach nearly every Internet user in the US."[1]

Toward that goal, Acxiom paid $310 million in cash in May 2014 for LiveRamp, a San Francisco–based company that enables marketers to use consumers' offline purchase and other transaction data to better target online ads to those consumers. According to the statement announcing the acquisition, Acxiom is in line "to reach more than 99 percent of the adult U.S. population . . . across all channels and devices."[2]

A brief explanation may be helpful here. To understand the scope of access to personal information under discussion, consider that offline data includes information from real estate and motor vehicle records, information from warranty cards filled out by consumers, homeownership and property values, marital status, annual income and education levels, travel records, ages of children in the home, and itemized store purchases made when a consumer swipes a loyalty discount card. In the latter case, a store can sell information regarding one's pharmaceutical purchases to a data broker that will then provide this information to a health insurance company, for example.

Government agencies participate in the data trade, too. In most states, the Department of Motor Vehicles can—and does—legally sell driver data, including driver names, addresses, car models, vehicle identification numbers, and license plate numbers. The relationship is symbiotic: government agencies like the DMV sell offline data to data brokers, and they often obtain online data from those same companies.

The Transportation Security Agency (TSA), for example, purchases data from data brokers to prescreen air travelers. Edward Hasbrouck, a consultant to the Identity Project, a nonprofit initiative that opposes identity-based domestic security programs, told the *New York Times* in October 2013 that "the best way to look at it is as a pre-crime assessment every time you fly. The default will be the highest, most intrusive level of search, and anything less will be conditioned on providing some additional information in some fashion."[3]

Stanford's Aleecia M. McDonald says that government agencies, as consumers of data broker- and corporate-gathered data, have little vested interest in regulation. "It's not just the NSA watching this go by. Governments are interested in things like tax fraud, so the IRS is interested in Facebook. Does it look like you're living the lifestyle you told the IRS? So, there are applications for this data that are not necessarily what they think, when they post, 'Yay! I just came back from a vacation in Jamaica!,'" she warned in an interview.[4]

The combination of offline data with readily available personal online data such as information from dating sites—including sexual habits, drug use, political affiliation—and a dizzying amount of other data explains how Acxiom can develop 1,500 data points on an individual. Your personal information is valuable fodder for intelligence agencies and money in the bank for such data brokers. It is also the bread and butter of almost every company that, to the average user, appears to trade in apps and email services.

ᶺᵛ ᶺᵛ ᶺᵛ

MINING DATA IS THE WEAPON OF CHOICE FOR THE MAD Men of our day because of its rapier-like accuracy in striking at the heart of our desires. Appropriately enough, *data mining* was originally statisticians' pejorative jargon describing the overuse of data to draw invalid inferences. The current, most commonly accepted definition of the term is the practice of automatically searching large stores of data to uncover patterns that cannot be discovered through simple analysis.

All previous means of advertising were crippled by the inaccuracy of blunderbuss ads incapable of the precise targeting that is the source of the corporate Internet's wild expansion. Nothing will

be allowed to blunt that accuracy and certainly not any si
shield of individual privacy.

That was the salient point of a different White House study
issued the same day as the Podesta report on big data. Described
as a technical assessment and produced by the President's Council of Advisers on Science and Technology (PCAST), it made
clear that controlling the profit-driven exploitation of consumer
data was not the purpose of the study. The working group that
prepared it included the ubiquitous Eric Schmidt, Google's executive chairman, and other tech industry honchos, and the focus
was one of protecting data mining rather than hindering it.

Not surprisingly, the report concluded with a solution that a
Google exec like Schmidt could easily accept. It suggested no se
rious restraints on companies' collection of private data by means
that often rely on subterfuge but, rather, focused on ways to
make the companies more responsible in how they use the data.
The assumption of the report was a convenient one for those in
terested in exploiting private data, for it assumes that consumers
have neither the expertise nor the inclination to monitor the use
of their personal information.[5]

This assumption—that consumers are relatively powerless in
understanding, let alone controlling, what data about them is collected or how it is used—is manifested by the de rigueur "agree"
button at the bottom of long terms-of-service agreements, clicked
by consumers eager to get on with their purchase or other service
and unwilling or unable to digest the dense, legalistic fine print.

One solution advocated by consumer privacy groups, including the Electronic Privacy Information Center and the Center for
Digital Democracy, would be to simplify the agreement language
to clearly ban resale of data to third-party brokers and advertisers,
unless a new agreement were required each time the data is used in

such a way.[6] That is the essence of "opt-in," putting the power in the hands of the consumer to give explicit permission for each new effort to exploit personal data, as opposed to "opt-out," which puts the burden on the consumer to learn how the data is being used and then to register an objection.

But the former arrangement will not happen anytime soon, if ever, because an opt-in requirement would seriously curtail the profitability of Internet business, which is built on the notion of using the provision of services such as email, buying guides, and even news to secure a maximum amount of personal data. No other source of comparable profit has been found on the Web, especially for the social networks and search engines that mostly offer their core software and service for free.

This is the quandary for even the best intentioned of those operating on the Internet, be it a charitable operation or a major news publication like the *New York Times,* which, as acclaimed technologist Jaron Lanier notes, "invokes a competitive swarm of more than a dozen tracking services."[7]

Digital-content sites like that of the *Times* are based on a complex ecosystem of data gathering and analysis. When any reader initially visits nytimes.com, the site sets what are known as first-party cookies. These bits of unique text allow the domain visited to identify you, and to track your activity on the site—permitting, for example, the paper to determine which articles are the most popular with which readers.

When you conduct a search of the site, information about that query is sent over to Google, which operates the search box at the top of the screen. After scrolling down the page, you might choose to play a video that appears in the middle of the home-page. That video, hosted by YouTube, a Google-owned company, sets cookies on your browser that send your search and viewing history to its parent company, which then stores it indefinitely and combines it with your other data, to compile a more complete picture of you.

Under that video and linked to each item of content on the site are social "widgets," the Facebook "Like" button and the Google+ button invariably among them. You may elect not to use those tools to share any *Times* item with your social media network. No matter; so long as you've used the widget hosts' services, these hosts will collect your data anyway and correlate it with the data they've gathered from your visits to other sites featuring widgets, which may range from shopping to porn sites. Facebook collected data from surfers who had never visited the social networking site (but had visited a page with a Facebook widget) until it discontinued the practice in 2011, under public pressure.

In addition, there is the plethora of advertisements that dot the edges of the site. The instant that you visit a page, advertisers bid in a real-time auction for the chance to appear on your screen. The ads employ a number of tracking mechanisms, many of which are difficult to block or delete. Those mechanisms, including third-party cookies—a unique string of characters used to identify users (sort of like a social security number) and set by a party that is not the Web domain visited—are used to track your online activities when you leave the first-party site.

Cookies may or may not fall out of use, but they will most definitely be supplemented with more advanced tracking mechanisms. As noted in the PCAST report, "most technologists believe that applications will move away from cookies, that cookies are too simple an idea, and that there are better analytics coming and better approaches being invented. The economic incentives for consumer tracking will remain, however, and big data will allow for more precise responses."[8] Indeed, three months after the publication of the report, technology writer Julia Angwin reported on a new, more invasive tracking tool billed as "a cookie alternative," called canvas fingerprinting.

The technology, first documented in July 2014 by researchers at Princeton University and KU Leuven University in Belgium, works, she explained in a *ProPublica* piece, "by instructing the visitor's Web browser to draw a hidden image. Because each computer draws the image slightly differently, the images can be used to assign each user's device a number that uniquely identifies it. . . . Device fingerprints rely on the fact that every computer is slightly different: Each contains different fonts, different software, different clock settings and other distinctive features. Computers automatically broadcast some of their attributes when they connect to another computer over the Internet."[9] These differences allow online advertisers to identify users more effectively than ever before. Aleecia M. McDonald, in an email, explained that "[as] users become more savvy and block or delete cookies, or their software tools do so for them, advertisers cannot reach users as well over years at a time. That's the reason to move on to new approaches for those users who are not being well tracked by cookies. This has been likened to an arms race, or to the arcade game whack-a-mole. Every time people try to protect their privacy, advertisers respond with a new way to get around the protections, all the while claiming users choose to be tracked."[10]

The industry leaders who wrote the PCAST report called this sort of rank exploitation of the naiveté of the unsuspecting customer a "market failure." At the same time, they produced a cop-out that, at first blush, seemed morally appealing until one realized that it simply disenfranchised the consumer. "The primary burden" of privacy protection, the PCAST report concludes, "must fall on the commercial user of big data and not on the consumer." This is an all-too-convenient way of saying the consumers will have no say over how their data is used.

This course of action—capitalizing on user ignorance—is troubling even to some of those who would benefit from it, but there are few alternatives. McDonald, who during the course of an interview in her Stanford office drew a chart resembling a tangle of spider webs—meant to illustrate the average news sites' data-sharing practices—said that sites like the *New York Times*'s are too entrenched to adopt alternatives, which are few in number anyway. As director of Cookie Clearinghouse, a Mozilla/Stanford project that provides online privacy protection to users, and former co-chair of The World Wide Web Consortium's effort to create an industry-wide standard for "Do Not Track" (a way for users to signal a preference for privacy, much like putting a "Do Not Disturb" sign on a hotel doorknob), McDonald has explored this topic extensively.

"Newspapers in particular have the following problem: before, there was scarcity for advertising. If I want to advertise the opera, . . . there are very few places, if we're in the print world, where I can advertise that. If it's online and I'm advertising to a particular individual, [the ad] can be anywhere. It can be in the archives from fifteen years ago for a particular article that I happen to be reading. There's no longer a scarcity, so that means that the price drops," she continued. "So, advertising online in comparison to advertising offline, even if you have more users, it's not going to [financially] support the same level of content."

A minority of computer scientists and privacy experts argue that online advertising doesn't necessarily have to be based on user tracking. The corporate Internet has been built with tracking at the center of its business model, but the model, some argue, can be reconstructed. Privacy experts like Ed Felton, professor of Computer Science and Public Affairs at Princeton, and Jonathan Mayer—a brilliant provocateur in his early twenties who has made a career of embarrassing tech companies and the NSA alike by exposing their lies through empirical research—argue that user privacy and company profits can be protected by targeting advertisements, rather than users.

The primary reason advertisers set cookies and other mechanisms to track users is to learn how many times a given user saw a particular ad, as well as to understand if it correlates to his or her interests, so the ads can be better targeted and monetized. Alternatively, by tracking advertisements, so that a unique identifier is stored in the ad rather than on a user's hard drive, third parties can still ascertain the unique relationship between user and ad.

Those cookies attached to the ads would not only be indicative of user interest—for instance, a person who sees many sports ads attached to sports stories would be a prospective buyer of football gear—but also would record the number of times the user has seen any given advertisement. McDonald likens the practice to putting the barcode on the ad instead of the user's forehead. This model would give the user significantly greater control over his or her personal data.

Los Angeles Times business consumer columnist David Lazarus gives two thumbs up to the Europeans on this matter of who owns one's data. "Europeans enjoy far more robust privacy protections than Americans and have long complained that their data are unfairly exploited by U.S. companies," he wrote on May 5, 2014. "The Europeans have it right. . . . 'Under EU law, personal data can only be gathered legally under strict conditions, for a legitimate purpose,' declares the website of the European Commission. 'Furthermore, persons or organizations which collect and manage your personal information must protect it from misuse and must respect certain rights of the data owners which are guaranteed by EU law.'"[11]

In that same month, the European Union's top court ruled in favor of a Spanish lawyer, Costeja González, who sued Google to remove from a search of his name an item from 1998 stating his home was being repossessed to pay debts. The court ruled Google was infringing on his privacy by making that information public on its site. This "right to be forgotten" ruling was hailed by some— and criticized by others as leading to censorship of the Internet.

One prominent critic was Google's Eric Schmidt, who spoke out against the decision at the company's shareholders meeting on May 14, 2014: "A simple way of understanding what happened here is that you have a collision between a right to be forgotten and a right to know. From Google's perspective that's a balance. Google believes, having looked at the decision which is binding, that the balance that was struck was wrong."[12]

Google's position on the issue is of little wonder. What the Podesta report got right is that Internet companies are engaged in nefarious activities that undermine the very concept of privacy. They have done it so effectively that the NSA and other government agencies could easily tap into their treasure trove of data in building the apparatus of the most far-reaching and intrusive surveillance state the world has ever known.

However—and this is the nub of the matter—while the government, and indeed any government, can penetrate those private data banks, the companies cannot desist from data collection without destroying their basic profit model. The dirty secret of Internet business is that it is privacy and not just advertising that is being sold.

✧ ✧ ✧

THE MAIN DRIVER OF PROFIT ON THE INTERNET IS NEITHER subscription income nor general space ads that have served to produce revenue in traditional print publications. Nor is it the general appeal to different demographics based on Nielsen or other crude audience surveys that bring in television ad dollars. What is truly revolutionary about the Internet is both the completeness of the profiles of the individual customers being delivered to advertisers and, most importantly, the ability to determine via click-through whether contact with a customer results in an actual sale. That is an accountability factor never before available to either the sponsors who paid for print ads or the salespeople representing traditional publishers and electronic news outlets.

Even more significant is that the contact with the customer is not passive, as when, for instance, a viewer or reader of so-called old media saw an ad for a new car and the retailer could only speculate as to whether an increase in auto sales was a result of the ad. Now, the contact is proactive on a level never before imagined for determining precisely which aspects of the ad—which words and images— moved the viewer to become a customer. In turn, those attributes of the sale can be heightened to make them even more effective. Indeed, the unique value of Internet data mining is this ability to fine-tune outreach and manipulation of individual desire based on the most intimate mapping of personal taste, fears, and aspirations.

This was a point driven home, at the very time the NSA scandal was roiling our consideration of privacy, when Facebook spent upward of $19 billion to purchase WhatsApp, a messaging app that had yet to demonstrate profitability despite its 450 million active users.[13] Particularly perplexing was the fact that WhatsApp customers paid a minuscule amount for the service (one dollar a year) after a long grace period, and the founders of the company had pointedly shunned advertising as a distraction to their customers' messaging experience.

Facebook CEO Mark Zuckerberg shrugged off that inconvenience and indicated that introducing advertising revenue would be a slow and not necessarily important part of profiting from this enormous investment.

Suddenly the cat was out of the bag: If ad revenue was not the profit inducement, what was?

The answer was the data itself, with which application-owning companies barter. Facebook—along with Google and many others—races to accumulate these applications, which are often offered to users for free, in order to expand their already vast troves of data.

But all of those bits of information that WhatsApp customers had turned over to the company had been surrendered under the formal assurance that advertising was not part of the deal. Facebook was reminded of that inconvenient commitment by the US Federal Trade Commission (FTC) in an agency advisory warning on mining the considerable WhatsApp store of consumer data in ways that violated the acquired company's compact with its users: "WhatsApp has made a number of promises about the limited nature of the data it collects, maintains, and shares with third parties," notes the FTC letter, which was addressed to both Facebook's chief privacy officer and WhatsApp's general counsel, "promises that exceed the protections currently promised to Facebook users. We want to make clear that, regardless of the acquisition, WhatsApp must continue to honor those promises to consumers."[14]

Herein lies the essential contradiction of Internet commerce. As is often the case, the self-imposed restrictions on sharing this data by WhatsApp had helped it become wildly popular, but they also help explain the company's meager revenue flow. Shunning advertising that is the basis of Facebook's revenue, WhatsApp had relied on a $1-a-year subscription base, which would take four decades of collections from its 450 million active users to equal the roughly $21.8 billion Facebook paid for the company ($4.49 billion in cash, the rest in Facebook stock).[15]

If advertising revenue based on the exploitation of personal data supplied by customers is the goal, then Facebook would be required, according to the FTC advisory, to fully inform the app's customers of the intended use of their data and obtain a specific opt-in authorization from each one of them. Otherwise, the commission would pursue one of the many avenues of recourse available to it, such as charging the company a heavy civil penalty fine or shutting down the operation.

Those customers who chose to opt-in would be giving their consent for WhatsApp to renege on its promise published before the acquisition to "not collect names, emails, addresses or other contact information from its users' mobile address book or contact lists other than mobile phone numbers."[16] The FTC reminded Facebook that it would also have to honor WhatsApp's promise that "[w]e do not collect location data" and that "[t]he contents of messages that have been delivered by WhatsApp services are not copied, kept or archived by WhatsApp."[17]

The words of warning from the FTC are quite unambiguous, but clearly Zuckerberg made the assumption that there would be a workaround to justify the acquisition cost. Either customers would opt-in for the mining of their data in order to continue using a low-cost service or the data could be exploited in less direct ways in marketing products on another Facebook-owned platform. But without data mining, there was no logical purpose in acquiring WhatsApp.

Facebook has been brilliantly successful in doing this sort of cross-fertilization, particularly across the three widely popular smartphone apps it now owns along with WhatsApp—namely,

Instagram, Facebook Messenger, and the parent Facebook. "Our vision for Facebook is to create a set of products that help you share any kind of content you want within the audience you want" is the way Zuckerberg put it in a call with analysts.[18] But this content sharing also allows for using data collected on one of those sites to more effectively run ads on the others.

Whether the purchase of WhatsApp turns out to be a wise move is less important than the forces that drove the move: ever-larger databases as the key to increasingly effective advertising and hence larger profit. The point is that data mining, inherently at the expense of privacy, is not some addendum to Internet business but rather its very lifeblood.

A judgment on Facebook's deal making was rendered by *Advertising Age,* the venerable chronicler of the advertising industry in an April 23, 2014 article. Under the headline "Facebook Ad Juggernaut Rolls on Amid Mega-Deals for WhatsApp, Oculus VR," the magazine reported: "Amid a big quarter of deals and potential distraction, Facebook is showing that its core business—advertising—is still very much on track. The social network's blockbuster acquisitions of WhatsApp for $19 billion and Oculus VR for $2 billion in February and March, taken together with its purchase of Instagram two years ago, make it evident that Facebook wants to be the Procter & Gamble of social."[19]

Of course, that is not the way Zuckerberg puts it, since a comparison with a marketing conglomerate that hustles soap sales would be unflattering to customers in the self-consciously hip world of the tech industry. But the analogy is accurate for Facebook as well as for Google and other giants of the Internet that have prospered by bringing masses of people together in artificial communities of common interest for one, and only one, serious purpose: to sell them stuff. As it was for radio, television, and, largely, print media before it, the advertisers, not the consumers, are regarded as the true customers.

ᴧᵛ ᴧᵛ ᴧᵛ

IN THIS MOST MODERN OF THE ADVERTISING-FINANCED platforms, the Internet is only the latest mass media incarnation to find "news" to be a lucrative platform for advertising. Evolving from an obligatory fifteen minutes to fulfill station-licensing requirements, television news on the local level soon became a major driver of revenue, especially during election cycles. As *Advertising Age* reported, "Facebook is showing fewer ads but making a lot more money from the ones it places in news feeds."[20] One reason is that the data-mining targeting of ads is easily directed to news content based on user profiles.

The fact that the ads pop up with all of the innocence of chance—as if by serendipity just the right ad encounters the perfect reader at the intersection of their mutual interest—can be compelling and effective in a way that pre-Internet advertising could only dream about. By comparison to the old-school models, Internet advertising of the sort Facebook and Google have mastered is more akin to a heat-seeking missile, with the targeting accuracy provided by that vast trove of mined data, than to the random targeting of old.

The world of primitive shotgun advertising is one to which the modern Internet billionaires never want to return. Their anger with the NSA is not that the government's tapping into their carefully curated profile databases was a violation of civil rights but, rather, that by getting caught they had frightened the customer base. In other words, the Snowden scandal was endangering the Golden Goose.

Before the Internet, if the government wanted to spy on the activities of its citizens, it would need to dispatch a police agent out to follow someone's movements, tap his phone lines after obtaining a warrant, intercept and read his mail, or eavesdrop on his conversations in a café. It was a cumbersome and costly activity, fairly easily noticed by the targets—who would then take evasive action to divert their pursuers. But that expensive cop has been replaced by cheap algorithms that can sift through data culled from commercial records of consumer transactions collected in the normal course of doing business.

Because this automated monitoring combines thousands of data points, from your GPS travels to the books you buy to the friends you text, it is more intrusive then the gumshoe surveillance of old. Highly effective and thorough tracking has been rendered invisible, and it will be made ever more so because it is the heart of the commercial enterprise.

The original intent of the proposed "Do Not Track Me" law, introduced by Representative Jackie Speier (D-CA) in the House in 2011, was to create an accessible way to block Internet detectives from following you. According to a 2012 Pew Internet & American Life survey, 68 percent of Internet users say they are "not okay with targeted advertising" because they "do not like having [their] online behavior tracked and analyzed."[21] But lobbying by Internet companies got the new law watered down beyond any semblance of effective privacy protection.

To be effective as a matter of law, when an individual clicks a command stating "Do Not Track," it should mean just that. But instead, the measure was rewritten to make compliance with the customer's request a matter of the company's discretion and not that of the user. The company would stop showing you personalized ads, but that was misleading, for it still had the right and, obviously, the means to keep tracking your personal information.

The bill actually made the whole process even more deceptive, because at least those personalized ads were a clear indicator that one's information was being mined. And, most importantly, for a government spy agency like the NSA, which can gain access to that data, this is a difference without distinction: they still get the information about your actions.

Quite telling of the attitude of some corporate giants was their negative reaction to Microsoft's decision to make the "Do Not Track" option the default setting in its Internet Explorer 10 browser. Strong opposition came from IBM, Intel, Dell, Visa, Verizon, Yahoo, and Wal-Mart. This was really just an inconvenience to those companies, since, even if a customer stuck with the default, the companies could, unbeknownst to users, still track their activities.

Yahoo, a partner of Microsoft and a self-proclaimed privacy proponent, stated soon after IE 10 was released that it would ignore the "Do Not Track" request, arguing on its policy blog: "Recently, Microsoft unilaterally decided to turn on DNT in Internet Explorer 10 by default, rather than at users' direction. . . . In our view this degrades the experience for the majority of users and makes it hard to deliver on our value proposition to them."[22]

This nonsense was a cover for Yahoo's argument that the real users of its services are not the people using its search tool or home page but, rather, the advertisers selling to them. Microsoft undertook the policy shift only because its own marketing surveys showed that 75 percent of the people using its browser in the United States and Europe wanted the "Do Not Track" set on default.

To understand just how dependent the commerce that sustains the Internet is on data mining, you need only look at the revenue stats. Then consider just how threatening was the possibility that the concern for privacy, stoked by revelations of government surveillance, would spill over into a more critical examination of corporate data-mining practices.

That is exactly the specter raised when the European Court of Justice, the European Union's highest court, slapped Google with a ruling that required the removal of personal data if an individual finds it objectionable. While the decision raised a host of questions about its feasibility and potential effects on free speech, what was most alarming to Google and others who traffic in personal data was the affirmation by the European Court that the misuse of personal data violates a fundamental human right.

In the case of Google, the company could not hide behind the defense that it was merely pointing its search engine at information previously published by third parties. Rather, the company had a responsibility not to invade the privacy of individuals by republishing erroneous or objectionable material.

There are obvious problems with the European Court's decision to grant individuals the "right to be forgotten." As a critical article in the *New York Times* put it, the ruling "rejected long-established notions about the free flow of information on the Internet." The *Times* quoted Harvard computer science professor Jonathan Zittrain as saying "I think it's a bad solution to a very real problem, which is that everything is now on our permanent records."[23]

What if that "everything" includes material that is untrue, or information that was presumed to be private? In the case of the former, libel laws in countries such as the United States would offer a means of clearing the record. For the latter, if the private information were obtained through electronic surveillance, as in a secret recording of a conversation, it would also represent an illegal infringement on one's rights.

In a fundamental shift, however, the Internet has steadily reduced the role of the publisher, who must operate under the constraints of legal liability, and created new beasts—content aggregators, social networks, forums, and chat rooms—that operate virtually without restraint or, for the most part, human intervention. This means that it is harder to find anybody to hold accountable. In its decision, the European Court, perhaps with wishful thinking, established Google as more of a traditional publisher, with concurrent obligations, than as a neutral transmission entity. "The court said search engines were not simply dumb pipes, but played an active role as data 'controllers,' and must be held accountable for the links they provide," the *Times* editorial warned, adding that the ruling could compel search engines to remove links to pages even when the information on those pages was lawful.[24]

That is a valid concern, smacking of censorship, although mitigated by the fact that the court did not assert any right to require a withdrawal of the original story were its publisher to post it online. What the court was challenging, perhaps clumsily, was Google's unchecked power in a market like Germany, where Google controls 90 percent of the search market, or France, where it controls 96 percent, to draw the defining portrait of an individual.

"In some ways," the *Times* reported, "the court is trying to erase the last twenty-five years, when people learned to check out online every potential suitor, partner or friend. Under the court's ruling, information would still exist on websites, court documents and online archives of newspapers, but people would not necessarily know it was there."[25]

While my own view is supportive of the *Times*'s editorial position, and I do believe that the truth of a journalistic assertion should be the standard of accountability, just as in US libel law, the court's decision is significant in calling attention to the imbalance of power between the individual and the Internet giants when it comes to defining reality. What recourse should the individual have when, as in the case of Costeja González, he believes his online profile, as defined by the Google search-engine algorithms, distorts the very essence of his existence by what it includes and excludes?

In an interview at his UC Berkeley office, Paul Schwartz, law professor and co-director of the Berkeley Center for Law and Technology, cited another instance when the European Court moved to correct this power imbalance.[26]

"There's a case law about the Google autocomplete function, involving the ex-wife of the former president of Germany, Vulff— V-u-l-f-f," he said as he reached for a document buried somewhere in the tall stacks of legal literature surrounding his desk. "Her name is Bettina, and when you typed in Bettina Vulff in Germany, it came up as the autocomplete function—you'd type 'Bettina V-u-l' and then it would finish 'Vulff' and say 'prostitute' in German. . . . Or it would say 'red-light milieu' . . . why? Because there are all these rumors that before she married the then-president of Germany she'd been a prostitute or an escort person in the red-light district."

Google denied responsibility for this unfortunate autocomplete suggestion, maintaining that it does not author items of information, or stories—in this case, about Bettina Vulff and her alleged past—but just finds and links them. "Google's argument was that they're just the mirror of a social discussion and not the authors," Schwartz explained. "They say they're pointing to the fact that there are blogs and articles that talk about whether or not she's a prostitute. Their algorithms pick up on that, they say. And German courts don't necessarily accept that, and they say 'No, there is this difference in degree if you reveal this information, if you organize it and package it and make it more accessible, the link is something else.' And so European courts are not necessarily always sympathetic to the kind of more American view, which is, the information's out there, and if you organize it you're just a machine."

Both of these decisions hinge on a European conception of privacy, fundamentally different from the American one. "In Europe, privacy very much rests on this notion of human dignity, and so we have this opinion about the right to be forgotten from the European Court of Human Rights. In the European Charter we have a right to human dignity, and privacy is related to that," said Schwartz in the interview. He continued:

> In the US, it's harder, because we really don't know—privacy is kind of everything. It can be a right to contraceptive freedom; it can be a right to hand out leaflets without announcing who you are . . . that makes it harder for us to discuss what it is . . . [whereas] in Europe . . . they know what they're talking about. . . . [T]hey go back to the central concept of dignity and human personality in a kind of Kantian sense, that we all have this innate personality, and the law is there to protect it and let it develop. If you discuss that with American judges, it can seem very nebulous. Because then what I think we do very intuitively get, and like, is free speech.

All of this prompts the question of whether there is an inalienable right to privacy and what its connection is to the proper functioning of a democratic society. To what extent does privacy matter? A great deal, if by privacy we mean the right to be unobserved by others, including, most importantly, the state.

As the next chapter examines, the basic assumption of our system of governance is that societal power arises from the power of the individual, and the freedom of the individual to experiment with ideas and associations within a protected zone is, for that reason, guaranteed by the Constitution.

four

Privacy Is Freedom

WHAT IS THE ROLE OF PRIVACY IN THE TWENTY-first century? To the leaders of Internet commerce, whose basic business model involves exploiting the minutiae of their customers' lives, the very idea of privacy has been treated as, at best, an anachronism of the predigital age. Meanwhile, those desiring to keep their personal data from prying eyes claim it as an unconditional constitutional right.

After making a pro-privacy pretense, in his company's early years, Facebook founder Mark Zuckerberg began steadily advancing the argument that privacy is a luxury being willingly tossed aside by customers preferring convenience. "People have really gotten comfortable not only sharing more information and different kinds, but more openly and with more people," he said while accepting a Crunchie award in San Francisco in January 2010. "That social

norm is just something that has evolved over time. We view it as
our role in the system to constantly be innovating and be updating
what our system is to reflect what the current social norms are."[1]

Instead of viewing the protection of privacy as a business's obligation to his customer base, Zuckerberg suggested that the very concept of personal privacy could be gradually disappearing. "[F]our
years ago, when Facebook was getting started, most people didn't
want to put up any information about themselves on the Internet,"
he told an interviewer at the Web 2.0 Summit in 2008.[2]

> Right? So, we got people through this really big hurdle of wanting
> to put up their full name, or real picture, mobile phone number. . . .
> I would expect that, you know, next year, people will share twice
> as much information as they are this year. And then, the year af-
> ter that, they'll share twice as much information as they are next
> year . . . as long as the stream of information is just constantly
> increasing, and we're doing our job, and . . . our role, and kind of
> like pushing that forward, then I think that, you know . . . that's
> just been the best strategy for us.[3]

In other words, let's keep pushing customers to give up a little
more privacy every day until they have none left. This has, of
course, been the norm in an industry based on customers clicking
an "agree" button to approve privacy terms and conditions contracts designed to be unreadable—and to go unread. (As Sun Microsystems chief executive Scott McNealy famously said way back
in 1999, "You have zero privacy anyway. Get over it.")[4]

Zuckerberg went further in his 2010 statement, chastising those
given to an older business model based on caution over privacy and
instead praising companies (like his) that could easily rise above
such obviously out-of date-concerns: "A lot of companies would

be trapped by the conventions and their legacies of what they've built, doing a privacy change. . . . But we view that as a really important thing, to always keep a beginner's mind and what would we do if we were starting the company now, and we decided that these would be the social norms now and we just went for it."

An even darker defense of the end-of-privacy doctrine had been offered a month earlier by Google's Eric Schmidt, who impugned the innocence of consumers who worry about snooping by Google and other companies. "If you have something that you don't want anyone to know, maybe you shouldn't be doing it in the first place," Schmidt stated in an interview for a December 2009 *CNBC Special*, "Inside the Mind of Google."[5]

The ability of the fast-growing Internet data-mining companies to trivialize privacy concerns succeeded because the target audience of younger consumers was either indifferent to invasions of their privacy or ignorant of the extent and depth of that data collection. It was remarkable that an American social culture that had for so long been moored to a notion of individual sovereignty predicated on the ability to develop one's identity, ideas, and mores in private, had, in a wink, become willing to surrender any such notion.

Americans had fought and died for the right to have privately developed papers, conversations, friendships, and diaries, especially in our homes. Yet here we were as a society voluntarily moving so much of that into digital spaces owned and managed by corporations we have no control over. This relinquishing of the most private information about one's essence and aspirations became the norm in a shockingly short period, examined only lightly and in passing. As we shared more and more with ever-widening social networks, it seemed okay as long as the companies securely stored this precious data, to be used only to enhance the consumer experience. We counted on the self-interest of the corporation not to harm us, not to bite the hand that feeds.

But the Snowden revelations changed all that by exposing how easily the government could access—and indeed was accessing—our personal info. That troubling confluence between the corporate world and the state caught the public's attention in a way that Internet companies feared might be game changing, threatening the culture of trust needed to continue gathering that data.

Also straining global confidence in Internet commerce was the shock of those outside the country who had bought into the myth that US-based multinationals were international in their obligations, but who now found them to be subservient to the whims of Washington.[6] That was a message that US companies, up against a saturated domestic market for their products, found particularly alarming, since they depend on global growth to please shareholders.

A suddenly anxious Zuckerberg felt compelled to communicate his concerns to the president as well as to the larger public. Ten months after the first Snowden revelations, Zuckerberg posted on Facebook the following cri de coeur to air his concerns over the enduring costs of the ongoing firestorm. It is long but worth reading as a coming-of-age manifesto from one of the Internet's *wunderkinder:*

As the world becomes more complex and governments everywhere struggle, trust in the Internet is more important today than ever.

The Internet is our shared space. It helps us connect. It spreads opportunity. It enables us to learn. It gives us a voice. It makes us stronger and safer together.

To keep the Internet strong, we need to keep it secure. That's why at Facebook we spend a lot of our energy making our services and the whole Internet safer and more secure. We encrypt communications, we use secure protocols for traffic, we encourage people to use multiple factors for authentication and we go out of our way to help fix issues we find in other people's services.

The Internet works because most people and companies do the same. We work together to create this secure environment and make our shared space even better for the world.

This is why I've been so confused and frustrated by the repeated reports of the behavior of the US government. When our engineers work tirelessly to improve security, we imagine we're protecting you against criminals, not our own government.[7]

He ended by stating that he had called Obama "to express my frustration over the damage the government is creating for all of our future," but there is no indication the president got the message.[8] Obama continued to let his national security adviser James Clapper lead him about by the nose while joining him in treating whistleblower Snowden, whose courage is the only reason we learned what was going on, as one of the nation's most dangerous fugitives. Obama's Justice Department had chosen to forget all about the Fourth Amendment that protects citizens against the unwarranted searches of both state and federal governments, as Zuckerberg's lawyers would soon point out in court filings.

Soon after Zuckerberg's post, his company was embroiled in a lawsuit with the district attorney of Manhattan, who had sought the private data of 381 of Facebook's customers. In this particular situation, Facebook took the high road in defending its customers' privacy, as the record of the company's court filings would indicate. But the disclosure of that exemplary role on the part of Facebook in June 2014 (discussed following) was drowned out by the clamor of stories about Facebook's own manipulation of its customers' data in ways that many thought shameful, if not criminal.

A thorough report by Robinson Meyer on June 28, 2014, in *The Atlantic* magazine revealed that Facebook permitted data scientists to manipulate the "news feed" of almost 700,000 of its users in a study to determine whether users' moods could be manipulated through "emotional contagion." As Meyer reported, "Some people were shown content with a preponderance of happy and positive words; some were shown content analyzed as sadder than average. And when the week was over, these manipulated users were more likely to post either especially positive or negative words themselves."[9]

The study in question, which took place the week of January 11, 2012, and was published in the June 17, 2014, issue of the prestigious *Proceedings of the National Academy of Sciences*, indeed showed that "emotions expressed by friends, via online social networks, influence our own moods, constituting, to our knowledge, the first experimental evidence for massive-scale contagion via social networks."[10]

The story in *The Atlantic* was shared by thousands of readers and elicited numerous angry comments. The *New York Times* story on the study captured the essence of the outrage in its opening sentence: "To Facebook, we are all lab rats."[11] More negative responses to Facebook poured in—proof, one could conclude, of the emotional contagion of anger and outrage.

In a post on Facebook on that same day in June, Adam D. I. Kramer, a Facebook data scientist, fell on his sword, conceding that he wrote and designed the experiment in addition to co-writing the study with Professor Jeffrey T. Hancock and then-doctoral student Jamie E. Guillory of Cornell University's departments of Communication and Information Science.

Kramer's claim for the study was that "we care about the emotional impact of Facebook and the people that use our product. We felt that it was important to investigate the common worry that seeing friends post positive content leads to people feeling negative or left out. At the same time, we were concerned that exposure to friends' negativity might lead people to avoid visiting Facebook. . . . And at the end of the day, the actual impact on people in the experiment was the minimal amount to statistically detect it. . . . [O]ur goal was never to upset anyone. . . . In hindsight, the research benefits of the paper may not have justified all of this anxiety."[12]

For its part, Cornell was prompted to issue a statement making clear that Hancock and Guillory merely analyzed the results of the research previously conducted by Facebook and did not have access to user data. "Their work was limited to initial discussions, analyzing the research results and working with colleagues from Facebook to prepare the peer-reviewed paper," said Cornell.[13]

But more disconcerting than the results of that study was the fact that Facebook had turned 689,003 of its 1.2 billion users into unsuspecting subjects in a deliberate attempt to manipulate their emotions. As *New York Times* tech writer Vindu Goel noted in his article, "The uproar highlights the immense control Facebook exerts over what its users see. When someone logs in, there are typically about 1,500 items the company could display in that person's news feed, but the service shows only about 300 of them."[14] That is, despite the company's endless turnout of tools that purportedly allow users to curate the content shown in news feeds, Facebook—not the user population—is the real author of our social media stories.

The totalitarian overtones of this thought-control experiment were more chilling after a year of discoveries of cooperation between the NSA and Internet companies like Facebook.

⁂

The news feed controversy exposed a Facebook reality its users might already have known if they followed the company's critics, or read its jargon-ridden 9,000-word terms-of-service agreement. But judging from the shocked reaction, few had thought analytically about the implications of Facebook's ordering of the data its users and advertisers generate. As Cornell communications scholar Tarleton Gillespie put it in the wake of the controversy, it left many users with "a deeper discomfort about an information environment where the content is ours but the selection is theirs."[15]

Gillespie spelled out the sea change in communications technology represented by social networks as a sharp break from previous models of the mass delivery of information. "On the one hand, there had been the safe and sound 'trusted interpersonal information conduits'—namely, the post office system and the trunk lines managed by telephone companies that were designed to be neutral carriers of information but not curators prioritizing the content via an algorithm of importance.[16] We expected them not to curate or even monitor that content," Gillespie wrote. "[I]n fact we made it illegal to do otherwise; we expected that our communication would be delivered, for a fee, and we understood the service as the commodity, not the information it conveyed."[17]

He continued to explain that the opposite was true for broadcast programming and the content of newspapers and magazines, which were explicitly curated offerings; we were consciously choosing—and often actually paying—to consume filtered presentations produced by professionals.

Social networks such as Facebook represent a confusion of the two, however, with users generally expecting the former and instead getting an automated version of the latter.[18] They are neither fish nor fowl, and while Facebook seems to be a neutral carrier of data, like the old post office system, it also dips into the "mail" and responds to its content by prioritizing future deliveries, attaching relevant advertising, and hiding what it considers junk.

The end result is that your information becomes the raw material for a new commodity the company manages for its own purposes—binding users ever more tightly to Facebook as their social home base on the Internet. But to monetize clicks, the company's research will most definitely also include exploiting purchasing tastes to benefit Facebook's true customers, the advertisers who want to sell you something. They are paying, after all; you are not.

Sheryl Sandberg, second in command at Facebook, admitted the news feed manipulations were an effort to improve commercial marketing (rather than a high-minded academic project). "This was part of ongoing research companies do to test different products, and that was what it was; it was poorly communicated," she said. "And for that communication we apologize. We never meant to upset you."[19]

But the message was clear that the heads of Facebook were embarrassed not by doing something creepy and manipulative but, rather, by having been caught. Of course, they never meant to upset Facebook users by making them feel they were part of some experiment in social control. Yet this was just business as usual, albeit not something on which they want the public to focus.

As Jaron Lanier warned in a *New York Times* op-ed published days after the release of the emotional-contagion study, "This is only one early publication about a whole new frontier in the manipulation of people, and Facebook shouldn't be singled out as a villain. . . . Now that we know that a social network proprietor can engineer emotions for the multitudes to a slight degree, we need to consider that further research on amplifying that capacity might take place. Stealth emotional manipulation could be channeled to sell things (you suddenly find that you feel better after buying from a particular store, for instance), but it might also be used to exert influence in a multitude of other ways. Research has also shown that voting behavior can be influenced by undetectable social networking maneuvering, for example."[20]

Undetectable, because the news feed feature of Facebook, notwithstanding the disclaimers of the wordy terms-of-service agreement, manages to convey a sense of automated neutrality, in much the same way Google and Yahoo do with their searches. There is a thumb on the scale that users are lulled into ignoring, "[a]nd Facebook is complicit in this confusion," said Cornell professor Gillespie, "as they often present themselves as a trusted information conduit, and have been oblique about the way they curate our content into their commodity."[21]

This presents a persistent contradiction for Facebook because its basic attraction is that it is simply a reliable communication tool for friends and family (admittedly an unrealistic expectation for a service that is provided free of charge), but the company's profit model requires it to find ever more ingenious ways to commodify a customer's curiosity or personal data.

Furthermore, the power of social networks to define reality makes them targets for governments that have their own stake in manipulating public opinion. (China, for example, has attempted to block the use of such networks inside its borders.) The ability to alter the thinking or emotions of large numbers of people would have obvious appeal to political demagogues, and some observers were quick to connect the Facebook experiment with the US Department of Defense's controversial Minerva Research Initiative.

Launched in December 2008 with $50 million, Minerva is a tool for the Pentagon to fund academic research by theoretically independent scholars on subjects it is interested in, such as China, terrorism, and political activism, "to improve DoD's basic understanding of the social, cultural, behavioral, and political forces that shape regions of the world of strategic importance to the US."[22]

Disturbingly, some of the research they commissioned seemed to be aimed at understanding how to control or prevent public dissent inside the United States through surveillance and manipulation of information flows, like those curated by social networks. When it turned out that one of those on the Minerva gravy train was the same Cornell prof who headed the analysis of the Facebook news feed study, warning flags were raised for civil libertarians.

While Cornell officials said that Jeffrey Hancock did not use his Pentagon funding specifically for the Facebook study, the "emotional contagion" survey was consistent with both his overall focus on "psychological and interpersonal dynamics of social media, deception, and language"[23] and the study the university spearheaded, which was managed by the Air Force and designed to develop an empirical model "of the dynamics of social movement mobilization and contagions."[24]

The Pentagon's project, slated to be funded through 2017, "aims to determine 'the critical mass (tipping point)' of social contagions by studying their 'digital traces' in the cases of 'the 2011 Egyptian revolution, the 2011 Russian Duma elections, the 2012 Nigerian fuel subsidy crisis and the 2013 Gazi Park protests in Turkey,'" reported global security scholar Dr. Nafeez Ahmed, writing in the *Guardian*.[25]

Hancock's work is a clear and ominous link between market manipulation of consumer taste, Facebook's bread-and-butter goal, and the potential ability to use those same tactics to engineer public consent for government policies. (The Air Force study focused on Twitter posts "to identify individuals mobilized in a social contagion and when they become mobilized.") Other Minerva-funded projects cover similar terrain; examples include a study awarded to the University of Washington to research the origination, characteristics, and likely consequences of political movements as well as a study titled "Who Does Not Become a Terrorist, and Why?" that, according to Ahmed, frighteningly conflated peaceful activists with "supporters of political violence."

Ahmed argues that NSA mass surveillance "is partially motivated to prepare for the destabilizing impact of coming environmental, energy and economic shocks." He finds support from other concerned academics, including James Petras, Bartle Professor of Sociology at New York's Binghamton University, who says that Minerva-funded social scientists linked to US counterinsurgency operations are involved in the "study of emotions in stoking or quelling ideologically driven movements," including how "to counteract grassroots movements."[26]

In the end, the motives of Internet companies engaged in the creative exploration of their customers' data, or those of the academics who facilitate this, may not matter very much if government agencies, in the United States or elsewhere, can simply seize that data and perform their own extensive exploration of the "contagions" involved, the better to cause or eliminate them.

In other words, the news feeds or timelines of social media can be surveilled to locate agitators and predict legal "rebellions," and, if the next logical step is taken, can be manipulated through deletion, addition, or changes in algorithms to block the spread of dissenting or "dangerous" ideas.

In June 2014, as Facebook was attempting to deal with the controversy over its own manipulation of news feeds, the company went into court to prevent the district attorney of Manhattan from taking similar liberties with the privacy of nearly four hundred site users who were unaware of the government's access to their data. Suddenly, Facebook, which had previously cooperated with various federal and state agencies, was on the warpath, ostensibly to protect the privacy of its clients in the post-Snowden era.

To read memorandums of law filed in support of Facebook's case against the attorney general's demand for data is to encounter a born-again belief in the intrinsic wisdom of the Fourth Amendment. "These warrants fail to include date restrictions or any other criteria to limit the voluminous data sought, nor do they provide for procedures to minimize the collection or retention of information that is unrelated to the investigation. The warrants' extraordinary reach and lack of particularity render them constitutionally defective under state and federal law and should be quashed," wrote Facebook's attorneys. "In the alternative, Facebook should be permitted to provide notice to the people whose accounts are subject to these warrants to afford an opportunity to object to the expansive scope."[27]

There is an inherent irony in this language made obvious when one considers that Facebook's own customers are never afforded an opportunity to know, let alone object to, the scope of the personal data that it has gathered on them. So, too, the fact that this vast trove of data the government is unreasonably demanding is already in the hands of Facebook, to be freely exploited for advertising sales and other sources of profit. But this irony disappears if one accepts Facebook's argument that the Fourth Amendment provides a restraint only against *government* searches and therefore becomes an issue only when its agents can invade their massive collections of data.

Crucially, Facebook invoked the Fourth Amendment's ban on warrantless searches, noting that the amendment was designed to prevent government and not corporate overreach. Clearly, if

Facebook had been transparent in collecting customer data, with individuals' explicit approval, then this would have been a matter of private consensual commerce that does not fall under the Constitution's protections.

But in fact it is a fit matter of government regulation of business behavior, as the Federal Trade Commission (FTC) pointed out in challenging Facebook's possible mining of the data acquired in the course of its purchase of WhatsApp.

WhatsApp customers had supplied their information on the basis of that company's privacy policy restricting such mining, meaning Facebook was possibly breaking fraud laws by violating that binding agreement. However, fraud is not a constitutional violation, and the WhatsApp customers could not claim to be suffering the loss of Fourth Amendment rights, since those apply only to intrusive or abusive government actions.

What the Fourth Amendment clearly does prohibit, as Facebook's lawyers pointed out quite strenuously in their briefs versus the New York district attorney, is warrantless general searches by the government, and that applies even if the route to that data is through the files maintained by a third party, which in this instance is Facebook.

In this particular case, the DA was on a fishing expedition to find evidence that people claiming medical disability were cheating, a search that should have required a specific warrant. Pointing out that they were appealing the warrant's demand that Facebook "collect and turn over virtually all communications, data, and information from 381 Facebook accounts," and that only the holders of 62 of those accounts were even charged with any crime, Facebook correctly argued that the prosecutor's overreach represented a clear violation of the Fourth Amendment protections to which Facebook's clients were entitled.

"The trial court's refusal to quash the bulk warrants was erroneous and should be reversed. The Fourth Amendment does not permit the Government to seize, examine, and keep indefinitely the private messages, photographs, videos, and other communications of nearly 400 people—the vast majority of whom will never know that the government has obtained and continues to possess their personal information," the brief stated. "Nor does the First Amendment permit the government to forbid Facebook from ever disclosing what it has been compelled to do—even after the government has concluded its investigation."[28]

That last objection, to a government agency being able to require that a private company not inform its customers of possible violations of their rights, is particularly crucial. By what perversion of the hallowed American concept of an informed citizenry ever vigilant to deprivations of their freedom could such a gag order not violate the meaning of the First Amendment?

Facebook was appealing to the New York State Supreme Court appellate division to overrule the decision of a lower trial court that held the gag order valid, but the same argument could be made against a similar order imposed on communications companies by the federal courts that prevented them from discussing NSA and other government-agency spying on citizens.

One key issue here is whether third parties like Facebook and Google have legal standing to protect their customers' constitutional rights. Facebook's lawyers argued that permitting the government to rummage through the data collected in Facebook accounts would be analogous to government agencies hiring a private contractor to conduct a broad warrantless search in someone's home, a clear violation of the Fourth Amendment: "The Government's bulk warrants, which demand 'all' communications and information in 24 broad categories from the 381 targeted accounts, are the digital equivalent of seizing everything in someone's home. Except here, it is not a single home but an entire neighborhood of nearly 400 homes. The vast scope of the government's search and seizure here would be unthinkable in the physical world."[29]

⁂ ⁂ ⁂

THIS EXTENSION OF THE CONSTITUTIONAL PROTECTION against unreasonable searches in the physical world to the digital world is, of course, the heart of the modern challenge to government surveillance overreach. Obviously, the founders did not have in mind a "digital home." However, in June 2014, the Supreme Court delivered a groundbreaking decision extending Fourth Amendment protection to the data on a mobile device found on or near an arrested person. This victory for civil libertarians clearly set a precedent for protecting other digital collections, including those housed on Facebook.

As Chief Justice John Roberts argued in *Riley v. California*, the information digitally housed on a mobile device—or, by extension, a Facebook page—is so vast that searching through it represents a warrantless search without probable cause that is banned by the Fourth Amendment. An individual therefore has a reasonable expectation that this material will be treated as private and searched only pursuant to a specific warrant alleging probable cause of a crime.

The lack of such specificity, obviously not present in the district attorney's broad scan of the entire data collection housed on almost 400 Facebook users' pages, denies the essence of the constitutional protections. As Justice Roberts wrote: "Modern cell phones are not just another technological convenience. . . . With all they contain and all they may reveal, they hold for many Americans 'the privacies of life.'"[30]

So, too, do Facebook pages represent revelations of the privacies of life. The Supreme Court marker on privacy established that the digital world, instead of reducing the constitutional protection of privacy to a quaint anachronism, has in fact rendered those protections far more compelling, due to the vast amounts of data in digital collections.

"Before cell phones," Roberts wrote, in an opinion with obvious ramifications for all other digital databases, "a search of a person was limited by physical realities and tended as a general matter to constitute only a narrow intrusion on privacy. . . . Today it is no exaggeration to say that many of the more than ninety percent of Americans who own a cell phone keep on their person a digital record of nearly every aspect of their lives—from the mundane to the intimate."[31]

This extension of the protections that the founders afforded to even the most meager of traditional homes—treating a hut as a castle in establishing privacy as a fundamental human right—to homes in the digital world is perhaps the most dramatic evidence that the Constitution is a living document, fully capable of being adapted to a vastly changed world. Not doing so, Roberts argued, "is like saying a ride on horseback is materially indistinguishable from a flight to the moon."

Instead of concluding that modern technology renders privacy demands untenable, Roberts argued that those protections had to be expanded to provide meaningful privacy protection in a technologically far more invasive era. "The sources of potential pertinent information are virtually unlimited," he wrote, noting that failing to restrict warrantless searches of the digital home "would in effect give 'police officers unbridled discretion to rummage at will among a person's private effects.'"

In their appeal, Facebook's attorneys demonstrated just how invasive that unbridled rummage could be. Even many of the

1.2 billion users of Facebook forget how much of themselves they are revealing:

> People use Facebook to share information about themselves, much of it personal. This information often includes:
> • The person's age, religion, city of birth, educational affiliations, employment, family members, children, grandchildren, partner, friends, places visited, favorite music, favorite movies, favorite television shows, favorite books, favorite quotes, things "Liked," events to attend, affiliated groups, fitness, sexual orientation, relationship status, political views;
> • The person's thoughts about: religion, sexual orientation, relationship status, political views, future aspirations, values, ethics, ideology, current events, fashion, friends, public figures, celebrity, lifestyle, celebrations, grief, frustrations, infidelity, social interactions, or intimate behavior;
> • The person's photographs and videos of: him- or herself, children/family, friends, third parties, ultrasounds, medical experiences, food, lifestyle, pets/animals, travel/vacations, celebrations, music, art, humor, entertainment;
> • The person's private hardships meant to be shared only with friends; and
> • The person's intimate diary entries, including reflections, criticisms, and stories about daily life.[32]

This is just the sort of personal information the Fourth Amendment was designed to protect against warrantless searches. But given Facebook's acknowledgment that it is in fact collecting and storing such information, one has to ask why? Why collect such detailed and intimate information if you have already learned that the federal government, as represented by the NSA and other agencies, can routinely tap into that information? What is the likelihood of governments abroad doing the same? If Facebook and other Internet companies cannot guarantee the security of the data they collect, or even, as this case demonstrates, alert their customers to the risks involved, why collect or store the data at all?

The answer becomes apparent in what we have learned of the basic business model that ensures the profitability of most Internet companies. The data is collected not because government agencies require it but, rather, because the companies themselves want to exploit it, for profit. Consider the ethical implications of doing just that under an overtly totalitarian government enabling a degree of surveillance of the individual of unprecedented proportions. Perhaps Facebook trusts the US government more, but isn't that a choice its customers should make about the use of their data? In any case, Facebook has already shown that it is in a position to manipulate the choices its customers make, and what assurance can the company provide that it is impervious to any government's use of that same set of manipulative tools?

While Facebook, Twitter, and other social media companies have been applauded for indirectly helping dissidents in countries like Egypt and Ukraine by providing a decentralized, free, "real-time," and difficult-to-disrupt alternative communication system, what assurance can they give that those activities have not been appropriated by the very governments the protesters sought to challenge?

The reality is that most of us spend our days freely surrendering personal data out of convenience, whether to enhance a shopping experience or to build a friendship, while in denial—or simply unaware—of the fact that at the same moment all of it is being made available to government officials whose motives are inscrutable and potentially repressive.

～～～

IN ORDER TO CONFORM TO THE FOURTH AMENDMENT'S restrictions on unreasonable searches, wiretapping phone conversations has long been carefully restricted by court rulings, whether conducted by private detectives or government agents. All of the world's democratic governments, even without the specific restraint of that amendment, manage to strictly regulate the physical taps placed on phone lines to listen in and record conversations.

In the predigital age, physical intrusion on phone lines was required to intercept calls, but, today, undetected copying of signals has made the process much easier. So much so that in 2007 Google, in the course of cruising neighborhoods with vehicles designed mainly to collect photographic images to complement Google Maps, also had the ability to pick up and record data from homes connected to Wi-Fi networks. Google's equipment was able to collect basic data from those network connections, "location-based" service IP addresses, and payload information including usernames, personal emails, passwords, and documents.

By May 2010, when confronted over this practice, Google admitted it had inadvertently collected six hundred gigabytes of such data in thirty different countries.[33] Several class action lawsuits were filed accusing Google of having violated the federal Wiretap Act. Google lost the case both in district and appellate courts, and in June 2014 the Supreme Court refused to overturn the lower-court decisions and allowed the case to proceed.

The Supreme Court decision, coming a week after its sweeping affirmation of privacy protection for mobile devices obtained by police during an arrest, was interpreted as a shift in direction by the high court toward a reaffirmation of the importance of privacy in the digital age. Its significance for Google was less about tapping into home networks with its Google mapping trucks, which the company had agreed to stop doing, and more about important projects the company was launching that had even clearer privacy issues. As the *New York Times* reported, the court's ruling "[undermined] the search company's efforts to put a troublesome episode to rest even as it plans to become more deeply embedded in consumers' lives."[34]

That last phrase is the rub. In an earlier time, the General Electric Company boasted that "progress is our most important product"; it can fairly be argued that a comparable slogan for Google today could replace *progress* with *intrusion*. Expansion plans at Google involve more effectively mining ever-larger collections of data. The *Times* report noted why the Supreme Court's increased attention to privacy came at an awkward moment for the company: "Google's annual developers conference last week showcased the company's wide-ranging agenda to expand its technology from desktop computers and mobile devices to the home, the body, and vehicles. Google's new devices will communicate and share data, requiring a great deal of trust by users that all this information will not be used in unauthorized or unexpected ways."[35]

This is a concern of consumers throughout the world, and it has been greatly enhanced in the aftermath of the Snowden revelations. Suddenly, the arrogant insistence of Google's Schmidt or Facebook's Zuckerberg about privacy being merely an anachronistic obsession of the technologically primitive, the perverted, or the outright criminal begins to ring hollow.

For much of human history, the line between the government and the private individual was quite clearly marked, whether under rule of the British Crown or in the new republic born in the rebellion of the colonies. Arguably, the clearest distinction between Anglo-Saxon legal experience and its alternatives resided in a profound respect for the innate rights of the individual against societal sources of power, be they derived from church or government.

The English common law that restrained the crown and informed the mindset of the American colonialists contained the seeds of a notion of individual space, an inviolate personal sovereignty that guided the writing of the Fourth Amendment into the Bill of Rights. One's house, as humble as that dwelling might be, was safeguarded from the warrantless searches by agents of the crown, and when that right came to be ignored by the English administrators over the American colonies, it sparked the revolution as much as any factor.

That was the judgment of no less an expert on the origins of the American Revolution than a young John Adams, who witnessed the patriot James Otis delivering a speech denouncing the British Crown's use of general warrants and writs of assistance to invade the homes of colonialists. Chief Justice John Roberts cited that incident as foundational in offering his majority opinion in the mobile devices decision:

> In 1761, the patriot James Otis delivered a speech in Boston denouncing the use of writs of assistance. A young John Adams was there, and he would later write that "every man of a crowded audience appeared to me to go away, as I did, ready to take up arms against writs of assistance." According to Adams, Otis's speech was "the first scene of the first act of opposition to the arbitrary claims of Great Britain. Then and there the child Independence was born."[36]

By positioning the right to privacy so clearly as a motivation for the break from English rule and the establishment of the republic, Roberts offered the clearest defense of a constitutional protection for privacy, a word actually absent from the Constitution itself. With that opinion a year after the first revelations by Edward Snowden regarding the enormous loss of privacy to government surveillance, a unanimous majority of the Supreme Court unexpectedly drew a firm line in defense of privacy as a constitutionally protected right.

The justices did this not by addressing the abuses of privacy by the NSA, which would have required significant self-criticism on the part of the court, since Chief Justice Roberts was responsible for appointing judges to the FISA court that approved the scope of NSA spying. Instead, this same Roberts wrote a dazzling opinion in the cell phone case that enjoyed unanimous support across the ideological divide that has defined this court in recent decades. His defense of privacy in the age of the Internet set as clear a standard on the subject as the nation has ever enjoyed through its judicial system.

Prior to the Roberts opinion, the perception had been growing in the burgeoning Internet industry—which profited so mightily from the exploitation of privacy—that the very notion of privacy was an anachronism. Since the massive flow of previously private data was essential to the new tools and toys provided free of charge by firms like Google and Facebook, the right to mine that data was simply their payment in return.

The corollary justification for the end of privacy was in part a technical one: the data stream would be too costly and difficult to restrict in the name of privacy; the very vastness of the data collected had become the compelling reason to ignore demands for protection of individual privacy by granting consumers meaningful control over their own data. That was a judgment made by most of the lower courts, including the two that had ruled in the cases reviewed by the Supreme Court that formed the basis of the Roberts opinion.

But what Roberts did, much to the surprise of industry lawyers, was to stand the complexity argument on its head. He asserted that it was precisely the scope of the data collected in the case of devices acquired by police during an arrest that made it unwise to allow those same police to search the phones' various stored databases. This landmark decision provides an unequivocal answer on the critical role of privacy in the conception of the Fourth Amendment. Roberts did this in his conclusion by reminding us that because of the most rapid of technological changes, the threat to privacy has never been greater.

The question that Roberts's decision left unanswered is to what degree this broad extension of cell phone privacy protection applies to the even larger collections of similarly personal data held by federal agencies, beginning with the NSA. Until the Snowden revelations, there was no serious national debate or understanding about the scope of the federal government's assault on privacy in the digital age. But now that issue, of far greater consequence but organically quite similar to the one dealt with by Roberts in his decision, strongly and clearly demands the court's attention.

five

The Military-Intelligence Complex

R EGINA DUGAN IS "A PIRATE WHO DOES EPIC SHIT." That's her description, and for all it conveys, it's an accurate one. For nearly two decades, she played the role in a pantsuit at a government office in the greater Washington area. That was when she worked at the Pentagon's Defense Advanced Research Projects Agency (DARPA)—the DOD technology research unit that brought us the Internet and GPS, as well as drones, "smart dust," and mind-reading binoculars. She traversed the domain from program manager charged with developing mine-detection technologies to helming the agency as its director. As program manager, the Cal Tech PhD swiftly developed a reputation as a gonzo-scientist with an impulse to get out of the lab. In 1998, the State Department once declared her missing-in-action while on a mine-clearing expedition in Mozambique, where she drove massive South African military-designed vehicles over land-mines that would often detonate at waist-level.[1]

When she was named director in 2009, Dugan, a forty-some-thing hotshot with a deliberate swagger and potty mouth that would make a real pirate blush, wasted no time spinning DARPA's public image from an abusive Big Brother bureaucracy into one of a group of creative tech-savvy rogues, more concerned with developing so-cial networks and tackling cyber security than spying on Americans. That involved reviving the agency's relationships with academics and, more importantly, Silicon Valley technorati.

With projects such as a nationwide balloon-hunting contest with its $40,000 prize to illustrate how social networks and the Internet can mobilize society, and Silicon Valley–style management practices, Dugan brought to fruition President Obama's oft-expressed desire to remake government in the image of a Silicon Valley company— Google, in particular. It was no surprise that she attracted attention on the Google campus, and her move to the tech giant, coordinated by Eric Schmidt, was easily portrayed by the media and the tech in-dustry as a natural transition for the DARPA head.[2]

In 2012, to little fanfare outside the industry, Dugan began her tenure as the first director of Google's Advanced Technology and Projects (ATAP) group, one of the company's more shad-owy projects whose exact function is seemingly impossible to pin down. ATAP doesn't have an official website but, rather, a Goo-gle Plus account that bears the only company description of the project online: "Google ATAP—We like epic shit.—The future is what we choose to make. We make what we believe in. Welcome to Google's Advanced Technology and Projects. A small band of pirates. Believers. Makers."[3]

Though ATAP's budget and majority of projects remain secret, the few details made public about the organization reveal that the future that members of its leadership "choose to make" is a creepy one. In a May 2013 industry conference, Dugan gleefully debuted before a live audience some of the technologies under development at ATAP:[4]

> We got to do a lot of epic shit while I was at DARPA. . . . I wanted to do more of that. . . . There are so many . . . opportunities that can be realized by the advances of tech here. Let's just take . . . authentication. . . . [T]hink of a means of identification that you can wear on your skin every day for a week at a time, say an electronic tattoo. . . . So I'm wearing one here on my arm.

Dugan extends her forearm to reveal what appears to be a large microchip embedded in the skin above a stack of bangles and bracelets.

> Now, it may be true that ten- to twenty-year-olds may not want to wear a watch on their wrist, but you can be sure that they'd be far more interested in wearing an electronic tattoo, if only to piss off their parents [laughter]. . . . [T]hat's something you wear, but you can also imagine including authentication in just your daily habits.
> So, I take a vitamin every morning; what if I just take vitamin authentication? I have one right here [pulls out a tablet]. This pill has a small chip inside of it with a switch. It also has what amounts to an inside-out potato battery. When you swallow it, the acids in your stomach serve as the electrolyte, and they power it up, and the switch goes on and off. It creates an 18 bit EKG-like signal in your body and essentially your entire body becomes the authentication token.
> That becomes my first superpower. . . . It means that my arms are like wires, my hands are like alligator clips when I touch my

phone, my computer, my door, my car, I'm authenticated in. First superpower. Like, I *want* that. . . . [W]e're not shipping that right away. . . . [H]ere's the thing, this is not science fiction. . . . [T]hat pill has been CE stamped and cleared by the FDA. . . . [W]e [Google] can tell that you've taken your pill.

These technologies sound an awful lot like those that Dugan, and her DARPA colleagues who followed her from the agency to Google's ATAP, had their eyes on when she was a government bureaucrat. Dugan is one of many Internet missionaries who have spun through the revolving door between government and Silicon Valley, convinced that their take on technology will save the world, not to mention enrich them in the process.

The proselytizing message of this group—and, in fact, the hallmark of the Internet revolution—is the idea that information is power. Much of the time, this appears to be an intrinsically liberating notion—except when it isn't. Information that enhances individual choice, whether in the form of shopping or voting, should obviously be celebrated. But in the hands of potentially coercive governments, massive collections of data and information represent a threat to our constitutionally guaranteed freedoms.

At the heart of the interconnected world, there is an inherent contradiction between the immense abilities to expand individual liberty and the equally immense abilities to undermine it. That tension has been apparent since the idea of an information Internet was born in DARPA—created in 1958 under the Eisenhower administration.[5] Although DARPA was an effort to dramatically improve the quality of scientific research and development within what Eisenhower would refer to in his farewell address two years later as the "military-industrial complex," he acknowledged that even such brilliant innovation carried with it the same risks as the most mundane enterprises in the bloated Defense Department budget. His historic warning that "in the councils of government we must guard against the acquisition of unwarranted influence, whether sought or unsought, by the military-industrial complex" applied very clearly to the ever-expanding scientific wing of that complex.

A half century later, that prediction rings eerily true when one surveys the military-intelligence complex, a collaborative creation of Silicon Valley engineers and Washington national security bureaucrats. The crown jewel of this venture was a program crafted in early 2002 by the scientifically brilliant but politically tone-deaf CalTech PhD admiral John Poindexter, former national security adviser in the Reagan administration.

The program was called "Total Information Awareness." Its objective, according to an archived version of the DARPA website, was to "revolutionize the ability of the United States to detect, classify, and identify foreign terrorists —and decipher their plans— and thereby enable the U.S. to take timely action to successfully preempt and defeat terrorist acts."[6] And that's not simple, the programs overseers warned. "Total Information Awareness of transnational threats requires keeping track of individuals and understanding how they fit into models." This would be accomplished by integrating existing government databases into a "virtual, centralized grand database" and developing data-mining and profiling technologies that could analyze the data housed in that system.[7]

The Orwellian title of "Total Information Awareness" was itself enough to rouse the media and most of Congress—that and the fact that the DARPA-funded program was the brainchild of Poindexter. Harebrained schemes had come to define the enduring image of Poindexter, who was charged with eight felony counts in the 1980s for his role in the secret arms-for-hostages deal with Iran known as the Iran-Contra scandal. He, along with TV personality and former Marine Lieutenant Colonel Oliver North, avoided prison time only because of the technicality of an immunity granted by Congress for his testimony about the affair.[8]

Contrary to the Supreme Court—which in *Riley v. California* identified privacy as a constitutional right, as discussed in the previous chapter—the Defense bigwig Poindexter stated that he believes privacy is "certainly not a constitutional right."[9] His surveillance system was evidently founded upon that belief.

"Remember Poindexter?" scoffed the late William Safire, who was at the forefront of the fight against this threat to privacy. "He had this brilliant idea of secretly selling missiles to Iran to pay ransom for hostages, and with the illicit proceeds to illegally support contras in Nicaragua."[10]

Before he became a highly regarded columnist, Safire had been a speechwriter for President Nixon. He seemed to have emerged from that disastrous administration as a born-again believer in the cause of protecting individual rights from the ravages of unbridled governmental power. An overzealous White House staff that had misused the power of the IRS, CIA, and FBI to harass those who were arbitrarily placed on Nixon's enemies list—and the subsequent cover-ups—had brought Nixon to ruin and Safire to a commitment to privacy.

As a *New York Times* columnist, Safire cut his teeth on the privacy issue in the 1990s, attacking the Clinton administration for passing radical financial deregulation that allowed banks, insurance companies, and investment companies to merge their operations and all of their clients' personal, financial, and medical records.[11] He eventually lost that battle to keep private data private, but, three years later, Poindexter's move to vastly expand the reach of the snoopers under the Bush administration gave the Republican Safire a chance to fight the good fight once again. In his widely syndicated *New York Times* column, he fired off a devastating takedown of Poindexter's Total Information Awareness plan:

> Every purchase you make with a credit card, every magazine subscription you buy and medical prescription you fill, every Web site you visit and e-mail you send or receive, every academic grade you receive, every bank deposit you make, every trip you book and every event you attend—all these transactions and communications will go into what the Defense Department describes as "a virtual, centralized grand database."
>
> To this computerized dossier on your private life from commercial sources, add every piece of information that the government has about you—passport application, driver's license and bridge toll records, judicial and divorce records, complaints from nosy neighbors to the F.B.I., your lifetime paper trail plus the latest hidden camera surveillance—and you have the supersnoop's dream: a "Total Information Awareness" about every U.S. citizen.
>
> This is not some far-out Orwellian scenario. It is what will happen to your personal freedom in the next few weeks if John Poindexter gets the unprecedented power he seeks.[12]

That critique from a writer with impeccable conservative credentials, combined with those of others from across the political spectrum, produced one of the few clear-cut (though temporary) victories for privacy activists when, in a rare flare of outrage over the stripping of personal freedom in the name of national security, Congress in 2003 passed legislation that dismantled the Total Information Awareness program. Poindexter, having been pushed into retirement by Congress, would soon vanish from the American political scene. But, first, he would use his still-considerable clout on the Hill to make sure that his hazardous plan would survive in some form or another, primarily through farming out the work to other government agencies, with much of the data mining conducted by private contractors.

As key elements of Poindexter's program were shifted to other governmental departments, the task of preserving its central purpose and supervising data-mining operations was passed from DARPA to the National Security Agency's strikingly similar technology innovation program, the Advanced Research and Development Activity (ARDA). Poindexter, without a doubt, left office with a public-image problem: he was the poster child for reckless and over-bearing government bureaucracy. He realized that his program, in which the intelligence agencies and the Defense Department had a great interest, would more easily be brought to fruition if he played a behind-the-scenes role. The name Total Information Awareness would disappear, along with its author, Poindexter, but the essence of the program, renamed Terrorism Information Awareness,[13] would be reincarnated as an alliance between the government and Silicon Valley for-profit companies.

It was a brilliant plan. In its new manifestation, the data collection, storage, and analysis operation was far less visible. With the original Total Information Awareness program, there was a clear line of responsibility, so that this entire data-gathering operation could be traced back to Poindexter's actions in the Pentagon. That explicit expression of big government spying, ingrained in the American mind as anathema to democratic governance, raised red flags; critics from across the political spectrum called attention to the obvious creepiness of this program.

Lori Waters, executive director of the Eagle Forum, a conservative political organization, told *Wired* that the Total Information

Awareness activity "goes against our very character as a nation to accept that anybody is guilty until proven innocent in America. . . . It makes us all summary suspects, and does so without any guarantee that it will catch the bad guys."[14] In turn, Hendrik Hertzberg, the *New Yorker*'s liberal political commentator, aptly compared ARDA to the tyrannical corporations of Philip K. Dick's dystopian pulp science fiction. Certainly, Hertzberg had no shortage of fitting sci-fi analogies to choose from. "The Information Awareness Office plays it so weird that one can't help suspecting that somebody on its staff might be putting us on. . . . Dr. Strangelove's vision—'a chikentic gomplex of gumbyuders'—is at last coming into its own," he wrote in 2002.[15]

The scheme to preserve ARDA, the guts if not the label of Total Information Awareness, came to rely upon the deflection of that concern by outsourcing design and execution of the data-mining programs—traditionally carried out by official government spy agencies—to private corporations. Enter Booz Allen Hamilton, "a leading provider of management consulting, technology, and engineering services to the U.S. government in defense, intelligence, and civil markets."[16] As one of the thousands of contractors of that firm, Edward Snowden, would reveal a decade later, the surveillance program rapidly mushroomed far beyond what even Poindexter had dared to envision.

ᴧᵛ ᴧᵛ ᴧᵛ

FOR MANY DECADES, BOOZ ALLEN HAD BEEN AMONG THE Defense Department's cast of supporting actors—for-profit military contractors—that employed many personnel from the armed services and other branches of government who had swung through Washington's proverbial revolving door. This outsourcing of intelligence represented a sharp break from the practices of most governments—including, until the late 1990s, the United States— as it meant entrusting for-profit contractors with access to the most carefully guarded of a nation's secrets. In addition, as this chapter will explore further, there is a serious conflict of interest when the contractors massaging the data to assess threats to the United States also profit from meeting that threat. Another glaring conflict of interest is that spy agencies, like the CIA and NSA, which are restricted from interfering in US domestic life, become players in that realm by virtue of their influence over private companies.

The outsourcing of defense and intelligence work had been controversial in political circles until the last years of Bill Clinton's administration, when the president authorized the CIA's creation of the first US government–sponsored venture capital firm, In-Q-Tel, designed to invest in cutting-edge Silicon Valley companies. The firm, named after Ian Fleming's fictional character "Q," who masterminds James Bond's spy gadgets, was founded on September 29, 1999, when the intelligence agencies came to realize they couldn't produce the technology required to make sense of the vast amount of data they had acquired.[17]

The firm's mission is to "identify, adapt, and deliver innovative technology solutions to support the missions of the Central Intelligence Agency and broader US community."[18] This process provided a way of tapping the resources and creativity of Silicon Valley—which undoubtedly had gained a technological edge over government in the post–Cold War period—without the burden of trying to directly recruit the free spirits of Palo Alto into government bureaucracy.

Washington Post business writer Terence O'Hara summarized In-Q-Tel's many inherent contradictions in a 2005 column. "It is independent of the CIA, yet answers wholly to it," he wrote. "It is a nonprofit, yet its employees can profit, sometimes handsomely, from its work. It functions in public, but its products are strictly secret."[19]

Under the guise of In-Q-Tel, the CIA has invested in hundreds of start-ups, including a company called Keyhole, whose satellite mapping software became Google Earth.[20] In-Q-Tel proved immensely successful in its first five years, bringing revenue into the agency and, more significantly, allowing it to discreetly co-opt technologies and companies that would exponentially enhance its spying capabilities without causing the public to ever raise an eyebrow.

The practice of tapping tech companies for government work, then, began to shed its taboo and appear increasingly attractive to other governmental entities. For example, NASA and the US Army, inspired by the success of In-Q-Tel, are currently planning to develop their own venture capital firms in its image.[21] Thanks in part to In-Q-Tel, the already substantial for-profit investment in the intelligence area, which included Booz Allen, was expanded significantly under President George W. Bush, such that it constituted about 70 percent of the intelligence budget by 2007.[22]

This was just the ticket for Poindexter to ride when Congress terminated his pet program in 2003.

In this burgeoning market of government/tech synergy—the core of the military-intelligence complex—for-profit corporations play a deceptively important role in disguising the extent of government spying on its own people. As is the case with the government's seizure and exploitation of the massive data collected by Google, Facebook, and other Internet companies, there is an illusion that this information is simply an enhancement for shoppers and social networkers, rather than the means by which our government keeps tabs on all of our activities—from the political to the most personal.

For that reason, when Poindexter was stymied in his effort to develop the Total Information Awareness program by a Congress concerned about big government's threat to privacy, it was a natural fit to turn to a private, clearly for-profit Silicon Valley start-up called Palantir, in part with CIA funding. Palantir is the premier company for unraveling and interpreting dense tangles of information—data sets—for intelligence and law enforcement agencies. It offers software that, in the company's own words, "connects data, technologies, humans and environments" and, as a bonus, a staff that pays house calls to clients' offices to customize its programs.[23]

But, as the ACLU notes,

> We don't know the degree of entanglement between the company and the agencies in terms of how the software is operated. And depending on the details of how it's used, its deployment could be anything between a good, efficient use of government resources, and a true totalitarian nightmare, monitoring the activities of innocent Americans on a mass scale, collecting the records of those activities and leaving them open for suspicionless exploration by government analysts. Unfortunately, everything we know suggests that it is likely close to the latter.[24]

Palantir, entrusted to mine that massive trove of personal data on behalf of both local and federal governments, was Poindexter's Total Information Awareness program renamed and repackaged. Sure enough, it would blossom without him, a testament to his doing more than anyone to make the nightmare of a Big Brother government that knows the desires, fears, and habits of each and every soul a frightening reality.

Palantir's work for the spy agencies is highly classified, and the company has a very active public relations operation aimed at creating a benign impression of its intentions and stressing its non-spy activity, which includes data integration of investment bank knowledge bases as well as "philanthropy engineering." According to the company, this engineering involves working on "creating slavery-free supply chains, addressing small-plot farmer food security, improving global health and fighting disease outbreaks, providing humanitarian relief in the wake of natural disasters, and more."[25] But it is clear that the company, from its inception, had made its primary function the designing of surveillance programs for the spy agencies. In fact, Palantir would not have managed to stay in existence were it not for a multimillion-dollar investment and substantial technical support provided by the CIA.

When the CIA and NSA first approached Palantir with funds and support in 2004, the Palo Alto–based "computer software and services company" was a fledgling start-up. Since then, as a contractor for top intelligence agencies—as well as some major private banks, like JPMorgan Chase, and multinational corporations—Palantir is valued at $9 billion and has become the most successful among the numerous CIA-backed data analyzation companies.[26]

Peter Thiel, whose PayPal investment had left him a billionaire, founded Palantir. He was convinced that the tactics that had allowed PayPal to predict credit card fraud would work in identifying terrorists. Other investors, however, were not as convinced, and by 2005, a year after Palantir was incorporated, the company was without a single customer or investor other than Thiel.

Palantir was rescued by a referral to In-Q-Tel, according to a feature story on the firm in *Forbes* magazine. It was that fortuitous contact that resulted in a $2 million CIA investment and the subsequent success of Palantir. But far more important than the CIA's injection of financial capital was its support—access to the CIA's secret databases, in-house technical experts, and a rolodex of prospective clients on the Hill. These would give Palantir the lift it needed over the next three years.

Forbes nicely summarized the intimate connection between this Silicon Valley start-up and its CIA sponsor. "From 2005 to 2008 the CIA was Palantir's patron and only customer, alpha testing and evaluating its software," wrote the magazine's Andy Greenberg and Ryan Mac. "But with Langley's imprimatur, word of Palantir's growing abilities spread, and the motley Californians began to bring in deals and recruits."[27]

Motley is an appropriate descriptor, capturing the laid-back style of the Silicon Valley entrepreneurs. That image, concocted by Palantir's robust PR operation, was eagerly lapped up by the mainstream press. The headline on the *Forbes* piece reads "How a 'Deviant' Philosopher Built Palantir, a CIA-Funded Data-Mining Juggernaut." That "deviant," as he refers to himself, is Alex Karp, Palantir's CEO, a hipster exec who obtained his PhD in philosophy at the University of Frankfurt (earned, he might remind us, under the mentorship of the eminent philosopher Jürgen Habermas) and a JD at Stanford Law School. He possesses "progressive" politics and software engineering ignorance. This eclectic persona is enormously useful to Palantir, which effectively plays the role formerly assigned to the Total Information Awareness program: a monstrous government snoop, mining our most intimate data.

This point was obviously not lost on Poindexter—seemingly the complete antithesis of Karp in terms of personal style and political outlook—as he was casting about to keep his program alive after Congress shut it down. According to an account in the *Washingtonian* by Shane Harris—who wrote in great detail about Poindexter's second Washington tour of duty in his book *The Watchers*[28]—it was neo-con guru Richard Perle who put Poindexter in contact with Palantir's Thiel and Karp even before they had made the CIA contact and when they were desperate for support from the Washington defense establishment.[29]

Perle had been a key, if ultra-hawkish, member of that establishment ever since the 1970s, when he worked for Senator Henry "Scoop" Jackson, the Democrat from Washington who was better known as the "Senator from Boeing."[30] In particular, Perle had been chair of the authoritative Defense Policy Board and was very influential in pushing the Bush administration into the Iraq invasion.[31] The account by Harris doesn't explain how Perle came to be involved with the Palo Alto entrepreneurs, but he does report that Perle invited Poindexter to his house to meet the two Palantir execs.[32]

The parallels between what Palantir wanted to accomplish with its sophisticated data-mining software and Poindexter's goals were obvious. "Karp says Poindexter was one of many experts whom Palantir's founders consulted in their early days," Harris reported.[33] Another expert consultant was George Tenet, a founder of In-Q-Tel and director of the CIA during President George W. Bush's first term in office. Tenet—given his position at the CIA and his affinity for Palantir, about which he is unreservedly vocal—undoubtedly helped arrange In-Q-Tel's funding of the firm.[34] After retiring from the CIA, he was named an adviser to Palantir, as was former Bush-appointed secretary of state Condoleezza Rice.[35]

In retirement, Tenet began to significantly bank on his connection to the Iraq war that was based on false intelligence. In addition to nabbing a $4 million book deal,[36] speaking gigs for which he charges up the wazoo,[37] a substantial government pension, and, reportedly, a six-figure salary from Georgetown University,[38] he earned a sizable income working for private corporations that provide the US government with technology and personnel used in the "War on Terror."[39] As Tim Shorrock noted in a piece for

Salon, Tenet "is a director and advisor to four corporations that earn millions of dollars in revenue from contracts with US intelligence agencies and the Department of Defense. . . . [A]ccording to public records, Tenet has received at least $2.3 million from those corporations in stock and other compensation."[40]

The former CIA director currently serves as director of Guidance Software, "recognized worldwide as the industry leader in digital investigative solutions."[41] According to the company website, Guidance Software's products are "used by numerous government agencies, more than 70 percent of the Fortune 100, and more than 45 percent of the Fortune 500, to conduct digital investigations of servers, laptops, desktops, and mobile devices."[42] Its clients include Facebook, Yahoo, and the CIA.

Tenet is also on the board of directors of L-1 Identity Solutions, a defense contractor with an annual revenue of more than $1 billion, specializing in biometric identification technology, including facial recognition systems and fingerprint scanners.[43] In addition to providing software, L-1 Identity Solutions offers a number of handy services such as "public and private partnerships, which provide government agencies and commercial enterprises opportunities to outsource identity-related tasks to ease burdens on staff and improve customer service" and "authorized channeling," which means that it is entrusted with and facilitates the exchange of private data of Americans. L-1 Identity Solutions' website boasts that it is "one of a few companies authorized for FBI Channeling, which means we can also now obtain FBI Criminal History Reports for . . . customers as well as submit fingerprints to the FBI as part of the vetting process."[44]

L-1 Identity Solutions has in recent years grown considerably through acquisition, bringing in many profitable defense contractors under its umbrella, including Analysis Corp., a company that designs terrorist watch lists used by the State Department and the intelligence agencies.[45] It happens to be run by an ex-CIA official, and the ubiquitous Tenet sits on its board.[46] In addition to that, he is on the board of QinetiQ. Like In-Q-Tel, it is named after "Q," the fictional secret intelligence engineer.

The *Forbes* reporters who profiled Palantir interviewed Rice and asked her "How did founders Karp and Peter Thiel work together so successfully when Karp considers himself a leftist progressive and Thiel a libertarian?"[47] This was just the sort of softball question a skilled corporate PR manager would plant on a tip sheet in a company's official press materials. The question— when posed to a company like Palantir—prompts the answer: that government snooping is one of the few wonderfully bipartisan activities, transcending stale political categories. Rice, who undoubtedly will do much to avoid answering questions about the legacy of lying, torture, and spying that so indelibly marked her time in the Bush government, was delighted to play along with the rising-above-politics angle: "One of the great things about Silicon Valley is that people don't allow political differences to hinder progress or the spirit of innovation. Instead, young entrepreneurs see differences as an opportunity to create an out of the box solution to fulfill a need. Alex and Peter's partnership stemmed from a common interest in creative and innovative tech solutions. This is the heart of the Valley."[48]

Certainly it wouldn't be anything as tawdry as making gobs of money. Peter was already a billionaire when he launched Palantir, and Alex was almost in that club at the time of the *Forbes* profile. Interestingly, both Thiel, the self-described libertarian, and Karp, the equally proud "progressive," while supposedly sharing a common opposition to big coercive government, managed to swallow such concerns while working for the CIA.

Palantir has a carefully honed image as a sort of countercultural spy outfit committed to privacy and individual rights in the pursuit of national security. The company's home page and other marketing devices reek of a virtuous win-win alternative, speaking to the concern imbedded in the Fourth Amendment to the US Constitution that spying on the citizenry is an intrinsically doubtful proposition in a free society and needs to be carefully regulated. Paying homage to that notion, Palantir makes much of its built-in "audit trail," which presumably prevents unauthorized use of private data by individuals working within a government agency. The company plays up the supposed virtues of this mechanism in the "privacy and civil liberties" section of its official website:

> Palantir's immutable and real-time audit logging technologies help ensure compliance with applicable policies designed to protect privacy and civil liberties. Palantir's audit logs can be configured to capture the information a particular customer requires in order to identify behavior that might indicate misuse of data. Audit logs can record everything from login attempts to specific user search queries to user views of individual records. . . . Using Palantir, an investigator is able to quickly sift through large amounts of auditing data, identifying suspicious activity, and drill down to that activity to determine whether there may have been a violation of law or policy.[49]

But the grievous problem with this formula is obvious on two counts. One is that using the audit trail to monitor a government agency's or private corporation's spying activity is totally self-enforcing. If a company decides to be indifferent to that trail, the Palantir system continues to mine the data just fine. However, a more serious concern is that it may not be an aberrant individual employee who is using the software to monitor a private citizen's activities but, in fact, the organization itself.

This is of course routinely true of the NSA, FBI, and CIA, as we have learned through the years from the revelations by whistleblowers of unauthorized spying activities. Consider, for example, the Church Committee's revelation that the FBI had been spying on the personal life of civil rights leader Martin Luther King in an effort to discredit and eventually destroy him. The director of the FBI, J. Edger Hoover himself, authorized that spying. In cases like this, where the unconstitutional practice is authorized by the agency itself, the audit trail on such spying will go unexamined since the agent in question is merely carrying out agency-approved practice. It is far more likely that the Palantir-designed audit trail will be used to identify not agency-approved practices that violate the law but, rather, that rare whistleblower within the organization who dares to tell the truth about such illegal practices.

∿ ∿ ∿

THAT THE PEOPLE AT PALANTIR, DESPITE ITS BOAST OF being countercultural and pro-privacy, represent a symbiosis of official government and corporate conformity was revealed in an embarrassing episode that threatened, for a moment, to derail the company's carefully constructed image. Thanks to the loot of a 2010 cyber attack by the loosely knit "Anonymous" hactivist network, the dark side of the Palantir operation was exposed.

This time, it would be difficult for the company to make the claim that it was compelled to engage in spying by government security agencies, because it—along with two other private security companies, HBGary Federal and Berico Technologies—was contacted on behalf of a hybrid lobbying and law outfit, Hunton

& Williams LLP. The law firm claimed to represent both the Chamber of Commerce, which was being challenged by a coalition of labor unions and civic organizations for their lobbying policy, and the Bank of America, which was concerned that the WikiLeaks organization had obtained internal documents that could embarrass the bank.

Hunton & Williams brought the private security companies—all of which were government contractors—together to dig up dirt that could be used to destroy the principals and supporters of both the anti-Chamber groups and WikiLeaks. The merry threesome—Palantir, HBGary Federal, and Berico Technologies—began referring to its coalition as "Team Themis."[50] It must have been the irony of the name that amused them. *Themis* is a reference to the Roman goddess of law and order, but the project was, in fact, devoted to disrupting legal organizations that dare counter the propaganda of the Chamber of Commerce, primarily US Chamber Watch, a pro-union nonprofit whose mission is "to promote greater transparency and accountability in American political processes by shedding light on the funding and practices of the largest private interest lobbyist in America, the U.S. Chamber of Commerce."[51] The purloined documents created a stir when it was revealed that Team Themis was planning to undermine not only organizations that dared challenge the Chamber and the Bank but journalist Glenn Greenwald as well, with "actions to sabotage or discredit" him in response to his support of WikiLeaks' leaking of the classified materials.[52]

We know of this episode—just as with the nasty stuff that has emerged about Rice's time in government—not because the principal people involved did any earnest soul-searching in interviews with reporters, but only because members of the "Anonymous" collective managed to obtain and expose HBGary's emails about this nefarious escapade. They're arguably the sort of "cybercriminals" whom those very companies and intelligence agencies would use Palantir's software to expose.

When the story first broke in February 2011 with the assistance of journalist Barrett Brown, who provided a link to the hacked files, it was treated by the media as something of a hactivist lark. "Hackers Reveal Offers to Spy on Corporate Rivals" read the outrageously misdirected headline in the *New York Times*. Moreover, the lead totally missed the point: "A fight between a group of pro-Wikileaks hackers and a California-based Internet security business has opened a window onto the secretive world of private companies that offer to help corporations investigate and discredit their critics."[53]

The lead that was buried was that those "private" companies all had lucrative contracts with the government and that the CIA initially funded the key company that provided the software for the enterprise: Palantir. As a matter of law the CIA is prohibited from being involved in domestic American politics. Yet neither the *New York Times* nor other major accounts raised the question of the possible illegality of a defense contractor funded and under contract with the CIA investigating and attempting to "discredit" critics of the Chamber of Commerce and the Bank of America.

The *Times* reported that some hacked documents proposed a plan "to embarrass adversaries of the Chamber of Commerce for an initial fee of $200,000 and $2 million later." The proposal was followed a week later when Aaron Barr, head of HBGary Federal, "submitted a detailed plan to Hunton & Williams for an extensive investigation into U.S. Chamber Watch and other critics of the Chamber, including the possible creation of 'in-depth target dossiers' and the identification of vulnerabilities in their computer networks that might be exploited."[54]

Indeed, the Justice Department not only failed to investigate this possible violation of the law but reportedly had recommended that the Bank of America hire the law firm that put this effort together, creating the appearance of complicity.[55] There were no indictments of anyone from these companies or the law firm that conspired to engage in cyber warfare against their clients' critics. However, the journalist Barrett Brown, who reported on the insidious Team Themis program, had the proverbial book thrown at him. He was indicted by the Justice Department on seventeen counts in a separate case months later related to sharing a link to records hacked from the server of Stratfor Global Intelligence, the US intelligence contractor. Those files documented potentially illegal activities including, among other topics, "opportunities for rendition and assassination" and, similar to the HBGary Federal's files, detailed "attempts to subvert journalists, political groups and even foreign leaders."[56] The hackers' clean sweep included tens of thousands of credit card numbers and their verification codes.

Brown had no role in the server breach at Stratfor or HBGary, and did not post the emails or credit card numbers, but he faced 105 years in prison and has spent more than 2 years incarcerated, awaiting trial. The government, in a plea bargain, accepted Brown's guilty plea on one count and dismissed all but four counts in March 2014; they carry a maximum penalty of 7 years in prison. He was to be sentenced on December 16, 2014[57] (after this book was sent to the printer). Brown's actions were no different than what good journalists do routinely, which is to study documents and follow leads. In early 2011, overwhelmed with the volume of seventy thousand emails to which he had been given access, Brown used a crowdsourcing site for journalists and others to review and report on the HBGary documents.

While three security firms—HBGary Federal, Palantir, and Berico Technologies—are the main focus of the emails, a fourth security firm holds a particular interest for Brown. That is Endgame Systems, a highly secretive company that has on its board of directors retired Lieutenant General Kenneth A. Minihan, a managing director at Paladin and a former director of the National Security Agency. Its chairman is Christopher Darby, the CEO of In-Q-Tel, the venture capital arm of the US Central Intelligence Agency. It all seems a bit incestuous, not to mention lucrative for the parties involved.

Endgame is intriguing not only because of its secrecy but also because of its capabilities and products, as described in a story on the investigative news website *Who What Why* by the site's assistant editor Christian Stork. The article is about Brown and his relationship to the well-known investigative reporter Michael Hastings, who died in a mysterious fiery single-car crash on June 18, 2013, around midnight. Just twelve hours earlier he had emailed someone (the name is redacted) under the subject line "Subject: FBI Investigation, re: NSA." He wrote that the FBI had been questioning "close friends and associates" and noted: "I'm onto a big story and need to go off the rada[r] for a bit." Stork reported that Hastings had been planning to meet with Brown later that month. He had been examining the HBGary files.

According to the HBGary email documents, without an explanation of what prompted him, the former Endgame CEO Chris Rouland asked an employee, John Farrell, to "Please let HBgary [*sic*] know we don't ever want to see our name in a press release." Farrell forwarded that note to HBGary Federal's then-CEO, Aaron Barr, along with his own:

Chris wanted me to pass this along. We've been very careful NOT to have [a] public face on our company. Please ensure Palantir and your other partners understand we're purposefully trying to maintain a very low profile. Chris [Rouland] is very cautious based on feedback we've received from our government clients. If you want to reconsider working with us based on this, we fully understand."

The reporter continues:

One look at Endgame's product line explains a lot about their wariness. Their premier software, "Bonesaw," shows what a powerful asset the corporation has become to America's intelligence agencies.

Bonesaw is a targeting application that tracks servers and routers around the world. It maps out all the hardware attached to the Internet. Through these access points, NSA and Cyber Command can hack into or launch attacks against adversaries. The Bonesaw program functions essentially as a user-friendly map.

That map has at its disposal the geolocation and Internet address of every device connected to the Internet around the globe. By designating a country and city—like Beijing, China for example—and the name or address of a target—say, a People's Liberation Army research facility—a user can find out what software is running on all of the computers inside the facility, what entry points to those computers exist, and a menu of custom exploits that can be used to sneak in.[58]

So while Barrett Brown sat in custody on inflated charges, and the late Michael Hastings believed he was being investigated (the FBI denied it), why wasn't the Justice Department as interested in investigating the actions of Team Themis as it was in its prosecution of a journalist? And if the CIA is an investor in Palantir through In-Q-Tel and granted the company access to highly classified files, shouldn't the Justice Department be concerned that the CIA is intervening in domestic American political life? And shouldn't the *New York Times,* in its report on this effort to destroy opponents of the Bank and the Chamber, at least mention that Palantir, one of what the paper refers to as a "trio of data-related companies," is connected with the CIA?[59] What about the fact that the real target of "Team Themis," as revealed in the emails leaked by Anonymous and obtained by the *New York Times,* was WikiLeaks, a publisher of documents exposing government overreach, as well as journalists like Greenwald who have dared treat these disclosed materials seriously in their journalistic reporting?

The *Times* did, however, in reporting on the schemes of "Team Themis," refer to a PowerPoint presentation, revealed by Anonymous, that suggests not only cyber crime but also an assault on the free-press guarantee of the First Amendment: "One idea was to submit fake documents covertly to Wikileaks, and then expose them as forgeries to discredit the group. It also suggested pressuring Wikileaks supporters by threatening their careers."[60]

This was also conveyed in an email from HBGary Federal's head, Aaron Barr, to the other two potential partners, Palantir and Berico Technologies: "I think we need to highlight people like Glenn Greenwald. Glenn was critical in the Amazon to OVH [data center] transition and helped WikiLeaks provide access to information during the transition. It is this level of support we need to attack. These are established professionals that have a liberal bent, but ultimately, most of them if pushed will choose professional preservation over cause. WikiLeaks would fold."[61] Matthew Steckman, a "forward deployed engineer" in Palantir's Washington office, responded: "We are the best money can buy! Damn, it feels good to be a gangsta."[62]

~ ~ ~

SO THERE YOU HAVE IT. SO-CALLED PRIVATE COMPANIES that either are directly funded by the US government or profit from US government contracts move to destroy organizations and individuals who dare to expose the reach of government and corporate power—a classic manifestation of the government's threat to our constitutionally protected freedoms. But because for-profit private companies are used as proxies to engage in such nefarious behavior, the government threat to freedom goes largely unnoticed. Hence the prowess and danger of the military-intelligence complex.

When the story broke, two of the three companies, Palantir and Berico, shirked responsibility and placed the blame on the third—HBGary Federal. Their assertion of innocence, however, is a hard case to make. These three companies, after all, claim to be the world's leaders in sophisticated spying; the notion that their potentially hugely lucrative deals just slipped below the radar is absurd—especially since, as the documents reveal, top executives knew about the deals. The emails released deeply involve at least two Palantir employees in the planning of this caper, and the company's logo appears prominently on the leaked material, as do those of the other two companies. In addition, Berico's co-founders, Guy Filippelli (former special assistant to the Director of National Intelligence) and Nick Hallan, said in a statement that Berico had been "asked to develop a proposal to support a law firm . . . on behalf of American companies to help them analyze internal information security and public relations challenges. . . . [W]e proposed analyzing publicly available information and identifying patterns and data flows. . . . Any subsequent discussions or proposals that attempted to extend the initial scope of work run counter to our organization's values."[63]

Palantir put one employee on temporary leave and, after the story died down, brought him back. Of course targeting individuals is what Palantir is all about, but the claim is that it is only after the terrorist bad guys. Karp, the CEO, issued a statement assuring the public that his other fellow "progressives" would never be the target of any destructive campaign:

> Palantir Technologies does not build software that is designed to allow private sector entities to obtain non-public information, engage in so-called "cyber attacks" or take other offensive measures. I have made clear in no uncertain terms that Palantir Technologies will not be involved in such activities. Moreover, we as a company, and I as an individual, always have been deeply involved in supporting progressive values and causes. We plan to continue these efforts in the future. . . . Furthermore, personally and on behalf of the entire company, I want to publicly apologize to progressive organizations in general, and Mr. Greenwald in particular, for any involvement that we may have had in these matters.[64]

Not long after making this statement, Karp made a personal phone call to the targeted journalist. Greenwald, with some annoyance, recounted that conversation in a 2011 *Salon* blog post. "Karp called me," he wrote. "[And he] seemed sincere enough in his apology, vowed that any Palantir employees involved in this would be dealt with the way they dealt with HBGary, and commendably committed to telling me by the end of the week whether Bank of America or Hunton & Williams actually retained these firms to carry out this proposal."[65]

Palantir, like many Silicon Valley companies, claims that its work, though partially motivated by profit, is for the public good—a conceit consistent with Google's unofficial slogan: "Don't be evil."

But, like Google and a number of other corporate entities discussed throughout this book, Palantir bent the rules when the government offered a compelling incentive—profit, contacts, a chance to be part of the Hill's elite club.

Palantir was not alone in its effort to bring down WikiLeaks. Only two months earlier, PayPal, MasterCard, and Visa went along with a government-instigated plan to destroy WikiLeaks by cutting off payments as punishment for its having released incriminating State Department cables to a group of news organizations, including the *New York Times*.[66]

Thiel prides himself on being a major libertarian believer in small government and the free market—a position he has been advocating ever since his days as a student publisher of a libertarian magazine at Stanford.[67] But his concern about big government obviously does not include the mainstay of Palantir's business: the military-industrial complex in general and its surveillance agencies in particular.

The PR fiction surrounding Palantir has been a most effective denial of the rather obvious reality that this company is a prime instrument of the military-industrial complex about which Eisenhower warned us. It involves the same corrupting connection between the national security state and the for-profit companies that produce the guns, planes, and other inherently destructive implements of war. The Silicon Valley spin-offs traffic in incredibly vibrant technologies, marked by a troubling duality: one facet is a liberating, educationally transformative world of open-access information and the other an intrusive marketing mechanism that feeds off the private and public sectors' worse impulses.

In the private sector, that trade-off, as long as it is truly transparent, is a matter of negotiation between the consumer and the

Internet entrepreneur as to the acceptable balance between privacy and convenience—say, in giving up your location to Yelp for a more relevant selection of restaurants. But owing to the demands of classification, in the world of national security, that trade-off is rarely transparent, and privacy invasion can threaten democracy's delicate balance between government power and individual rights. This distinction between data mining in the world of commerce and data mining in the world of national security is one that a company like Palantir, which does both, seeks to blur. Consider the mission statement carried on the company's home page:

> Since its inception, Palantir has invested its intellectual and financial capital in engineering technology that can be used to solve the world's hardest problems while simultaneously protecting individual liberty. Robust privacy and civil liberties protections are essential to building public confidence in the management of data, and thus are an essential part of any information system that uses Palantir software.[68]

What is one to make of this statement other than to view it as a stunning example of cognitive dissonance? Surely anyone familiar with the origins of the company know that its CIA investor was Palantir's only paying client during the first three years "since its inception," when its engineering technology was explicitly refined under the tutelage of the CIA's experts. "Robust privacy and civil liberties protections" were the least of the agency's concerns. Simply read the summary of the Senate Committee report on the CIA's torture program (cited in Chapter 6) that was blocked from being made available to the public by the agency for five years until the Obama administration reluctantly agreed to a heavily redacted version.

The core argument of the CIA is that whatever sacrifices of privacy and civil liberty the agency made were necessary to protect Americans from a terrorist attack after 9/11. Yet Palantir on its home page categorically denies the essential rationale for the CIA's ultra-secret practices throughout the agency's history: "Some argue that society must 'balance' freedom and safety, and that in order to better protect ourselves from those who would do us harm, we have to give up some of our liberties. We believe that this is a false choice in many areas. Particularly in the world of data analysis, liberty does not have to be sacrificed to enhance security."[69]

This notion is unquestionably consistent with the assumptions of a society based on limited government, transparency, and an informed citizenry. It is also one that Palantir's clients at the CIA, NSA, and FBI have, in practice, consistently undermined.

None of the vital details about what Palantir or, for that matter, any other private contracting company does for our government spy agencies are available to the public. These companies are part and parcel of a national security establishment that has rarely been held publicly accountable for its activities. The exceptions—instances when democratic accountability called for in our Constitution is respected—occur most often when individuals working for government agencies, as a matter of individual conscience, report on the questionable activities of those government agencies. It is only through the action of those whistleblowers that a national debate about the alarming reach of the surveillance state—which many now realize threatens the foundations of representative government—emerged.

six

A Whistleblower Shall Set Us Free

THE SCENE COULD STAND AS A THEATRICAL SET PIECE illuminating the workings of a totalitarian society: secret police arrive with sledgehammers and proceed to smash the printing presses. Only, in these modern times, the presses are computer hard drives and, in place of hammers, power drills, and angle grinders are the destructive tools of choice. The goal is the same, however—a government seeking to summarily destroy, in the ultimate act of censorship, data it deems too dangerous for public viewing.

This update on a classic historical scenario actually took place on July 20, 2013, in the mostly deserted basement of the *Guardian*'s Kings Cross office in London. Instead of secret police, three staff members—clad in white dust masks and safety goggles—were wielding the aforementioned tools under the direction of two intelligence officials from the Government Communications Headquarters (a British intelligence agency known as GCHQ, analogous to the United States' NSA). As the spies took notes and photographs of the scene, "the . . . staff fed crushed bits of computer into a degausser, a microwave-like device intended to irreversibly erase data," the Associated Press reported.[1]

It was nearly seven weeks after the *Guardian*, along with the *Washington Post*, published the first batch of US and British intelligence files revealed by Edward Snowden, and almost a month after the paper initially got word from the GCHQ that the agency wanted this material destroyed.

After great deliberation, the *Guardian*'s leadership decided to do the deed themselves. It was better than what they believed to be the alternative: face litigation that would halt their publication of the Snowden documents. Editor Alan Rusbridger made it unequivocally clear that he would rather destroy the copied files than hand them back to the NSA and GCHQ. The process took three hours of determined smashing, grinding, and zapping to complete.

It might appear odd that it was British and not American authorities that were going through all this trouble, given that Snowden was a contract employee of an agency of the NSA. That the situation went down that way is an ironic leftover of British colonial rule; the American colonists had, once upon a time, been so outraged about the agent of the crown seizing their papers that, upon gaining independence, they enshrined strict limits on the actions of their new government's reach. The First and Fourth Amendments would have made such a move legally awkward in the United States, but it was acceptable in the United Kingdom, at least in the eyes of the courts.

In the end, the *Guardian* data sweep was totally ineffective, as mindlessly vindictive as it was beside the point, because the doc-

uments on those hard drives now existed in many other digital locations. "This is stupid, I was shocked that the U.K. government
would go so far for so little," said Snowden in a *Guardian* interview
a year after the raid. "It should have been obvious to anyone who
works with data or journalism that . . . you can't grind data out of
existence when we have a global interconnected Internet." Indeed,
"[i]t seemed like a clear intent to intimidate the press into pulling
back and not reporting," he concluded.[2]

Since the incident, Rusbridger has carried a shard of pulverized
computer in his inside pocket "rather as a medieval pilgrim would
cherish a saint's bone," writes *Guardian* correspondent Luke Harding in *The Snowden Files*. "It's a sort of artefact, a symbol of the role
of the state versus the journalist," he quotes Rusbridger as saying.[3]

Thus, fortunately, the editors of the *Guardian* were apparently
not cowed. The paper's US edition, based and edited in New York,
along with the *Washington Post*, continued to report extensively
on the Snowden material and both papers were rewarded with the
Pulitzer Prize for Public Service, the highest American journalism
award.

Snowden himself also seemed unbowed. After a year on the
run, trapped in Russia after his passport was revoked while in transit, he exhibited a remarkable calm in his July 2014 interview with
the *Guardian*. He explained that he had intentionally distributed
the documents to respected news sources and others who would
guard them, while carrying nothing on his person. As an engineer,
he said, what you worry about most is a "single point of failure" in
any system—a weakness that, if exploited or triggered, will bring
an entire program to a halt.

"If the government thinks you're the single point of failure,
they'll kill you," he noted grimly, in describing his modus ope-
randi.[4] Presumably the next-best thing was to kill those hard drives,

bolically speaking—although the Americans tried to distance themselves from this event. At first they denied any knowledge that the Brits had forced such a destructive act, and White House press secretary Josh Earnest expressed cautious disapproval.

Discussing the likelihood of this type of action occurring on US soil, Earnest said, "It's very difficult to imagine a scenario in which that would be appropriate." Behind the scenes, however, some in the administration did know in advance that the *Guardian* hard drives would be smashed—and expressed their delight at the prospect.

The convenience of having the Brits act as surrogate press-basher was noted by NSA leaders in documents that came to be released in response to a Freedom of Information Act (FOIA) request made by the Associated Press in July 2014. The office of National Security director James Clapper denied that any such messages existed and had earlier blocked an identical request, but emails were eventually produced that contained revealing snippets.

"Good news, at least on this front," wrote Richard H. Ledgett, leader of the NSA task force responding to the Snowden leaks, in an email to the agency's director, General Keith B. Alexander. The email was titled "Guardian data being destroyed" and was sent before the hard drives were ground to bits. Clapper was also on the email chain and responded, "Appreciate the conversation today."[5]

In response, a spokesperson for the *Guardian* stated, "What's perhaps most concerning is that the disclosure of these emails appears to contradict the White House's comments about those events last year, when they questioned the appropriateness of the U.K. government's intervention."[6]

The documents that were finally released were heavily redacted, with even key pieces of the metadata in the headings obscured. The official defense of blacking out so much of the material, given by an administration whose president had promised transparency, was the desire to protect the privacy of government officials—a bizarrely ironic concern for a government that had been exposed as invading the privacy of billions of people around the world.

As Glenn Greenwald reported on the significance of the new information:

> At least as notable as what the Obama administration disclosed in response to AP's FOIA request is what they suppressed. Look at the documents the administration produced: Virtually all of it censored, even though it pertains to discussions by public officials of the U.K. government's attack on *The Guardian*'s news gathering process. We are permitted to see only the smallest snippets; virtually everything in this email chain is concealed, once again making a complete farce not only out of FOIA but also Obama's self-glorifying claim that he presides over the Most Transparent Administration Ever.
>
> Also recall how we have constantly heard from people like Senator Dianne Feinstein and even the president himself that when the government collects "only metadata" that does not even constitute real spying (it "is not surveillance," Feinstein wrote; "we don't have a domestic spying program," proclaimed Obama). Yet here the administration is concealing not only virtually all of its own email content but also substantial portions of the metadata of those emails.
>
> In justifying its concealments, the administration has the audacity to claim the disclosure "would constitute a clearly unwarranted invasion of privacy." So the Obama administration is apparently capable of recognizing how invasive metadata can be when it comes to its own. Thus we are not permitted to know which of our public officials participated in this little celebration over British attacks on press freedom, let alone what they said.[7]

It was, the *Guardian* noted, "[o]ne of the stranger episodes in the history of digital-age journalism" and may stand as a depressing marker in the decline of free journalism in the West.[8]

In sum, the cause of a free press had survived the British Keystone Kops routine, an object lesson in the irrationalities of power, but the signal sent was ominous. "Both the 1917 U.S. Espionage Act and the 1911 British Official Secrets Act—each with roots in wartime sedition and spy fever—cast a long shadow," noted Rusbridger in the *New York Review of Books*.[9]

That long shadow is unusually threatening in the information age, when the spooks, even the well-intentioned ones, are empowered with a technology of surveillance that enables them to not only observe but distort human reality in ways both effective and subtle. It is a power to control global information flows, which those mired in the old technology, like Senator Feinstein—the member of Congress most responsible for monitoring the NSA—barely seem to comprehend.

But it is a reality Snowden is painfully aware of. As he warned in a video interview with the *Guardian*:

> The storage capability of these systems increases every year consistently by orders of magnitude to where it's getting to the point— you don't have to have done anything wrong. You simply have to eventually fall under suspicion from somebody, even by a wrong call. And then they can use this system to go back in time and scrutinize every decision you've ever made, every friend you've ever discussed something with. And attack you on this basis to sort of derive suspicion from an innocent life and paint anyone in the context of a wrongdoer.[10]

To which Snowden added, in explaining his own decision to risk all: "You realize that that's the world you helped create and it's going to get worse with the next generation and the next generation who extend the capabilities of this sort of architecture of oppression."

That's an appropriately grim view of where this new technology is taking us, and it is difficult to understand why that prospect is not more alarming to officials operating within a democratic society that is based on the efficacy of individual freedom and limited government power. Why do they treat respect for individual privacy and government transparency as a costly indulgence that weakens our national security?

The basic assumption of Western Civilization for hundreds of years has been that a free people in a self-governing republic is stronger rather than weaker when bad ideas—like, say, secret police destroying a news organization's hard drives—are rejected in an atmosphere of unfettered debate. And yet, after 9/11, the United States quickly came to abandon it. As a consequence, we are dependent upon a few brave individuals like Snowden who are willing to risk everything to tell us the truth about the world and our own government.

࿔ ࿔ ࿔

THE WORK OF WHISTLEBLOWERS IS DANGEROUS AND thankless, and the investigative reporters who abet their truth telling also risk their own credibility and careers to do so. While both play a crucial role in the healthy functioning of a democracy and the creation of effective foreign and domestic policies, the powers that be are seldom appreciative of their efforts, to put it mildly.

This is old news to the whistleblowers who have attempted to sound the alarm about the increasingly invasive sprawl of the surveillance state and been harshly condemned for their efforts—not only by an administration maneuvering to keep the public in the dark while maintaining a guise of openness but also occasionally by the so-called guardians of the Fourth Estate, who ostensibly exist to maintain an informed citizenry.

For example, in 2013, the *New York Times* editorial board condemned Russia for granting asylum to Snowden and argued that he should be extradited,[11] while that paper's former executive editor, Bill Keller, criticized Greenwald for his NSA reportage.[12] Ad hominem attacks on whistleblowers came from many commentators in the traditional media, and some implied that the journalists who carried their story should be arrested.

Luckily, however, even in a weakened and corporatized media environment, some real reporting is still undertaken. In 2005, for example, the *Times* published an exposé by investigative reporters James Risen and Eric Lichtblau on the Bush administration's warrantless wiretapping of Americans. This first big hint at the vast expansion of government snooping into the lives of the citizenry after 9/11 was delayed for a year and vastly underestimated the extent of the NSA program, yet it began to shine some essential light on the issue.

"Months after the Sept. 11 attacks, President Bush secretly authorized the National Security Agency to eavesdrop on Americans and others inside the United States to search for evidence of terrorist activity without the court-approved warrants ordinarily required for domestic spying, according to government officials," reported Risen and Lichtblau.[13]

Their story referred to an executive order Bush signed in 2002, without providing its name or quoting the text. That order, it was later revealed by Lichtblau and Scott Shane, was Executive Order 12333 and, in comparison to other extensions of the NSA's power to conduct domestic surveillance under Section 215 of the Patriot

Act and the Foreign Intelligence Surveillance Act (FISA), it was not as readily subject to overview by the other two branches of government, the judiciary and Congress.[14]

This turned out to provide an enormous loophole for the NSA to avoid established restrictions on its surveillance of communications within the United States. Under this order, all the NSA had to do to avoid the limits of the Fourth Amendment was claim it did not intentionally target an American and that the surveillance was conducted from a point outside our borders. Whereas that latter condition might once have been a technical showstopper, it is now relatively simple for the government to have the huge telecoms like AT&T and Verizon, which proved to be eager accomplices, route domestic communications traffic to foreign storage locations where they could be mined by the NSA.

This reality was exposed in another story the government attempted to suppress, one first investigated by the *Los Angeles Times* in 2006. A senior technician at AT&T revealed to reporters that the phone company was routing phone and Internet traffic offshore. The NSA managed to pressure the LA paper to kill the story but, facilitated by legal filings by the Electronic Frontier Foundation (EFF), the *New York Times* did eventually break it, based on the insider knowledge of whistleblower Mark Klein.

The technician, who had worked at the telecom giant for twenty-three years, told the papers he had been startled to discover the NSA had installed equipment in a mysterious room at a San Francisco AT&T building. "The equipment, which Mr. Klein said was installed by AT&T in 2003, was able to select messages that could be identified by keywords, Internet or e-mail addresses or country of origin and divert copies to another location for further analysis," the *New York Times* reported.[15] This story crucially corroborated the earlier *New York Times* account reported by Lichtblau and Risen, yet the Bush administration denied its significance and took legal action to prevent the EFF from getting the program killed by the courts on constitutional grounds. In 2008, Congress passed an amendment to the original FISA that granted immunity to telecom companies from lawsuits relating to their turning over information to the federal government.

These news reports from the mid-2000s, while raising vital awareness that the NSA was engaging in domestic surveillance, greatly underestimated the scope of that snooping. The first *New York Times* story stated that, "[w]hile many details about the program remain secret, officials familiar with it say the NSA eavesdrops without warrants on up to 500 people in the United States at any given time."[16] The Snowden revelations made it clear that this was an absurdly low figure. Yet even the lower figure used by the *Times* elicited a denial from the Bush administration that anything was seriously awry.

The *Times* said its report was based on anonymous interviews with "nearly a dozen current and former officials," but none stepped forward with permission to use their names or provided documents to support their assertions. Thus, despite the fact that a large number of people in both the government and private sectors had significant knowledge of the NSA's vast, unconstitutional program of spying on Americans, few were prepared to publicly reveal the truth.

One of the exceptions was Thomas Drake, an NSA analyst and decorated Navy vet whom the Obama administration targeted in only the fourth prosecution under the Espionage Act in US history. The charges, filed in 2010 and carrying a possible thirty-five-year sentence, were dropped a year later—but Drake's career was already destroyed. In June 2013, he was asked on the *Democracy Now!* radio show for his response to the Snowden revelations. Drake was blunt. "My reaction? Where has the mainstream media been? This is routine. These are routine orders," he said. "This is nothing new. What's new is we're actually seeing an actual order. And people are somehow surprised by it. The fact remains that this program has been in place for quite some time. It was actually started shortly after 9/11. The Patriot Act was the enabling mechanism that allowed the United States government in secret to acquire subscriber records [from] any company that exists in the United States."[17] Drake was clearly acting in the classic mode of the whistleblower, believing Americans and their elected representatives needed to know that a less costly program for conducting electronic surveillance, and one that was simultaneously protective of privacy, had been shelved in favor of a far more costly and ultimately unworkable program with insufficient privacy protections.

Under the Bush administration, Drake's home, as well those of two other NSA officials and a staff member of the House Intelligence Committee, were invaded by federal agents, but no prosecutions ensued. That is, until more than a year later, when the Obama administration's Justice Department was seeking to appear more vigorous in prosecuting such cases. Drake came to be indicted under the Espionage Act and other felony acts. But it turned out that most of the information he supposedly passed on was not classified. All ten felonies were dropped when Drake, drained of resources, agreed to a misdemeanor charge of "exceeding his authorized use of government computers."[18] He was sentenced to 240 hours of community service and a year of probation.

The prosecution was blasted by federal judge Richard D. Bennett, who termed the government's case "unconscionable" and a violation of the Fourth Amendment.[19] Berating both the Bush and Obama administrations for the "four years of hell" they put Drake through, the judge did not hold back, noting that at the heart of the case was "the very root of what this country was founded on"—the stand against general warrants of the British.

Michael Hayden, who was CIA director when Drake passed on information to the *Baltimore Sun,* told Leonard Downie, Jr.— former executive editor of the *Washington Post*—that he disagreed with the original decision to prosecute Drake under the Espionage Act, saying that, instead, "[h]e should have been fired for unauthorized meetings with the press. Prosecutorial overreach was so great that it collapsed under its own weight."[20]

While one can appreciate Hayden's relative candor after the fact, the question remains as to why a whistleblower should be fired for talking to the press after, as had happened in Drake's case, he had taken up his complaint within the proper NSA channels and to a relevant congressional intelligence committee. He had evidence of a crime—subversion of the Constitution and violation of FISA—and it was information the public had a right to know. Where else left to take that complaint but to the press?

An even more important question is why the Obama administration felt the need to prosecute a Bush-era whistleblower. As Downie concluded after investigating the case: "Whatever his role in the NSA's internal rivalries at the time, Drake appears to be a whistleblower whose information about the secretive agency's telecommunications surveillance methods should have resulted in greater government accountability at the time, rather than a criminal prosecution for spying."[21] One wonders why the Obama administration brought these charges, if not to set an example in order to silence other potential whistleblowers.

✵ ✵ ✵

ON HIS FIRST DAYS IN THE OFFICE OF PRESIDENT, OBAMA
had acted boldly to make good on his campaign promise to increase
the pace of declassification and other measures of a more open administration. He issued directives to streamline the processing of
Freedom of Information Act requests to make more government
data readily available to the public, for example, citing his putative
belief that "[g]overnment should be transparent." Yet his administration soon betrayed this commitment, ultimately exceeding his
predecessor's assault on press freedom.

The presidential candidate who had been so successful in cul-
tivating a reputation for accessibility—while portraying himself as
the herald of constitutional restraint—didn't seem to fully grasp
that as president he would also be judged on his ability to deliver
on those promises tangibly, beyond the effectiveness of his rhetoric. In response to press criticisms, in fact, he seemed surprised and
even hurt to discover that his declaration of good intentions was
not given precedence over his administration's aggressive attempt
to silence government whistleblowers.

While Obama campaigned against the "excessive secrecy" of
the Bush administration and on his first day in office directed government agencies to create "Open Government Initiative" websites, the appearance of transparency was deceptive. The substance
turned out to reflect a more manipulative aspect of the Obama
campaign than had been evident to many of his supporters.

"The government websites turned out to be part of a strategy,
honed during Obama's presidential campaign, to use the Internet
to dispense to the public large amounts of favorable information
and images generated by his administration, while limiting its exposure to probing by the press," Downie observed.[22]

Specifically, Obama was the first president to fully grasp the potential of targeted emails much amplified by the brave new world of

social media presented by Twitter, YouTube, and Facebook post-
ings. However, to stay on message with that sort of propaganda, the
White House also had to effectively block more critical reporting. It
did this brilliantly. As the online magazine *Politico* put it,

> One authentically new technique pioneered by the Obama White
> House is extensive government creation of content (photos of the
> president, video of White House officials, blog posts written by
> Obama aides), which can then be instantly released to the masses
> through social media. . . . [The aides] are more disciplined about
> cracking down on staff that leak, or reporters that write things
> they don't like. And they are obsessed with taking advantage of
> Twitter, Facebook, YouTube and every other social media forum,
> not just for campaigning, but governing.[23]

But while all leaders attempt to control their message, what has
made the Obama administration uniquely successful provides an
ominous model: the fevered pursuit of increasingly important new
media that could be exploited at a time of marked decline in the
strength of traditional journalism.

Downie, who was perfectly positioned at the center of Washington journalism to witness this transition of power, ruefully quoted a
senior White House official telling him that "[t]here are new means
available to us because of changes in the media, and we'd be guilty
of malpractice if we didn't use them."[24] That official offered the example of the Obama White House instantly communicating news
briefs to more than 4 million Twitter followers of @whitehouse.

What is alarming about this situation is that the historic check
on the government's power to manipulate the public, enshrined
in the First Amendment's protection of a free press, is simultaneously at risk.

The information world of the Internet, promising in so many diverse ways, lacks the authority of a recognized, professional press that can aggressively maintain its constitutionally protected right to report the news. Bloggers do not have that authority and, while their free speech is also ostensibly guaranteed, it is not the same as the traditional and powerful credibility bestowed upon the organized press by laws and courts, even in the worst of times in our history.

For example, in the landmark whistleblower case of Daniel Ellsberg's release of the Pentagon Papers, a history of the Vietnam War that the public had every right and need to know about, it mattered that a paper with the reputation of the *New York Times* attempted to publish it. And when that was stymied in the courts, another heavyweight, the *Washington Post,* stepped up to the task.

This history was echoed in the more recent example of the Snowden leaks, where, again, the credibility of two major newspapers, the *Guardian* and the *Washington Post,* was invested in the vetting and publication of revelatory documents. They also took responsibility for defending the legitimate news value of the material.

In the past, presidents have attempted to break that link between the press and its sources, as Richard Nixon did in attempting to prevent the *New York Times* from publishing the Pentagon Papers. A strong legal tradition blocking prior restraint of the press has allowed the media to prevail in the US courts when challenged. However, the repressive alternative tactic of threatening the sources themselves, punishing them for giving information to reporters, has been much more successful.

"We make an effort to communicate about national security issues in on-the-record and background briefings by sanctioned sources," Ben Rhodes, the deputy national security adviser in the

Obama White House, told Downie. Rhodes seemed genuinely surprised that the press was not fully sold on the White House version of
the truth. Despite those official briefings, Rhodes complained, "we
still see investigative reporting from non-sanctioned sources with
lots of unclassified information and some sensitive information."[25]

And that is the crux of the problem: the government leaks its
version of the truth all the time and, through background briefings by its sanctioned sources, has no compunction about sharing
ostensibly classified information on a selective basis that makes
the government or particular branches of it look good, while aggressively suppressing information that doesn't paint as pretty a
picture. That is business as usual, and none of those officials doing
the leaking are ever punished for violating the rules of classification
that their administration insists on imposing on everyone else.

For example, on June 24, 2011, when Leon Panetta was head
of the CIA, he provided a detailed description of the capture of
Osama bin Laden to an audience at CIA headquarters that included Mark Boal, the screenwriter of the 2012 movie *Zero Dark
Thirty*.[26] The writer was not cleared to receive that information but
was considered sympathetic to the agency—and, not surprisingly,
the movie he was working on would end up tacitly endorsing the
false notion that torture had been necessary to elicit information
essential to the capture of bin Laden.

Yet when John Kiriakou, a veteran CIA agent who had led the
team that captured top al Qaeda operative Abu Zubaydah in 2002,
went public with his view that waterboarding was torture and
should not be used, he was treated by the CIA as a pariah. When
he persisted in his criticism, after retiring in 2004, the government
accused him of leaking information to the press and charged him
with three counts of espionage. Kiriakou compared his fate to that
of Panetta: "The confirmation in December that former CIA Di-

rector Leon Panetta let classified information slip to *Zero Dark Thirty* screenwriter Mark Boal during a speech at the agency headquarters should result in a criminal espionage charge if there is any truth to Obama administration claims that it isn't enforcing the Espionage Act only against political opponents."[27]

More detail on the *Zero Dark Thirty* leak was provided by a June 14, 2013, report of the Inspector General of the Department of Defense. It confirmed that a top aide at the White House, as well as Panetta (who, according to his aide, wanted to be played by Al Pacino in the movie), were actively providing the filmmakers top-level access to those with knowledge of the deadly bin Laden raid, including a "Special Operations Planner" who had helped coordinate it.[28] An admiral's memo shows that Boal and director Kathryn Bigelow were, at a meeting on July 15, 2011, even given this planner's name, a clear violation of classification that could theoretically endanger the life of an operative.

An even more blatant violation of the law occurred at the June 24 meeting at CIA headquarters honoring undercover operatives involved with the bin Laden raid. The operatives were using their own names, believing no outsiders were present, yet screenwriter Boal was there despite having no special clearance.

"We found no precautionary measures were taken to protect special operators from being identified by the Hollywood executive at this event," said the Inspector General report. "Further, [Admiral William H. McRaven] and the former Chief of Staff at USSOCOM [United States Special Operations Command] told us that the protection of the names associated to this mission was a top aspect of the UBL [Usama Bin Laden] raid they wanted to protect from public disclosure."[29] The admiral reported that he and the special operators present were all "universally surprised and shocked" that a Hollywood executive attended the ceremony.

Clearly, the names of the personnel on the raid who killed bin Laden are highly classified for their protection. But the report makes clear that there was no adverse consequence experienced by anyone in the chain of command who compromised their security. "I'm one of the people the Obama administration charged with criminal espionage, one of those whose lives were torn apart by being accused, essentially, of betraying his country," said Kiriakou. "The president and the attorney general have used the Espionage Act against more people than all other administrations combined, but not against real traitors and spies. The law has been applied selectively, often against whistleblowers and others who expose illegal, corrupt government actions."[30]

In short, we have a clear case study of the double standard on secrecy. On the one hand, a filmmaker the CIA was courting is given classified access in the hopes that his movie would be good pro-Agency propaganda. On the other, Kiriakou, an agent who had risked his life for the country, was charged with violating the Espionage Act for giving the name of a colleague to a reporter, Scott Shane of the *New York Times,* who never even made it public.

After he blew the whistle on the CIA's waterboarding torture program in 2007, Kiriakou was the subject of a years-long FBI investigation. In 2012, the Department of Justice charged him with "disclosing classified information to journalists."[31] Shane, who has done significant reporting on the CIA, wrote, "In more than six decades of fraught interaction between the agency and the news media, John Kiriakou is the first current or former C.I.A. officer to be convicted of disclosing classified information to a reporter," adding that Kiriakou had received many commendations in his fifteen years as an agent.[32]

The irony in this case is that Kiriakou, the whistleblower on torture, is the only person in the US intelligence community in any way connected with that hideous stain on American history to be punished. The significance of this contradiction was not lost on Bruce Riedel, who was once Kiriakou's boss and had conducted an Afghan war review for President Obama—and even turned down an offer to be considered for head of the CIA. "To me, the irony of this whole thing, very simply, [is] that he's going to be the only CIA officer to go to jail over torture," even though he publicly denounced torture, said Riedel, who called Kiriakou "an exceptionally good intelligence officer."[33]

As Drake had done, Kiriakou, with his career and finances in tatters, accepted a deal and pled guilty to violating the Intelligence Identities Protection Act by passing the name of an agent to the media. The Espionage Act felony charges were dropped and Kiriakou was sentenced to thirty months in prison.

The fierce dedication of this White House in attempting to punish those claiming to be doing their duty to the Constitution as whistleblowers had the expected consequence of chilling the national debate. Former *Washington Post* executive editor Downie, whose newspaper had been challenged by no less hostile a president than Nixon during Watergate, described the far-ranging impact:

> In the Obama administration's Washington, government officials are increasingly afraid to talk to the press. Those suspected of discussing with reporters anything that the government has classified as secret are subject to investigation, including lie-detector tests and scrutiny of their telephone and email records. An "Insider Threat Program" being implemented in every government department requires all federal employees to help prevent unauthorized disclosures of information by monitoring the behavior of their colleagues.[34]

Downie's conclusions were echoed in July 2014 with the release
of a joint report, based on interviews with dozens of reporters and
lawyers, by Human Rights Watch and the ACLU, "With Liberty
to Monitor All: How Large-Scale U.S. Surveillance Is Harming
Journalism, Law, and American Democracy." As the report's author, Alex Sinha, summarized in an interview with Amy Goodman: "[W]e finally have documentation of concrete harms that
flow from large-scale surveillance."[35]

One of the reporters quoted, Brian Ross, chief investigative
correspondent for *ABC News*, said, "We sometimes feel—or I feel,
at least—like you're operating like somebody in the Mafia. You've
got to go around with a bag full of quarters and, if you can find a
pay phone, use it, or use, like drug dealers use, you know, throw-
away burner phones. These are all the steps that we have to take to
get rid of an electronic trail."[36]

Jonathan Landay of the McClatchy News Service noted that
"[w]hat we found out through the Snowden disclosures is that the
United States government is collecting all of our metadata, which
shows who your social and professional networks are, who your
connections are, where you are at a particular time, where perhaps
a source is. They don't need to know what you were talking about.
They've got enough to be able to go to your source and say, 'Why
were you talking to this journalist?'"[37]

National security reporter Jeremy Scahill was even told by officials that his calls were being monitored in what he referred to as
the US version of the "war on journalism around the world":

> When we spoke to the National Counterterrorism Center the other
> day, one of the things they said early on, in the call is, "Jeremy,
> we know you've been making a bunch of phone calls throughout
> Washington, D.C., today." And I'm like, "Well, I mean, thank you

for acknowledging that," but it's like—you know, I mean, I think that they basically—the Obama administration's posture is that only state propaganda belongs in the public domain, and if you want to cultivate your own sources and you want to challenge assertions made by officials in Washington by developing your own sources, we're going to go after you with the full extent of the law.[38]

For ABC's Ross, this is clearly abusive. "To have to take those kinds of steps [to avoid surveillance] makes journalists feel like we're criminals and like we're doing something wrong," he told Sinha. "And I don't think we are. I think we're providing a useful service to Americans to know what's going on in their government and what's happening."

❧ ❧ ❧

"WHEN YOU'RE AN NSA ANALYST AND YOU'RE LOOKING for raw signals intelligence, what you realize is that the majority of the communications in our databases are not the communications of targets, they're the communications of ordinary people, of your neighbors, of your neighbor's friends, of your relations, of the person who runs the register at the store," Snowden told the *Guardian*. "They're the most deep and intense and intimate and damaging private moments of their lives, and we're seizing them without any authorization, without any reason, records of all their activities—their cell phone locations, their purchase records, their private text messages, their phone calls, the content of those calls in certain circumstances, transaction histories—and from this we can create a perfect, or nearly perfect, record of each individual's activity, and those activities are increasingly becoming permanent records."[39]

Snowden continued: "The people that are staffing these intelligence agencies are ordinary people, like you and me. They're not moustache-twirling villains that are going, 'ah ha ha that's great,' they're going: 'You're right. That crosses a line but you really shouldn't say something about that because it's going to end your career.' We all have mortgages. We all have families. And when you're working for a national security system that has these official secrets acts that means . . . you can be prosecuted for it, you can lose your job over it."[40]

Despite the erroneous claims of President Obama and others that Snowden could have availed himself of whistleblower protection and communicated his concerns through official channels, it's not true that those protections extend to private contractors. And as Snowden points out, even senior NSA staffers like Drake and William Binney, who attempted to file a complaint about the wasteful and privacy-shattering Trailblazer program (as discussed in Chapter 2), ended up suffering mightily.

In fact, Snowden took a harsh lesson from Drake's experience at the hands of the NSA, since "rather than having those claims investigated, rather than having the wrongdoing remediated, they launched an investigation against [Drake] and . . . all of his co-workers. . . . They pulled them out of the shower at gunpoint, naked, in front of their families. They seized all of their communications and electronic devices, they interrogated them all, they threatened to put them in jail for life, for years and years and years, decades, and they destroyed their careers."

For Snowden, the government's message was clear: "The public should not know about these programs. The public should not have a say in these programs and, for God's sake, the press had better not learn about these programs or we will destroy you," he said.[41]

Government secrecy, and any repression of debate and transparency in a society, limits the ability of citizens to make good collective decisions based on the best information and analysis available. Whistleblowers are far from a luxury. We desperately need them, even if they must break laws, if we are to be successful and free as a nation.

seven

Foreign Policy: A Tissue of Lies

O UR GOVERNMENT, LIKE OTHERS THROUGHOUT
history, tells us that repressive, invasive, and paranoid
national security policies are for our own good, especially
in terms of our safety. Yet where do the prerogatives of a surveillance state driven by fear and governed by secrecy really take us?
The reality is that these procedures not only are unconstitutional
but all too often lead to bad government policies, both at home and
abroad.

One need only review the invasion of Iraq to see the folly of
toppling a regime that was an implacable enemy of al Qaeda—an
invasion driven by a fear of weapons of mass destruction that free
access to the available data would have discounted. The direct result, billions of dollars and hundreds of thousands of deaths later,
is a fractured Iraq that, at the time of this writing a decade later,

seems to be in a constant state of bloody division. Or as veteran correspondent Patrick Cockburn summarized in the *London Review of Books* in 2014, after the extremist Islamic State of Iraq and Syria (ISIS) seized huge swaths of both countries:

> For America, Britain and the Western powers, the rise of Isis and the Caliphate is the ultimate disaster. Whatever they intended by their invasion of Iraq in 2003 and their efforts to get rid of Assad in Syria since 2011, it was not to see the creation of a jihadi state spanning northern Iraq and Syria run by a movement a hundred times bigger and much better organised than the al-Qaida of Osama bin Laden. The war on terror for which civil liberties have been curtailed and hundreds of billions of dollars spent has failed miserably.[1]

The obvious lesson of that debacle, and others like it, is that an informed public with access to accurate information—even when the facts are embarrassing to the government—is the best safeguard against such errors. Aren't we better off knowing when our freedoms are threatened or we are being lied to, even by our own leaders, so that we can rectify such policies?

In other words, didn't Edward Snowden, regardless of the legality of his actions, actually make us safer?

Consider the case forty years earlier, when another great national security whistleblower, Daniel Ellsberg, revealed the Pentagon Papers—a secret history detailing how the public had been lied to about the reasons for the Vietnam War. That conflict, which took the lives of nearly 4 million human beings, was later deemed by historians—and even by its architects, such as Robert McNamara—as an abject disaster.

In his interview from Moscow with the *Guardian*, Snowden mentioned that he was reading Ellsberg's memoir *Secrets*.[2] The parallels between the experiences of the two men are strong: both were private-sector contractors at the moment they gave classified government information to journalists, and both ended up being charged with violating the Espionage Act. (Ellsberg's trial ended in a mistrial over prosecutorial misconduct and the legal issues were never resolved.)

Ellsberg has made the point that "[w]hen I released the Pentagon Papers and survived, I expected others to follow my example, but I had to wait for forty years for that to happen."[3] That it took so long, and still happens so rarely, is an enduring mystery of our culture, given the 1.3 million[4] who had the same top-secret security clearance as Snowden. What was so unusual about Snowden's situation was not that a twenty-nine-year-old contract employee could have access to the most intimate data concerning millions of ordinary people but that he chose to do something about it.

To return to the case of the occupation of Iraq, it was over-classification of the relevant information of what our government really knew that allowed opportunistic politicians in both parties to deceive the public into granting unquestioning support for the reckless and ultimately disastrous scenario.

In Leonard Downie's scathing indictment of the Bush administration's co-option of the media, he demonstrates how some journalists finally rediscovered their purpose and exposed the lies about Iraq, as well as the systematic use of torture at Abu Ghraib prison and CIA "black site" secret prisons throughout the world and the initial reports on NSA mass spying.

The result was an intensified search by the Bush administration for the sources of those stories and an aggressive confrontation with an increasingly critical press. However, no one was prosecuted for leaking news contradicting the administration's narrative, noted Downie.

Interestingly, despite the (well-earned) reputation of Vice President Dick Cheney and others in the Bush administration as manipulative, secretive warmongers, Downie quotes many journalists as saying that the situation, ironically, became much worse under Obama. "The Bush administration had a worse reputation, but, in practice, it was much more accepting of the role of journalism in national security," claimed *Washington Post* executive editor Marcus Brauchli, according to Downie.[5]

Ellsberg was the first to be charged under the Espionage Act for revealing classified national security information, and, as mentioned, there were only two other cases prior to Obama's presidency. The United States does not have an equivalent to the British Official Secrets Act, which provides criminal penalties for all unauthorized disclosures of classified government information. The intent of the Espionage Act when it was passed in 1917 was clearly to punish the transfer of government secrets to foreign enemies, not to block the release of information that might better inform the American public.

As Ellsberg himself has pointed out, the only time Congress passed legislation that approached the severity of British laws, it was vetoed by President Bill Clinton, who quoted Justice Potter Stewart's opinion in the Pentagon Papers case. Nevertheless, Ellsberg said in an interview at his home in Northern California that "President Obama's Department of Justice has now set a repeated precedent of acting as if it did have such a legislative basis of prosecution of classified leaks" as that provided in the British Official Secrets Act, "in the form of the 1917 Espionage Act." In the three cases previous to the Obama presidency, the Supreme Court has never ruled on this use of the Espionage Act.

"My case, the first such prosecution for a leak ever, was dismissed for governmental misconduct before going to a jury in 1973," Ellsberg wrote in an unpublished manuscript. He added:

The third, brought under George W. Bush, was withdrawn by prosecutors after a judge's rulings that effectively rewrote the law to protect it from unconstitutionality. The appeal on constitutional grounds by the single defendant so far found guilty by a jury, Samuel Loring Morison, was denied [certification] by the Supreme Court, which has never yet addressed the issue of the constitutionality of the Espionage Act, or any other legislation in a leak case.

Thus, there has been a nearly 90-year tradition of non-prosecution of classified leaks: with only three exceptions, despite leaks occurring—and being condemned by successive presidents—nearly every other day since World War II. The striking lack of prosecutions before the present administration has reflected a long-held belief that the First Amendment bars a law intended to criminalize the disclosure of such a vast amount of information as is covered by the actual classification system. . . . That traditional interpretation of the First Amendment has been decisively abandoned under President Obama, with his eight indictments so far, nearly three times those of all previous presidents combined.[6]

It was only three months into the new administration when its first Espionage Act prosecution was instituted, against Shamai K. Leibowitz, a Hebrew translator who worked as a contractor for the FBI and was accused of giving a blogger classified information concerning Israel. No details were made available and Leibowitz received a twenty-month sentence after pleading guilty.[7]

The next two cases were handed down a year later involving investigations that had been launched under George W. Bush. The first involved Thomas Drake for allegedly retaining and disclosing classified information to a *Baltimore Sun* reporter, who detailed

NSA mismanagement, waste, and legally questionable activity in a series of stories.

Given the prosecution of Drake, who had gone through proper channels originally, there was every reason for Snowden to eschew raising questions internally and instead take that evidence of wrong-doing and make it as widely available as he responsibly could.

That lesson was lost on both Obama and his former secretary of state Hillary Clinton, however. They claimed that if Snowden were serious about blowing the whistle on wrongdoing, he would simply have taken his case to the proper authorities—his supervisor, the NSA, the Department of Defense Inspector General, or the internal counsel. "If he were concerned and wanted to be part of the American debate, he could have been," Clinton stated. "I don't understand why he couldn't have been part of the debate at home."[8] This from a high-ranking member of an administration that had sent the FBI to invade Drake's home before charging him under the Espionage Act. Both Obama and Clinton made much of the protections they insisted existed for genuine whistleblowers, but both knew that those protections applied only to government employees and not to private contractors like Snowden. What is more, even employees of the defense agencies found those protections to be of little value in attempting to make their case that they were serving the public interest by leaking to the press; the Obama Justice Department even tried in court to prevent Drake from using the words *whistleblower* and *First Amendment*.[9]

Snowden was in a far weaker position, a point made by Ellsberg in a column for the *Washington Post,* drawing on his own experience as a contract worker for the RAND corporation.[10] Regardless of employment status, however, the more fundamental question the Obama administration is not willing to answer is this: Why is whistleblowing required at all?

In Ellsberg's case, the secret documents he revealed to an entire nation not only detailed how we came to be involved in a brutal and failed war but also showed that our government did not believe the faulty narrative it was pitching to its citizens. The Pentagon Papers included information the public needed to have in order to properly assess the wisdom of sending their children to die and kill halfway around the world.

Even influential members of Congress were in the dark. J. William Fulbright, the chairman of the Senate Foreign Policy Committee, for example, said he didn't have access to the crucial analysis and data he read in the Papers. He admitted later that if he had, he would not have introduced the enabling Gulf of Tonkin resolution President Lyndon Johnson would claim as congressional authorization for the war against North Vietnam.[11]

And just as the Papers pushed the Vietnam War debate to new heights, Snowden's documentation has clearly provoked a meaningful debate on the threat to privacy that even the president acknowledged was long overdue.

Of course, in both situations, many inside and outside of government did announce immediately that the release of secrets greatly aided our enemies. However, in the decades since Ellsberg's disclosure, it is quite clear that the claims made at the time by the government that he was endangering national security were without merit. While it is much earlier in judging the case against Snowden, there is already ample evidence to conclude that the material he turned over to the press—leaving the *Post* and the *Guardian* to make the publishing selections—did not, in any significant way, put America at risk.

A lack of evidence did not slow down the hyperbole, though.

"I think turning over a lot of that material—intentionally or unintentionally, because of the way it can be drained—gave all kinds of information, not only to big countries, but to networks and terrorist groups and the like," insisted Secretary of State Clinton, essentially shooting the messenger.[12]

The issue is a classic Catch-22: How can the public be expected to rationally consider the need for invasive surveillance if they are left in the dark about whether such programs even exist?

Speaking of Snowden, Clinton said, "When he emerged and when he absconded with all that material, I was puzzled, because we have all these protections for whistleblowers. . . . If he were concerned and wanted to be part of the American debate, he could have been. But it struck me as—I just have to be honest with you—as sort of odd that he would flee to China, because Hong Kong is controlled by China, and that he would then go to Russia, two countries with which we have very difficult cyber-relationships, to put it mildly."[13] Now, Clinton knew very well that Snowden did not flee to either of those countries and that there is no evidence, nor has there ever been a charge from the US side, that he gave any information to either. The Chinese did not grant Snowden asylum, and he was in transit at the Moscow airport when the US State Department lifted his passport so that it would be impossible for him to move on to one of the countries that had offered him asylum.

Admiral Michael S. Rogers, who became the head of the NSA after spending three months assessing any damage from the Snowden leaks, summarized his findings in an interview with the *New York Times* under the headline "New N.S.A. Chief Calls Damage from Snowden Leaks Manageable." In contrast to Clinton's "Chicken Little" imitation, the *Times* reported that while Rogers "has seen some terrorist groups alter their communications to avoid surveillance techniques revealed by Edward J. Snowden, the damage done overall by a year of revelations does not lead him to the conclusion that "the sky is falling."[14]

History always seems to land on the side of those who speak truth to power. Already, by March 2014, a *Huffington Post/YouGov* survey concluded that over half of Americans believe "we have a right to know about the surveillance programs Snowden revealed" and more than a third thought Obama should pardon him.[15] Today, you would have to dig under many rocks to find anybody who believes the release of the Pentagon Papers endangered the security of the nation, rather than strengthened it. In the not-too-distant future Snowden will be at least as highly regarded for his efforts to tell us what we needed to know.

⚡ ⚡ ⚡

PERHAPS THE MOST IMPORTANT CONSEQUENCE OF THE leaks Snowden engineered will be the development of global standards of privacy protection. That was the point made by Navi Pillay, the UN High Commissioner for Human Rights, who in July 2014 praised Snowden as a defender of human rights who should not be prosecuted. "We owe a great deal to him for revealing this kind of information," said Pillay. The recognition of Snowden's enormous contribution in sparking debate and understanding was validated by the release of a major report by her commission, "The Right to Privacy in the Digital Age."[16]

As Mona Rishmawi, the head of the UN High Commissioner's law branch, put it: "In this particular case, the way we see the situation of Snowden is he really revealed information which is very, very important for human rights. We would like this to be taken into account in assessing his situation."[17]

In underscoring the universality of privacy as a human right, it is significant to note that Pillay is from South Africa and began her legal career defending anti-apartheid activists. "Those who disclose human rights violations should be protected: we need them," Pillay told a press conference. "I see some of it here in the case of Snowden, because his revelations go to the core of what we are saying about the need for transparency, the need for consultation. We owe a great deal to him for revealing this kind of information."[18]

To be sure, we Americans do frequently pay lip service to the idea that a free people's access to information and right to dissent is the best barrier to tyranny and corruption. That is, until the specter of some all-knowing and all-threatening enemy is invoked, be it communism or terrorism. Rarely considered is how odd it is to assume our enemies are easily understood, and that a simplistic analysis of these scourges, uninformed by the complexity of fact and logic, is the best way to deal with them. But in fact, informed public debate frequently increases government and even military effectiveness, rather than hindering it.

Case in point: our shallow, broad-stroke analysis of international communist movements throughout the middle to late twentieth century. This process, largely left unchallenged in a culture of paranoia and accusation, led us to make terrible strategic mistakes (which then, ironically, stirred a renewal of citizen skepticism and challenge). Specifically, the misrepresentation to the American people that communism was an undifferentiated and internationalist enemy missed the nationalistic nuances of an ideology with a different interpretation and history in each locale—most famously manifested in the Sino-Soviet split, which defied the conventional wisdom.

Not that those inside the citadel were necessarily caught napping. For example, the Pentagon Papers contained the analysts' wisdom, kept secret from a public the American government apparently didn't trust with the truth: that the Vietnamese Communist Party was highly nationalist—and so was predictably going to develop a conflict with its historic rival (and former occupier), China. Americans, who were told to believe that the war in Vietnam was about blocking the creation of a monolithic communist Asia, were understandably baffled when a border war broke out between China and Vietnam soon after US withdrawal. Even today, both countries, still ruled by communist dictatorships, fight over fishing and oil rights while simultaneously courting capitalist investments from their former enemies.

The so-called War on Terrorism has similarly floundered in a sea of deliberate ignorance. Most of the 9/11 attackers happen to have been subjects of the tight-knit Sunni theocracy of Saudi Arabia, and yet we focused our ire, and massive firepower, on overthrowing rivals to that kingdom in then-secular-run Iraq, while isolating and harassing Shiite Iran. This is not the place to revisit all the historical circumstances or policy decisions that made the Middle East a far more dangerous and unstable place than ever before. Yet it is safe to say that fear mongering and excessive classification of facts—facts that can potentially lead to understanding and effective policy—have not made the world safer for us or anybody else.

Indeed, the underpinning rationale of a surveillance state is the consolidation of knowledge in the hands of an elite that has every reason to perpetuate fear and to deny that knowledge to the public. However, in practice, even the elite are largely kept in the dark by the guardians of state secrecy, who routinely exceed the mandate of their appointment by distorting or suppressing information (sometimes in order to allow vulnerable leaders so-called plausible deniability).

As *Guardian* editor Alan Rusbridger points out, for example, the elite in the English government were deliberately kept ignorant of the most questionable programs revealed in the Snowden leaks. Rusbridger quotes Chris Huhne, a Liberal Democrat who was in the cabinet, as saying he had never heard of the NSA's Prism program and GCHQ's Tempora programs, which collected vast amounts of private information on millions of people in England and throughout the world. "The cabinet was told nothing about . . . their extraordinary capability to vacuum up and store personal emails, voice contact, social networking activity and even internet searches," as Huhne put it.[19]

That's in England, but what about top officials in the United States? There were a few members of the Senate Intelligence Committee who indicated they knew something was dangerously amiss with the activities of the NSA and other agencies they were charged with supervising, but even they couldn't go public.

Senator Feinstein, the Democrat who chaired the committee during the time of the Snowden disclosures, was quick to condemn him as a traitor rather than a whistleblower. But she has also continuously denied the negative consequences of surveillance programs she either hadn't known existed or didn't fully understand. She was at great pains to discount the intrusive impact of the vast collection of metadata or anything else done under her supervision—the collection of programs Snowden refers to as possessing the "architecture of oppression."

Others in Congress have grown less sanguine. Much of the spying by the NSA has been justified by the Patriot Act, authored by Republican congressman Jim Sensenbrenner, then-chair of the House Judiciary Committee. Yet, after the Snowden revelations, Sensenbrenner told the European Parliament that the trust his bill had placed in the US executive branch had been betrayed. "The NSA abused that trust," he said. "It ignored restrictions painstakingly crafted by lawmakers and assumed a plenary authority never imagined by Congress. Worse, the NSA cloaked its operations behind such a thick wall of secrecy that even if our trust was restored, we would lack the ability to verify it."[20]

That is a terrifying concern because it means that the nation's top spy agency has been found to be totally unaccountable to the branch of government that legislated it into existence and is charged with supervising its activity.

With a few notable exceptions, the Senate Intelligence Committee, which was originally created to provide a serious oversight function, has failed miserably to do so even—or, rather, particularly—after the Snowden revelations. Oddly enough, while other congressional critics like Sensenbrenner and Senate Judiciary chair Patrick Leahy, a Democrat from Vermont, were sufficiently moved by the new information on the vast reach of government spying to attempt to curtail it, the Democratic chair, the Republican second in command, and the majority of the other members took the tack of shooting the messenger—Snowden—while heaping praise on the heads of the spy agencies that had in fact deceived them and the American people.

࿔ ࿔ ࿔

THIS SITUATION POINTS TO THE ALL-IMPORTANT SEPARATION-of-powers construction of the American political system. The intelligence committee was formed through an act of Congress in response to the misuse of the intelligence agencies by the executive branch under President Richard Nixon. Further questions were raised concerning the political interference of those agencies after a much-publicized *New York Times* exposé by Seymour Hersh showed that the CIA had for a decade been violating its charter by engaging in domestic spying.[21]

After those revelations, the Senate voted by an overwhelming 82–4 vote on January 27, 1975, to establish a new select committee investigating federal intelligence operations to determine "the extent, if any, to which illegal, improper, or unethical activities were engaged in by any agency of the Federal Government."[22]

The committee, then headed by Senator Frank Church (D-ID), conducted a far-reaching investigation of the work of the CIA, FBI, Internal Revenue Service, and National Security Agency. The investigation made headlines revealing, among other things, a CIA program to assassinate foreign leaders and the FBI's COINTEL-PRO covert action program "designed to disrupt and discredit the activities of groups and individuals deemed a threat to the social order" (which included civil rights and peace organizations as well as individuals who critiqued US foreign and domestic policy, including local, state, and federal elected officials).

After an exhaustive investigation involving eight hundred witnesses and lasting over a year, the committee concluded that beginning with Franklin Roosevelt in the 1930s there had been a persistent pattern of "intelligence excesses at home and abroad" that were not the "product of any single party, administration, or man" but were a by-product of America's rise as a superpower during the Cold War.

"Intelligence agencies have undermined the constitutional rights of citizens," the committee's final report concluded, with words relevant to our more recent period, "primarily because checks and balances designed by the framers of the Constitution to ensure accountability have not been applied."[23]

There were ninety-six legislative and regulatory recommendations in the final report intended "to place intelligence activities within the constitutional scheme for controlling government power." Stating unequivocally that "there is no inherent constitutional authority for the President or any intelligence agency to violate the law," the committee recommended stronger oversight of the intelligence agencies.[24]

Toward that end, in 1976, the Senate passed Resolution 400, which established the Senate Select Committee on Intelligence to provide "vigilant legislative oversight over the intelligence activities of the United States to assure that such activities are in conformity with the Constitution and laws of the United States." Two years later, Congress passed and President Jimmy Carter signed into law the Foreign Intelligence Surveillance Act (FISA), establishing the FISA court that would have to approve all executive branch warrants for wiretapping and surveillance purposes.

In other words, Congress and the president had imposed strong demands for transparency and privacy on the spy agencies at the height of the Cold War, a time when the United States was locked in a power struggle so precarious that the fate of the entire world was literally in the balance. The Soviet Union possessed an enormously sophisticated military arsenal and intelligence apparatus and, according to the assessment of the CIA, a vast array of surrogates and allies, willing to act on its behalf in nations throughout the world. There was also Maoist China, which, while not militarily a superpower, certainly had the proven troops to confront the United States in regional warfare.

Meanwhile, aside from the Cold War confrontations, there were plenty of other political revolutionaries, religiously motivated "terrorists," and rogue nations that threatened what the spy agencies' claimed were our vital interests. At the time the Church Committee issued its damning indictment and the Senate set up its permanent committee to critically regulate the intelligence community, there were regional wars and terrorist incidents throughout the world. When Carter signed the Foreign Intelligence Surveillance Act, requiring a prior judicial warrant for all electronic surveillance in which communications of US citizens might be intercepted, those threats were at a high-water mark in places that now concern us again, including Afghanistan and Iran.

So how in the world did 9/11 and the threat of al Qaeda come to be perceived by an American president and much of the political class as a more pressing threat, one justifying a sacrifice of our individual freedoms? After all, by the time of the attack on the World Trade Center and the Pentagon, the Cold War had come to an end, with Russians and Chinese now our trading partners.

*** *** ***

KHALID SHEIKH MOHAMMED, IDENTIFIED IN THE 9/11 Commission Report as the sophisticated and complex hijacking plan's mastermind, was an engineering student at a North Carolina Baptist college who exhibited no particular hostility toward his American hosts. Despite his having been waterboarded close to two hundred times, or perhaps because of it, there is not a single piece of information made public, which explains where and why he became so hostile toward the United States.

The 9/11 commissioners, despite possessing very high security clearances, were never allowed to interview him or any other key witnesses; nor could they speak directly to those who did—leaving us in the dark, essentially, about what this terrorist enemy was all about, even as we devote so many resources to fighting it that the functioning of our democratic society is jeopardized.

That ignorance, unparalleled in any modern nation's preparation for a major "war"—as we have described the struggle to prevent terrorism—was on full display at a critical hearing of the Senate Intelligence Committee on January 29, 2014. Chairwoman Feinstein, who had quickly labeled Snowden a traitor only days after he accepted responsibility for the NSA leaks, warmly welcomed the heads of the intelligence agencies. Her effusive, even fawning testimonial to their work was obviously shared by a majority of the committee (although not by many in the public audience, whom Feinstein admonished to put away signs and threatened with ejections should they speak out).

Despite the theatrics, the session is worthy of detailed examination by anyone seriously concerned about the state of the intelligence apparatus—a collection of agencies the Snowden leaks revealed has a combined secret budget of over $50 billion a year, yet which Director of National Intelligence James Clapper was repeatedly at great pains to complain is underfunded.

After stating that, largely due to the wonderful efforts of the intelligence agencies, there had been no terrorist attacks "in the United States since our last threat hearing," Feinstein hastened to add that she is "concerned that this success has led to a popular misconception that the threat has diminished. It has not. . . . In fact, [the] terrorist [threat] is at an all-time high, if you include attacks by groups like the Taliban against the United States military and our coalition forces."[25]

There are many bad things one can say about the Taliban, a group that originated from anti-Soviet forces the United States recruited and trained, which has been preoccupied with reestablishing a theocratic state in Afghanistan (not all that different from, or necessarily more threatening than, that of our longtime ally in Saudi Arabia). But they are not a viable international threat. And when Feinstein in part attributed increased "terror" threats to "the instability that spread through North Africa and the Middle East during the Arab Spring"—an odd reference to what has been generally interpreted as a movement toward democracy led by young people—she showed just how elastic the term *terror* can be in the hands of national security opportunists.

However, this hodge-podge of exaggerated concerns was only the prelude to the big new terror threat that Clapper made the centerpiece of his case for additional funding—the real motive for holding the hearing in the first place.

The big new threat, he said, comes from extremist Sunni rebels in Syria (soon to be known to the world as the Islamic State of Iraq and Syria, or ISIS). Yet neither he nor Feinstein nor the intelligence experts arrayed before her ever once mentioned the inconvenient truth that the United States had only recently supported the rebellion and the destabilization of Syria, just as it had the anti-Soviet rebellion in Afghanistan more than four decades earlier that gave rise to both the Taliban and al Qaeda. In CIA terms, this is called blowback.

True, there are other terrorists to worry about, Feinstein assured:

> But I think the most notable development since last year's hearing is actually in Syria, which has become a magnet for foreign fighters and for terrorist activity. . . . Because large swaths of the country of Iraq are beyond the regime's control or that of moderate—excuse me—of Syria are beyond the regime's control or that of the moderate opposition, this leads to the major concern of the establishment of a safe haven and the real prospect that Syria could become a launching point or way station for terrorists seeking to attack the United States or other nations. Not only are fighters being drawn to Syria, but so are technologies and techniques that pose particular problems to our defense.[26]

Feinstein's statement raises the key issue about intelligence gathering that all the furor over Snowden's revealing of classified information ignores: the intelligence we need most is not revealed in the "noise" of all those endless emails and phone conversations that the intelligence agencies mine. America needs to comprehend its enemies, not just monitor them. The fact is that, despite pouring billions of dollars into black budgets and undermining our constitutional safeguards, we keep misunderstanding the world in terribly destructive ways—without examining why. We hope to eradicate our foes without stopping to carefully assess why they are our enemies in the first place.

For example, who are these Syrian rebels that now trouble Feinstein and the intelligence officers that testified before her? Where did they come from, what motivates them, and, most important of all, why did our intelligence community not warn our president that the policy of undermining the basically secular government of Assad—and the basically secular government of Saddam Hussein in Iraq ten years earlier—was doomed from its inception?

Both Assad and Hussein were, after all, implacably and brutally hostile to al Qaeda and other Sunni-led fanatical movements. One could have—should have—known that, both from reading publicly available press and scholarly reports about the political struggles in those countries and from doing the in-country detective work of talking to locals in the know. Instead, our intelligence juggernaut focuses on quantity over quality—or even makes the facts fit the narrative that Washington has already embraced.

Intelligence should be about learning what you need to know and don't already, not just about sucking up unmanageable gigabytes of minutiae everywhere in the world, which has been the NSA's enormously costly and ineffectual game of choice.

As NSA whistleblower William Binney put it, "There are ways to do the analysis properly, but they don't really want the solution because if they got it, [the NSA] wouldn't be able to keep demanding the money to solve it. I call it their business statement, 'Keep the problems going so the money keeps flowing.' It's all about contracts and money."[27]

WE ARE A NATION THAT HAS LONG CELEBRATED DISSIDENTS throughout the world who dare, often at great risk, to expose the secret actions and challenge the legitimacy of repressive governments. In some cases, we even provide legal sanctuary or asylum for such people. However, when Americans dissent in such radical ways, the opposite is often the case—they are vilified as disloyal and as a threat to our collective security or stability. The assumption, embraced so widely, must be that our system never requires such a fundamental challenge to its authority, as represented by the actions of a Daniel Ellsberg, Thomas Drake, Chelsea Manning, or Edward Snowden.

We know, however, from so many historical examples—the Roman Empire, Nazi Germany, the Soviet Union—that unchallenged authority not only will violate human rights but also will ultimately sow the seeds of its own ruin, increasingly blind to its own limitations and flaws. Despite our historically innovative constitutional checks on government power, we are nevertheless always flirting with imperial hubris. We see this clearly in the pattern of lies that defined US foreign policy after 9/11; it is quite apparent that leaving those lies largely unchallenged in the name of classification seriously weakened the position of the United States in the world.

eight

How the Digital Cookie Crumbles

W HILE THE HORRIFIC 9/11 ATTACKS ACCELERATED the acceptance of surveillance culture, large-scale government surveillance was already under way. Back in October 2000, in a cover story on privacy for the magazine *Yahoo! Internet Life,* I described how new communications technologies were being exploited by overeager government agencies to rapidly erode our privacy:

> The point of Aldous Huxley's *Brave New World* was that the public would come to accept totalitarian intrusion as a part of the normal fabric of life, as something that was actually good for them. We are fast approaching the point where we're inured to the cameras that record us when we enter stores, to the telephone company that asks for reams of information before connecting

our service, to the hospital social worker who needs to know more about your personal habits than you have thought about yourself. All that data, collected from the most disparate sources, is then recycled into recognizable clumps of information about you, to be devoured by others.

It's true that snooping has been with us from the earliest gossip grapevines linking our grass huts. And we've endured modern forms of surveillance such as wiretaps and bugs. But those methods tended to be obvious—picture a couple of bored cops sitting over their coffee, listening on their earphones, transcribing tapes, filing folders. It was labor-intensive and tedious. But what we have today is different by several leaps and bounds. Old spying had to be selective, targeted. New spying is like a high-powered vacuum cleaner; one that scoops up every bit of information it comes across, even the extraneous or incomprehensible stuff.[1]

At that time, in the pre-Snowden world, the government surveillance programs I wrote about had different names, such as the NSA's Echelon and the FBI's Carnivore, but the pattern was the same: a reckless disregard for Americans' right to privacy in the name of our security. Less than a year later came the September 11 attacks, the perfect rationale to dramatically ramp up both domestic and international spying to a magnitude that portends nothing less than the end of this nation's grand experiment in democracy.

Now, nearly a decade and a half later, we are clearly losing the continuing battle between individual freedom and collective conformity that has marked the history of human society. The right to be left alone—to think, to experiment, to contemplate—has been essential to the development of individual personality. The private space, protected from the intimidating observation of others, is the sacred ground where self-discovery occurs, and to the degree that external forces intrude, whether of the state, church, or marketplace, the sense of self will wither.

The information revolution that has been properly celebrated for irrevocably destroying the parochial restraints of language, society, and religion, while exposing much of the world's population to a boundless world of universally shared information, is at the same time stripping both passive and active participants of their privacy in ways most don't comprehend.

No dictator or intelligence agency, with its network of spies, could ever have hoped to obtain such access to the thoughts and aspirations of their subjects that today's off-the-shelf information technology so easily provides. This is the great contradiction of our time: the unprecedented liberating power of the supercomputer combined with the worldwide Internet—credited with facilitating such dramatic expansions of the democratic experience as the Arab Spring—also contain the seeds of freedom's destruction because of the awesome power of this new technology to support a surveillance state that exceeds the wildest dream of the most ingenuous dictator.

Do I exaggerate? Don't take my word for it; let the toolmakers tell you. In a burst of public honesty, Google executives Eric Schmidt and Jared Cohen wrote in April 2013: "Despite the expense, everything a regime would need to build an incredibly intimidating digital police state—including software that facilitates data mining and real-time monitoring of citizens—is commercially available right now. . . . It's the digital analog to arms sales."[2]

Of course, none of this is a complete surprise. Privacy is inevitably linked to technology, because anything that extends the reach of the eye, ear, or nose threatens intrusion into another's personal space. The ability of the first primitive telescope would allow a snooper to check on your bedroom antics, for example, and the ability of the first camera to record your activities—and the press that allowed publication of those images for the entire world to see—was what initiated the first sweeping defense of privacy in the United States.

That defense came in a forceful affirmation of the right to privacy in a *Harvard Law Journal* article by future United States Supreme Court justice Louis Brandeis in 1890. It vastly extended the reach of the Fourth Amendment, which protects one's personal freedom in the home, in papers, and in movement, but it also assumed a static and immediate point of intrusion, as befitted the limited technology of the day.

The freedom to be left alone, simple though it may sound, embodies the most basic of human rights. If the individual cannot find sanctuary in his home and person, he is easy prey for avenging governments, rapacious mobs, and exploitive robbers. Some call it the right to privacy, which puts the emphasis on seclusion for personal activity, but the framers of the Constitution used the stronger concept of security, as in creating a strong barrier to the intrusions of outside power. That's why the Constitution's protection of individual space in the wording of the Fourth Amendment stresses physical security, but its intent, certainly as interpreted by the courts, is broader: to form a cocoon of safety around the individual, which over the years we have come to associate with the word *privacy*.

Brandeis was concerned about technology-driven threats to one's privacy that by the late nineteenth century were becoming more invasive, particularly the use of the telephone. His article titled "The Right to Privacy," co-authored with Samuel Warren, is widely considered to be the decisive factor in establishing a broadened constitutional protection. "Political, social, and economic changes entail the recognition of new rights, and the common law, in its eternal youth, grows to meet the demands of society," wrote the lawyers. "Thus, in very early times, the law gave a remedy only for physical interference with life and property. . . . Gradually the scope of these legal rights broadened."[3]

Brandeis went on to join the Supreme Court, where his famous dissenting decision in *Olmstead v. United States* (1928) provided a landmark warning on privacy threats posed by technological advances: The government was identified as a potential privacy evader because "discovery and invention have made it possible for the government, by means far more effective than stretching upon the rack, to obtain disclosure in court of what is whispered in the closet," he wrote.[4]

Thanks to advances in technology that Brandeis could not have imagined, the reach of government and private corporations now extends far beyond the whisper in the closet. The basic economic model of the Internet—the sticky adherence of advertising to one's comments and curiosities—leaves exposed, for example, not only purchase histories but also random keystrokes and scattered drafts of one's flights of fancy. Overhearing conversations that the participants are lulled into assuming are private, when they are anything but, is the advertising model of the Internet.

Facebook, as far back as July 2010, according to *USA Today*, had over 500 million members who would upload more than 25 billion pieces of content each month.[5] Twitter has more than 200 million active users, and the Library of Congress recently announced that it will be acquiring and permanently storing the entire record of public Twitter posts.[6] As the *New York Times* noted on July 19, 2010, in reporting that factoid, "the Web means the end of forgetting."[7] Whether it also means the end of privacy depends on what control individuals have, and are able to regain, over how their personally generated data is compiled and disseminated.

ᴬᵛ ᴬᵛ ᴬᵛ

IT WASN'T UNTIL THE FIRST WEEK OF JUNE 2013, HOWEVER, that the nation's media finally caught up with the news that for a decade Americans had abjectly surrendered their historic respect for individual privacy to the chimera of national security. That week, the NSA files leaked by Snowden revealed that the federal government has full access to all phone records and to the vast trove of presumably private personal data posted on the Internet.

The most sacred tenet of American individualism, the right to be left alone, had been squandered, almost without notice. In the wake of the 9/11 attacks, a snooper state had come to be accepted as the norm in which an already robust corporate intrusion into our privacy came to be conjoined with the heightened obsession with security at all costs. A new military-intelligence complex had come into its own based on the unprecedented power of spy agencies, unleashed by the urgency of a so-called War on Terror, fused with the previously unimaginable intrusion into private space wrought by the Internet revolution. The Constitution's Fourth Amendment guarantee of the sovereignty of the individual—"The right of the people to be secure in their persons, houses, papers, and effects, against unreasonable searches and seizures, shall not be violated"—was being treated as an irrelevant relic of a bygone civilization.

It was a perfect storm. The snoopers, both state and corporate, now had the capacity for massive storage and search functions, able to move far beyond the level of surveillance ever deemed permissible, or even possible, by the constitutional framers. Now the government, rationalizing the excessive use of state power with a hysterically defended claim that the very existence of our country was threatened by terrorism, merged the private and the public data fields in order to create instant, absurdly detailed portraits of any citizen "of interest." One's most intimate habits, from private correspondence, book pages read, and lists of friends and phone conversations, can be seamlessly merged with a detailed map of an individual's DNA, both biological and social.

The radical transformation of technology today has turned the NSA "into the virtual landlord of the digital assets of Americans and foreigners alike," a *New York Times* editorial aptly stated in response to the disclosures of the monitoring of commercially based data by the nation's most invasive security agency.[8] The mainstream media had finally began to focus seriously on the loss of privacy, which was old news to a brave group of government whistleblowers who had attempted to sound the alarm and been severely punished for their efforts to hold their government accountable.

The boldest justification for unfettered government intrusion in our privacy came back in October 2001, when, without hearings or even serious discussion, Congress rushed to pass "an Act to deter terrorist acts in the United States and around the world, to enhance law enforcement investigatory tools, and for other purposes." With less consideration than two months of fleeting thought in an atmosphere of panic could provide, two centuries of constitutional law had been swept aside with only sixty-six dissenting votes in the House and one in the Senate. President Bush signed the measure into law on October 26, 2001. Laws regarding wiretapping, searches of homes, examination of mail, the right to due process, and even freedom from arbitrary and secret arrest were suddenly neutered.

The power of the Patriot Act to undermine our freedoms was evident as a nagging thought even in the minds of some members of Congress who voted for its far-reaching provisions. They assuaged their conscience by scheduling the act to expire in four years. In March 2006, however, President Bush signed new legislation passed by Congress that reauthorized the most controversial provisions, and on May 26, 2011, President Obama, while traveling in France, used an autopen to extend the reach of onerous provisions of the act another four years.[9]

As when the colonists championed the principles that became the Fourth Amendment during their war of independence against the British Crown, individual rights are most severely tested when foreign policy and national security are at the fore. Hunts for spies or subversive plots become more compelling under such circumstances and are generally backed by wartime laws based on the idea that the present crisis demands special measures.

The targets may be scapegoated citizens with some "foreign" attachment, as in the case of Japanese Americans interned in camps during World War II or, today, those Americans accused of terrorist ties or aspirations—usually Muslim—who can be arrested and even executed abroad without the restraint of due process or any sort of judicial procedure.

In July 2014, Human Rights Watch released a devastating report on the anti-Muslim bias in terrorism prosecutions.[10] The lengthy report, written in collaboration with the Columbia University Law School's Human Right Institute, showed that the FBI entrapped Muslims with mental and intellectual disabilities to appear to be engaged in planning terrorist actions for which they were then arrested. "The report clearly shows, in many respects, the American public is being sold a false bill of goods," said Andrea Prasow, one of the Human Rights Watch report's authors. "To be sure, the threat of terrorism is real," she said. "But in many cases we documented, there was no threat until the FBI showed up and helped turn people into terrorists."[11]

Wartime, and that includes any period of extreme fear of an enemy, including the irregular forces of terrorism or other subversion, is in every nation the great enabler of suppression of freedom—and it begins with the invasion of privacy, in order to collect the evidence of attacks, plots, or rebellions. It is also a time when governments can act with the impunity afforded by the secrecy that wartime demands, as the concealment of government's purposes and evidence becomes formalized through classification of documents and communications. That, in turn, becomes the excuse for denying the sovereign rights of the individual.

As in other nations when citizens have traded freedom for security, throughout our history our safety is the excuse to weaken or destroy the freedoms of speech, press, and assembly our Constitution asserts as fundamental rights. And what that venerable yet resilient document could not anticipate is both the immense promise and the chilling threat to those freedoms posed by life in the digital age.

Suddenly, people anywhere, or at least those in the wired world, could view any document challenging the government's case for going to war. Consider the attack of 9/11 as a marker in that information revolution, when, like no time before, the public could be riven by debates over what it takes to destroy a skyscraper, the political and religious motives of its destroyers, and the history of their connections with various governments. And when the Bush administration chose to invade Iraq in response to that attack, its claims of a connection between that country and al Qaeda, as well as the presence of weapons of mass destruction, were quickly exposed by documentary evidence, never before so readily and widely available, that contradicted the official narrative.

Of course, fomenting healthy debate is only the first step to making good decisions, and in this case the Bush administration,

with the cover of powerful Democrats like Senators Hillary Clinton and John Kerry, pushed through a war regardless of the facts.
Meanwhile, the mainstream media, never consistently brave in
wartime, seemed cowed by the blind rage spawned by 9/11 and
provided only minimal resistance to the tsunami of cherry-picked
evidence Bush officials Dick Cheney, Colin Powell, and others used
to intimidate Congress, the UN, and a good chunk of the public.
(Or, as in the infamous case of Judith Miller, then of the *New York
Times,* touted sightings of Iraqi weapons of mass destruction that
turned out to be nonexistent.)

At the same time, and in the media's defense, the Internet had,
indirectly but devastatingly, weakened the traditional press, long
led in content, if not audience, by daily and weekly print publications. Without glamorizing an often sordid, rancorous, or erratic
industry, it must be remembered that the United States has an
established and venerated tradition of muckraking, independent
journalism going all the way back to the barbed commentary the
founders themselves had squirmed under but which they nonetheless felt was necessary to protect. Undermined economically
by everything from Craigslist (no more classifieds!) to the flatten-
ing power of search engines and news aggregators, the biggest reporting machines were suddenly operating under much-reduced
budgets with smaller readership and reach, and competition from
nontraditional—and free—news and content recycling sources
like blogs and Twitter.

But two other factors also emerged—factors of great consequence in weakening the role of the traditional media's ability to
cover national security issues. One was that the government had a
much-increased ability to use new media to propagate their message,
bypassing the tough questions from traditional media. The other was
that the modern technology of surveillance allowed the government

to spy on independent reporters and their sources to a degree never before imagined, even in overtly totalitarian societies. This dangerous confluence of new surveillance technologies, combined with the hyping of a never-ending but shadowy terrorism "war," ushered in a dangerous threat to freedom—particularly that of the press.

One of the best surveys of that transformation came in October 2013, in the form of the aforementioned report for the Committee to Protect Journalists written by former *Washington Post* executive editor Leonard Downie, Jr.[12] As discussed in Chapter 6, Downie was a leading journalist who had steered the *Post* through some of that paper's most legendary investigative exposés. His report was informed by interviews with some of the most accomplished veterans of that sort of journalism. It provides a chilling marker in the deterioration of press freedom in the surveillance age.

The report's conclusions also delineated how scrambled the political spectrum had become regarding the protection of personal and press freedom. Although the report is quite tough in its criticism of the Republican President Bush in seizing upon the trauma of the 9/11 attack to justify a vast increase in the prerogatives of the national security state, his administration was actually less damaging to press freedom than that of his Democratic Party successor, according to Downie. Writing under the subheading "Leak Investigations and Surveillance in post-9/11 America," Downie argued:

U.S. President Barack Obama came into office pledging open government, but he has fallen short of this promise. Journalists and transparency advocates say the White House curbs routine disclosure of information and deploys its own media to evade scrutiny by the press. Aggressive prosecution of leakers of classified information and broad electronic surveillance programs deter government sources from speaking to journalists.[13]

As we have seen in earlier chapters, even before the Snowden bombshell there had been a series of cases brought by the Obama administration against reporters and their whistleblowing sources that illustrated just how effective massive electronic surveillance was in preventing them from conducting private conversations unless they deployed extraordinary encryption tools. These captured communications were already showing up as evidence in government legal proceedings against journalists and their sources with such regularity as to clearly reflect the use of a new—and massive—surveillance mechanism. The Snowden revelations, Downie wrote, confirmed this, adding a chilling caution to the relationship between reporter and source.

"Compounding the concerns of journalists and the government officials they contact, news stories based on classified documents obtained from Snowden have revealed extensive surveillance of Americans' telephone and email traffic by the National Security Agency," Downie continued. "Numerous Washington-based journalists told me that officials are reluctant to discuss even unclassified information with them because they fear that leak investigations and government surveillance make it more difficult for reporters to protect them as sources."[14] What that last sentence captures is the essential role of privacy as the elixir vital to the "big picture," in that it allows the processing of random facts, bits of conversations, undeveloped thoughts, and all of the other fragments of knowledge that form the raw material collected by journalists in pursuit of an investigative article on government actions that the public has a right and need to know about.

For many liberals, the realization that Obama has doubled down on intimidation of journalists is tough to swallow. Nevertheless, it is an undeniable reality after a term and a half under the former constitutional law professor. "It's hypocritical," said James Risen, the Pulitzer Prize–winning *New York Times* reporter. "[A lot of people] don't want to believe that Obama wants to crack down on the press and whistle-blowers. But he does. He's the greatest enemy to press freedom in a generation."[15] Risen has personal experience of this, under another president. Having accurately reported a story on a failed US government effort to thwart Iran's alleged nuclear program that backfired, he found himself put under legal threat by the Bush administration to turn over his alleged source to support a criminal prosecution. While such a repressive reaction fit the liberal critique of Bush, civil libertarians were shocked when Obama's administration renewed the persecution of Risen in 2009.

"A lot of people still think this is some kind of game or signal or spin [on the part of the Obama administration]," Risen told his colleague Maureen Dowd in the article dated August 16, 2014, referring to the fact that he faces possible jail time for refusing to reveal his source. Continuing his criticism of Obama, he pointed to "recent stories about the administration pressing an unprecedented initiative known as the Insider Threat Program, which [the] McClatchy [news service] described as 'a government-wide crackdown on security threats that requires federal employees to keep closer tabs on their co-workers and exhorts managers to punish those who fail to report their suspicions.'"[16]

Of course, all of this is much bigger than the president. Whatever he may or may not feel in his gut, we know, as with so many officials functioning in societies who proclaim their commitment to the utility of freedom, it is harder to walk the walk than to talk the talk. The assumption of such cultures is that even the well-intentioned—some would argue, particularly the well-intentioned—have the capacity to overreach the limits of reason, fact, and fairness, and to do harm. Leaders' good intentions are no assurance of responsible governance; only an independent, questioning public willing to act on its sense of grievance can protect us from state abuse. Yet when people attain power in any society, as Lord Acton famously warned, that power tends to corrupt as remaining true to their espoused values becomes increasingly inconvenient.

Perhaps that explains Obama's retreat from his bold stance as a presidential candidate, when he pledged to reverse Bush's pattern of official lies and secrecy. "Transparency promotes accountability," he stated on the White House website, after he was inaugurated, adding logically enough that "[transparency] provides information for citizens about what their government is doing."[17]

However, in the wake of the Snowden revelations, even small steps in the right direction have been stymied by the administration. For example, a review group that Obama appointed recommended several changes to limit the potential abuse of massive loopholes provided by Reagan-era Executive Order 12333, which allows so-called incidental collection of US citizen communications if they are swept up abroad.

According to an August 13, 2014, *New York Times* report by Charlie Savage on State Department whistleblower John Napier Tye, the review group suggested that analysts should purge citizen data from the "12333 storehouse upon detection, unless they have foreign intelligence value or are necessary to prevent bodily harm"; that analysts should not use any "12333 intercepts of Americans as direct evidence in criminal proceedings against them"; and that "analysts should not search the storehouse for an American's messages unless a court finds probable involvement with terrorism."[18]

These reasonable safeguards, however, were rejected by the administration, sparking Tye to file whistleblower complaints with the NSA and Congress based on Fourth Amendment violations inherent in the 12333-allowed programs. Tye, who himself may end up being targeted for prosecution, went public as Congress was considering changes to the Foreign Intelligence Surveillance Act. However, these changes, should they even happen, would not affect Order 12333—which Obama, or his successor, could lift instantly with a signature. "We are at an inflection point in human history," Tye told Savage. "It's a problem if one branch of government can collect and store most Americans' communications, and write rules in secret on how to use them—all without the oversight from Congress or any court, and without the consent or even knowledge of the American people."[19]

With an executive branch that seems to seek increased powers regardless of which party is in charge and a historically paralyzed and ineffective Congress, it is hard to know where meaningful reforms will come from. The European model for seeking to push back the frontline in the battle over what is public likely won't work in the United States, since it would threaten our First Amendment rights, while technological fixes like encryption may only slow rather than halt our loss of privacy.

One way or another, however, we have to begin building firewalls, circuit breakers, protected zones—whether legal, digital, or based in government policy.

⁂

IN THE PRE-INTERNET AMERICAN JOURNALISM WORLD OF the twentieth century there were many traps of corrupting purpose that continuously threatened the integrity of the newsgathering enterprise. Advertising as a major source of revenue was certainly the major potential moral pitfall, in that those who could pay for the ads had agendas—mostly sales- and profit-related, but sometimes explicitly political—that could undermine the integrity of the project. Pressure also came from powerful religious, cultural, and political institutions, both locally and nationally, and the publisher, network, or station owners would be under pressure to mollify the concerns of those interests while preserving editorial independence.

In response, evolving and solidifying over time, there came to be the notion of a metaphorical "wall" between editorial and publishing, between the journalists and the businesspeople. Over time, the strength of this wall came to be the bellwether of integrity for traditional news enterprises in the United States. While it would be naive to presume the wall wasn't occasionally breached, sometimes all too easily, there was nonetheless a standard whose violations could be noted, publicized, and challenged internally or publicly.

The Internet has no such walls. Formed initially at government instigation to provide an alternative means of communication in the event of nuclear war or some other earth-threatening catastrophe, this stupendous invention was not thought of initially as either a profitmaking or newsgathering enterprise. But today it is certainly the dominant means of purveying news and fast becoming the all-encompassing means of commerce. Indeed, the success of both of these is at the heart of the destruction of traditional print and even commercial television and radio news operations.

In this new wired world, where news and profit are comingled like never before, the notion of a wall between the two has been treated as an anachronism of a simpler, bygone time. So, too, has the concern over the separation of newsgathering from the pressures of government and large economic enterprises that the news is expected to critically and honestly cover.

As a potent symbol of how those once clearly separated activities are now intricately entwined, consider the example of Amazon. Jeff Bezos, the online superstore's founder and major owner, is now also the owner of the *Washington Post*—the paper most significant for its daily, in-depth coverage of the federal government—while, at the same time, his company has a contract to build a $600 million cloud to store the data that the seventeen US spy agencies are collecting on the world's population.[20]

With such a massive conflict of interest, will Bezos's *Post* continue to run exposés of the surveillance state as it did as one of the main publishers of the Snowden leaks? Will Amazon, with near-monopoly dominance, be influenced in its marketing of books, music, or movies critical of the government, or of big corporations like itself?

For those given to a myopic view of the intentions of their own nation's government and corporations, perhaps it is better to think of examples of such comingling of enterprises in other nations. That must be a concern of any multinational corporation whose profit base by definition crosses a sharply divided, global cultural, religious, and political terrain.

The lesson of the US experience, from a nation that is much advertised in its commitment to limited government and individual freedom, is hardly reassuring on such matters. Prior to the Snowden and other leaks, a fiction had developed that only bad guys and bad governments abuse the freedom of the Internet to invade the privacy, and hence the freedom, of its citizens. Or that at least in a society that has the markings of freedom, such abuse will be quickly discovered and corrected. But the opposite may be the case. No government has been more far-reaching and effective in invading the private space of the individual than our own, and disclosure of that fact resulted not from the ordinary checks and balances of our political system but, rather, from the all-too-rare example set by a few brave truth tellers risking imprisonment or worse.

Consider how little we knew about our own government's spying on us, until Snowden came along. And he, even by his own reckoning, knows about only a small part of the assault on our individual space by a government that cannot control its invasive impulse.[21]

Whether we are at a tipping point, or have slid far past it, remains to be seen. In any case, as Thomas Jefferson noted, "even under the best forms of government those entrusted with power have, in time, and by slow operations, perverted it into tyranny," and so we can claim no inherent immunity to authoritarianism simply because we hold elections.[22] Jefferson also once hoped "our wisdom will grow with our power, and teach us that the less we use our power the greater it will be," a hope so far unfulfilled.[23]

Yet, as a dictum commonly attributed to Alice Walker goes, "The most common way people give up their power is by thinking they don't have any."[24] If we persist in apathetically accepting the privacy invasions of corporations and the predations of our own government—perhaps believing the war is already lost—our dystopian future is clear: a world where our private and public spheres are one and the same, where any agency or business or even individual who can afford the fee can scrutinize us at their leisure, and penalize us for any perceived defect or nonconformity.

Epilogue

ISTANCED FROM THE HUBBUB OF SAN FRANCISCO'S
Market Street, where the likes of Twitter, Square, and Microsoft have set up shop, and tucked away from the overwhelming air of tech fetishism in bustling San Jose, whose main
draws include the Googleplex and the Tech Museum, lies Palo
Alto—a quiet, well-manicured suburb that at first glance could
be mistaken for any other in the state. But in fact, it is the heart of
Silicon Valley, as subdued in its presentation as it is earthshaking
in its power and impact.

There are few emblems of that status on the route between San
Francisco and Stanford. Cruising up Willow Road in adjacent
Menlo Park, where the landscape is flat and nondescript, a giant
white and cobalt blue thumb, surrounded by photo-snapping tour-
ists, pops into view. It is the iconic symbol of the Facebook "Like"

button, marking the company's office; super-sized, it looks like a piece of oddly placed architectural kitsch, reminiscent of Claude Bell's full-size concrete dinosaurs that greet visitors to California's desolate Coachella Valley desert from miles away.

Facebook's headquarters is the backyard of Stanford University, the citadel of the tech capital. The campus includes a compound of Mission-style sandstone buildings from which have emerged nearly forty thousand companies including Hewlett-Packard, Google, LinkedIn, Intuit, Yahoo, and Sun Microsystems, according to the university's "Stanford Facts" pamphlet. It also notes that these companies, "if gathered collectively into an independent nation, would constitute the world's tenth largest economy."[1] Indeed, Stanford both generates and nets enormous wealth. It has raised more money than any American university over the past decade and set a single-year record in 2012, raising more than $1 billion, mostly in alumni donations.[2] That is partly due to the longstanding relationship between the tech industry and the university's powerhouse president, John L. Hennessy, a former Stanford professor of electrical engineering and computer science and director of its Computer Systems Laboratory. It was under his mentorship that Stanford grads Larry Page and Eric Schmidt birthed a formerly Stanford-owned technology, Google, for which Hennessy now serves as a director. He is also a director at Cisco Systems and a founder of MIPS Technologies and Atheros.[3]

Among the faculty members and students engaged in a fevered pursuit of money and patents are a small number of techies and technophiles with a social conscience; they give high priority to civil liberties and privacy preservation, sometimes at a personal or professional cost. The Stanford Center for Internet and Society employs a number of these people, all of whom work in Silicon Valley or closely with those who run it. This includes Director of

Privacy Aleecia M. McDonald, whose small office in the Stanford Law School building barely seats three people.

In an interview, McDonald vacillated between patient teacher and rhapsodizing advocate for Internet privacy. When asked "How many *'yous'*—privacy advocates—are there?" she replied that there are many different types of groups that have fought for privacy reform and progress. But, she says, "put all those types of groups together and you wouldn't even fill the smallest of lunchrooms at Google."

These groups come up with many important ideas, some of which have been or can be reasonably implemented, about how to design law and technology as a means of preserving privacy—and, by extension, other democratic values—rather than crushing it. Nobody among them will find a panacea for digital privacy problems because there isn't just one. Instead, engaged citizens will have to rely on privacy *scrum*, a software development term referring to a flexible, holistic strategy whereby multidisciplinary team members work as a unit to reach a common goal.

As McDonald put it, "[W]e need to do everything all at once, because the problem is that big. We need to be doing policy. We need to have new laws. We need to have user education. We need to have people angry and pushing back in some cases and in some cases not. In some cases we need paternalism, and in some cases we don't, and it's okay to leave things to user choice. It's going to be a mix of approaches; some of them are highly contextual."

As she speaks, scholar, lawyer, and Stanford lecturer Jonathan Mayer can be seen darting around the narrow hallways just outside McDonald's office. "You have academics who are very pure; they want to sit in their offices and think. Then you have academics who are basically advocates who happen to get tenure," says McDonald. She and Mayer are somewhere in between. Their work has focused on lessening the privacy effects of user tracking through legislation, federal regulation, and industry self-regulation. Mayer put regulatory agencies like the FTC on guard when he blew the whistle on Google for circumventing Apple's Safari privacy features, resulting in the largest FTC fine in history, $22.5 million.[4]

Many of these individuals have at some point been connected to the Electronic Frontier Foundation (EFF), the leading nonprofit organization defending privacy and civil liberties in the digital realm. The EFF, with its team of lawyers, technologists, and activists, advises policymakers and educates the press and the public. Founded in the early days of the Internet by a group of cypherpunks and libertarians, including writer John Perry Barlow and activist John Gilmore, the organization started out with a focus on government issues and kept a distance from business. But, as outlined in previous chapters, the EFF and other such libertarian organizations necessarily took up work concerning the private sector, as the government and big tech got increasingly cozy with one another.

As with the ACLU, the EFF's primary weapon against governmental privacy invasion is the law. Its courtroom efforts have set legal precedents protecting digital communications from government intrusion. For example, its victory against the Secret Service established that it is illegal for law enforcement to access and read private electronic mail without a warrant.[5] In addition, the EFF established that computer code is speech and shielded the developers of privacy-protecting software from government censorship.[6]

The EFF and its offshoot, the Freedom of the Press Foundation (FPF), which boasts Edward Snowden, Daniel Ellsberg, Glenn Greenwald, and Laura Poitras on its board, also promote aggressive, public interest journalism that takes aim at excessive government secrecy. Toward that end, they've developed and managed encryption technologies such as SecureDrop, an open-source software platform that allows whistleblowers and journalists to securely transmit documents.[7] A directory of media users and their Web links on the EFF includes *Forbes*, the *Washington Post*, *ProPublica*, the *New Yorker*, and others.[8]

SecureDrop, originally designed and developed as DeadDrop by Aaron Swartz and Kevin Poulsen, famed hacker and now digital security journalist, is also accessible to average users through FPF's education initiatives.[9] The widespread use of encryption technology—tools that allow the digital scrambling of information so that only authorized parties can decipher it (though often not foolproof)—can make government snooping on our data increasingly difficult and expensive.

Micah Lee, a twenty-eight-year old cryptologist for the Freedom of the Press Foundation and a "digital bodyguard" for Greenwald and Poitras's *The Intercept*—an investigative reporting venture founded to "provide a platform to report on the documents previously provided by NSA whistleblower Edward Snowden"—is an important figure in the world of technologists who work to strengthen and protect the security of the digital tools we use every day.[10] Lee was hired to pore through the Snowden documents to help decipher some of the more technical material and also to protect the documents from being hacked.

"We can take huge steps to put the genie back in the bottle" through use of encryption," Lee said in an interview. "But I don't know how likely it is that we'll completely succeed at any point. . . . I think it's possible to make mass surveillance not nearly as valuable as it currently is, so when mass surveillance is conducted, they don't get as much useful information; they'll have to do more targeted surveillance. . . . Encryption is the crux of it."[11]

Lee cited "Yahoo and Google," which "are now working to build end-to-end encryption into their email services. That's an example of how we're making mass surveillance much less effective. Suddenly, in 2015 or 2016, when Yahoo and Google finish with these services, it'll be much harder for these companies to read their users' emails. Therefore, it will be much more difficult for a Yahoo or Google to take those emails and hand them to the government when they're forced to."

"The fact that encryption is possible is one of the marvels of our universe and of mathematics, the language that our universe is written in," he continued. "We're living at a technological crossroads. The Internet could still yet wind up being the greatest tool for human liberation or the greatest tool for ubiquitous surveillance and oppression that civilization has ever seen. But if we're clever enough we can win. The laws of physics are on our side, if only we accept their help."

↝ ↝ ↝

IT'S NOT ONLY STRICT PRIVACY ADVOCATES WHO SUPPORT privacy reform, but also Silicon Valley techies, who have come up with alternatives to big tech's data-vacuuming search and communication services. They include entrepreneurs like Gabriel Weinberg—founder of DuckDuckGo, a search engine that doesn't track users—and others who create viable alternatives to big tech search engines and communication services. Weinberg bills his product as the alternative to Google's services, and it has taken off since Snowden's revelations.

Another example is Ladar Levison, a computer programmer who founded and operated Lavabit, a secure email service that used an elaborate encryption system to protect its users' communications. Levison shut down the enterprise in 2014 when the Supreme Court compelled him to turn over the site's master encryption keys for its entire system in order to facilitate court-approved surveillance on a single user—Snowden.

A number of big tech companies have hired legions of privacy teams, composed mostly of technologists. Likewise, some Internet companies have found a market advantage in offering tools that their customers can use to restrict the tracking of their journey as they browse the Web. These companies were in part pushed by customer concerns for privacy overseas, particularly in Europe.

The European reaction to privacy invasions not only had an enormous effect on industry regulation of big tech, which counts Europe as a large piece of its market share, but also influenced how Americans think about privacy. Rules and regulations originating from the European Union's headquarters in Brussels have penetrated many aspects of economic and cultural life within and outside Europe, a phenomenon referred to by scholars as "the Brussels effect."[12] The European Union and independent governments are seeking to protect the privacy interests of their citizens by requiring greater transparency on the part of Internet corporations.

The assumption increasingly being made is that an individual's data is in fact a private possession to be guarded rather than exploited. The pressure on Google from the EU to allow individuals to delete its posted search results on them, enforced by a court decision, is a strong reminder that multinational corporations such as Google must operate in a political as well as a commercial market in which consumer rights need to be accommodated. Google has been on the receiving end of much of the European Union's criticism of its practices in Europe—the company commands more than 90 percent of the search market, even greater than the two-thirds dominance that Google enjoys in the United States.[13]

The challenge for Google and other immense US tech firms is to demonstrate that they are truly multinational companies fully capable of serving their worldwide customer base with equal consideration despite being US-based and enjoying a special connection to the company's home government headquartered in Washington. But those foreign governments have power over Google's operations in their countries, and, as a result, the activities of Google's street-view cars have elicited fines in Germany, Italy, and France.[14]

The suspicion that Google has moved far afield from its original "Don't Be Evil" start-up days has become widespread, as the company enjoys massive monopoly power. "We are afraid of Google," Mathias Döpfner, CEO of Germany's largest publisher, Axel Springer AG, wrote to Google executive chairman Eric Schmidt. "I must state this very clearly and frankly, because few of my colleagues dare do so publicly."[15] Hachette, another huge European publisher, has taken a similar stance in its much-publicized dispute with Amazon over profit distribution from the sale of its books by the US-based giant.

As mentioned earlier, in 2013 Amazon snagged a $600 million contract to provide cloud service to the US intelligence community. This development confirms that US multinational corporations, while international in their business operations, are at the same time deeply entwined with the nationalistic concerns of the US government. In fact, when that government sounds the alarm of national security, invalid or not, US companies simply cave. This contradiction represents an ever-widening threat to the worldwide growth that US-based companies require to maintain their profit margins.

Criticism of the overreach of US multinational corporations appears around the world and is troubling to American-based companies that face saturated markets at home and depend upon foreign sales for profit growth. In that contest, it is a matter both of non-American versus US-based companies and of customers' confidence in the latter's willingness to preserve their privacy. Consumers do still have choices, after all.

Whereas Google is dominant in Europe, for example, it is virtually nonexistent in China, the world's fastest-growing market. And although Google deserves credit for refusing to go along with the Chinese government's insistence back in 2010 on censoring search inquiries, it is also true that Google and other internationally successful American companies have found resistance from Chinese consumers. Due in part to obvious advantages enjoyed by Chinese companies, beginning with language, the homegrown companies now command a market comparable to the worldwide operations of their American rivals.

Three Chinese-based companies—Tencent, Baidu, and Alibaba—are among the top six most valuable Internet companies in the world, based on projected stock market capitalization, with Alibaba ranking third behind Google and Facebook.[16] With the Chinese companies now buying up US- and other foreign-based firms, the great rivalry for Internet commerce is shaping up as a battle between those three Chinese companies and three US-based competitors, Google, Facebook, and Amazon.

This could be a healthy development if the Chinese companies are forced to compete with their US counterparts in providing Internet services that favor consumer rights, beginning with privacy protection. But that would mean challenging the power of a company's home government, the still free speech–adverse rulers in Beijing. In any case, to date the advantage is with the US companies, which also happen to have a better track record in this regard, despite a record compromised, as delineated in previous chapters, by evidence of deference to the demands of US spy agencies.

In the best of all worlds, these companies, no matter their host location, should be truly multinational, meaning that they must be free to serve the demands of their consumers before catering to those of the governments of the countries in which they operate. That balancing of power across national lines may well define the battle for human freedom in an increasingly interconnected and wired world.

That is certainly, as earlier chapters indicate, a prime consideration for the executives of US-based companies as they have pushed back on Washington with their common statement in response to the Snowden revelations. After those revelations showed that most tech companies had gone along with the NSA's Prism program, their commitment to foreign consumers was seemingly compromised.

Most of these companies claimed they did so reluctantly, but it was only in September 2014 that 1,500 pages of FISA court documents from 2008 were finally released, vindicating the claims of one of those companies, Yahoo.[17] As Yahoo general counsel Ronald Bell noted, "The released documents underscore how we had to fight every step of the way to challenge the US Government's surveillance efforts."[18]

Yahoo unsuccessfully challenged the constitutionality of the government's intrusion into its customers' privacy and was rewarded with the threat of a $250,000-a-day fine.[19] After Yahoo lost its case, Google, Facebook, Apple, AOL, and most other tech companies went along with the government's demand. Microsoft was the one major company that surrendered without even waiting for the FISA court's decision.

No wonder Bill Gates condemned Snowden for his embarrassing disclosures—embarrassing because Snowden allowed Microsoft's customers to witness the company's craven capitulation to a government that was intent on spying on its citizens.[20] Evidently, Gates's ethical philosophy is that what we don't know doesn't hurt us. While Microsoft might have been the worst offender in its failure to protect its consumers' right to know, it is also quite clear that none of the above-mentioned tech companies was prepared to be honest with its customers until Snowden's leaks forced the issue. By that cynical calculation, their marketing experience had proved them right.

The commercial collection and mining of consumer data have come to define the basic business model of the Internet. It is that massive trove of personal data collected for commercial purposes that the government systematically plundered with the Prism program in the name of national security. The Yahoo example, and the lesser resistance of the other tech companies, confirms their statements after the Snowden releases that they consider that the Prism program and other government violations of their customers' privacy undermine their business model as well as democracy. Undoubtedly, there is a growing consensus among tech companies that privacy, or at least a veneer of it, is an essential ingredient of the product they are selling in order to garner consumer trust.

For example, Apple, with its long history of privacy breaches—including a September 2014 leak of nude celebrity photos stored by its iCloud service—was forced by mounting consumer backlash to engage in the debate about privacy protections in a far-reaching manner when it held its September 2014 press conference on its impending release of the new Apple iWatch and Apple Pay service. For the first time, Apple was entering the top tier of companies that profit from data mining, primarily dominated by Google and Amazon.

The proud boast of Apple had long been that, as opposed to those other companies, its profits derived predominantly from the creation and sale of physical products rather than from targeted advertising. As the *New York Times* reported, "Timothy D. Cook, Apple's chief executive, said in an interview that in contrast to companies like Amazon and Google that relied on tracking user activity to serve ads or sell things, Apple still primarily made money from selling hardware. With Apple Pay, which will be available next month, Apple does not store any payment information on the devices or on Apple's servers. It simply acts as a conduit between the merchant and bank."[21]

In a sneer at the aforementioned competition, Cook told the *Times,* "We're not looking at it through the lens that most people do of wanting to know what you're buying, where you buy it, how much you're spending and all these kinds of things. We could care less."

Another top Apple official announced that the company would not allow app developers for the new Apple Watch to use iCloud, presumably more vulnerable to hackers, to store sensitive health information, and that the data stored on the watch itself would be encrypted. Similar protection was assured regarding the financial data logged by Apple Pay, which will employ the more secure chip-based Europay, Mastercard, Visa (EMV) technology that relies on changing numbers assigned to each purchase instead of the old-fashioned magnetic-strip technology that had proved vulnerable to theft at stores.[22]

But none of this was quite true, and little of the boasting stood up to scrutiny, since the apps that had made the iPhone so profitable were most often dependent for their profitability on the harvesting of individual location and other data. With the new Apple iWatch collecting an individual's health data and Apple Pay recording a record of credit card purchases, Apple is suddenly wading in the deepest waters of sensitive personal data collection.

A few years ago, with privacy concerns largely dormant in the mainstream political discussion, this product-line shift from a prominent company did not raise many questions from the public, but in the post-Snowden era, Apple was forced to directly confront the problem. The good news is that once consumers have been warned about the glaring threats to their private data online, companies will be forced to tighten those protections in order to maintain their customers' trust in the process. The bad news is that those same companies have been loathe to inform consumers of the risks they face for fear that doing so will jeopardize a profit model based for most Internet companies on targeted advertising.

"The Achilles heel for privacy and consumer protection are apps connected to marketing, where information can be gathered and used," noted privacy advocate Jeffrey Chester of the Center for Digital Democracy, adding, "I do not believe safeguards are in place to protect consumer health information that will be gathered for profiling and targeting."[23]

The overall pitch of those who run Google, Facebook, Apple, Amazon, and the rest is: trust us and trust market forces to keep us straight when we stray from the proper course. This is, after all, a basic conceit of free-market capitalism—as long as the game is not rigged by crony capitalists gaining an advantage from the government to distort the market to their benefit. If consumers are alert and companies forthcoming as to the privacy implications, the threat to privacy is a manageable problem to be resolved between entrepreneurs and their customers, arriving at a more or less mutual satisfaction.

But then came the Snowden revelations of an alternative universe in which those companies were not simply governed by the rules of a free market but were instead adjuncts of the US government and, by extension, of the governments of other nations where they do business. When it came to protecting consumers' personal data, what ensued was no longer a negotiation between those companies and their customers as to what was acceptable but, rather, a more or less contested struggle between the companies and those governments that could control their performance.

It is reassuring that major US companies, particularly Yahoo, recognized the threat of this bulk surveillance not only to their business model but also to democracy—yet also quite depressing to realize that, for all of their wealth and prestige, they were totally ineffectual in attempting to hold the government to honor reason or the Constitution.

As this book goes to press, Congress is working on a bill that would limit the Patriot Act of 2007, under which Yahoo and the other companies were compelled to turn over not just "metadata" records of communications but the full text of emails.[24] That reform effort, despite having been initiated by the Patriot Act's original author, Representative James Sensenbrenner (R-WI), shows few signs of significantly altering this dangerous law.

Why all this matters to the health of a democratic society was laid out quite persuasively in Yahoo's original brief in 2007: "The issues at stake in this litigation are the most serious issues that this nation faces today—to what extent must the privacy rights guaranteed by the United States Constitution yield to protect our national security."[25]

⚡ ⚡ ⚡

WE MUST CHALLENGE THE ASSUMPTION THAT PROTECTING national security requires sacrificing the constitutional rights of the individual. As pointed out in this book, the Fourth Amendment does not contain an absolute ban on searches and seizures but, rather, requires a court-authorized warrant based on probable cause of a crime before invading an individual's private space. All Yahoo was asking of the court was that the searches of its company's customers meet this requirement. Instead, the government responded that the so-called War on Terrorism could not be won on that basis, and the secret FISA court endorsed the view.

As Stewart Baker, the former NSA general counsel and Homeland Security official in the Bush administration, told the *Washington Post* after the Yahoo case documents were released: "I'm always astonished how people are willing to abstract these decisions from the actual stakes." He went on to say that "[w]e're talking about trying to gather information about people who are trying to kill us and who will succeed if we don't have robust information about their activities."[26]

As demonstrated in previous chapters, however, there is simply no serious evidence that the mass surveillance program initiated under President Bush provided the sort of "robust information" Baker claims was required to identify the people "trying to kill us." Yet, as this book goes to press, we have been presented with still another case study in the rise of a terrorist movement—the Islamic State of Iraq and Syria (ISIS), whose members are creating considerable mayhem in Iraq and Syria—for which the mass surveillance techniques of the NSA left us totally unprepared.

They appeared suddenly, startlingly so, these black-clad men of ISIS, beheading journalists and others[27] as they formed their proclaimed Sunni Caliphate over a broad swath of Syria and Iraq.[28] Once again, as with the al Qaeda attacks of 9/11, the fearsome spectacle of a terrorist enemy drove reason from the stage and the chant of war was in the air. The *New York Times* carried the text of Obama's speech to the nation on September 10, 2014, in which he vowed to "destroy the terrorist group."[29] Defense Secretary

Chuck Hagel said that ISIS poses an "imminent threat to every interest we have."[30]

Suddenly, all the arguments for peace and restraint were cast aside and the defense of privacy and civil liberty seemed an unaffordable indulgence in the rush to combat an enemy of such awesome power and mystery. Lost in the moment of fear-induced passion was the fact that these men of ISIS who so alarmed us, like their cousins in al Qaeda, were hardly unknown or mysterious beings, but instead monsters partially of our own creation.

Adam Gopnik reinforced this point in an August 2014 article in the *New Yorker*. "ISIS is a horrible group doing horrible things, and there are many factors behind its rise," he wrote. "But they came to be a threat and a power less because of all we didn't do than because of certain things we did do—foremost among them that massive, forward intervention, the Iraq War. (The historical question to which ISIS is the answer is: What could possibly be worse than Saddam Hussein?)"[31]

Now, once again—and this time as compared to 9/11, when the public was so ill-served with alarmist information about the extent of the terrorist threat—the president was presumably in possession of that vast trove of intelligence data collected by the NSA and analyzed with the brilliant software of the best Silicon Valley data-mining companies such as the media-celebrated Palantir. And yet there is no evidence that this costly and intrusive effort was the least bit useful in predicting the rise of ISIS.

Clearly, there is a disturbing disconnect between the zeal with which big data is collected and the lack of scientific precision in utilizing that data to make sound policy decisions and to inform the public as to the necessity of action. It is also difficult to see just how that data, based as it is on the minutiae of the lives of much of the world's population, is useful to an understanding of this threat.

This book explains the continued rise of a military-intelligence complex that, through the assertion of a pressing danger to national security after 9/11, made an unfettered and largely unchallenged claim upon the vast amount of private data collected in a wired world by government and private enterprises. It is a claim based on the unquestioned assumption that what passes for military intelligence is sufficiently and uniquely productive of useful insight to warrant the costs to our democracy as well as our federal budget, and that less invasive means of research such as scholarship, journalism, and traditional shoe-leather spy and detective work are inherently inadequate to the task of protecting us in a cyberworld. It is a commonly persuasive argument and difficult to challenge given that the high-tech surveillance is cloaked in such tight secrecy.

In the wake of the Snowden revelations, when there was a much-heightened public awareness of the threat to privacy and a willingness, even on the part of Congress, to address the issue more vigorously, all it took was the appearance of a renewed terrorist threat to develop anew a consensus that privacy needed to be surrendered as an unaffordable risk to the nation's security.

Just the opposite is the case. What now passes for military intelligence is a tech-driven oxymoron that denies the place of historical contemplation, cultural and religious study, political complexity, and ethical restraints in assessing dangers to a nation. Never has our nation's foreign policy been so poorly served as in the era of the Internet, with its enormous potential to enlighten us; but the collusions of war-mongering fanatics and profiteers are beyond the comprehension of even the most powerful machines.

They must not be beyond the purview of public awareness, however. A fully informed public is the best safeguard against the hazardous foreign entanglements that our founders warned were the main threat to the health of the republic. That is why they enshrined the constitutional protections against unbridled government power they believed would subvert the American experiment in representative governance.

We must heed the wisdom of the EFF's senior attorney Lee Tien, who as much as any constitutional lawyer has battled on behalf of those rights. As he summed up in an interview: "We need to fix the national security classification system that has classified so much information that we don't know what's going on. It's hard to know what we should do, but we should all agree that knowing what's happening is the first step. It's dangerous to propose a solution when you don't know what the extent of the problem is. If you asked me before the Snowden revelations, my answer would be different. There are no personal solutions to this; there is nothing we can do individually."

"This is a systemic problem," he continued. "It's an institutional problem, it's a political problem. There can only be collective action. That's it. That means we need to call on all of them—individuals, Internet companies, politicians, the government—to fix it, and we need to organize. You can't have a democracy if you don't have sufficient information. We're fighting for the soul of this democracy."

Acknowledgments

M Y SCHOOLING IN THE BEST TRADITIONS OF CONVENTIONAL journalism began in earnest in 1976, when I went to work for the *Los Angeles Times* after a boisterous career in alternative media. That was when I encountered the formidable force of Narda Zacchino, a young reporter at the paper who rose to become the associate editor and a vice president. She never lost her commitment to journalistic excellence and her concern for society's underserved. In our four decades of marriage and professional collaboration, Narda has never failed to call me out when I got it wrong. With this book, she has once again held me accountable to her high standards.

Much thanks are owed to former Nation Books editor Carl Bromley for seeing the potential in the idea for this book and also to Daniel Lo-Preto for stepping in to make that idea a reality after Carl became an editor at New Press. Dan has been a tough, creative editor in every respect, and the book bears the defining marks of his superb professionalism. Dan will surely appreciate why Sara Beladi's name appears on the cover page, for he witnessed her tireless and always excellent contribution to

213

the interviews and writing that went into this book. Sara's profound understanding of the issues involved and impressive literary skills informed this project throughout. My agent Ronald Goldfarb, a knowledgeable Washington lawyer and important columnist, has also been very supportive. I want to thank Alessandra Bastagli, for seamlessly guiding this book through the production process after she took the reins as editorial director of Nation Books. I am also grateful to Melissa Raymond, managing editor of PublicAffairs and Nation Books, and copy editor Christine Arden, for their patience and professionalism.

The book is dedicated to my three sons, Christopher, Joshua, and Peter, who, while often challenging me in ways that made thinking harder, could not have been more constructive. Christopher did a major edit of the entire manuscript, and his writing and thinking did much to enhance this book as they have with my other writing. It pays to have children who are smarter than you, as my dependence on Christopher attests. That also goes for Joshua, who did much of the original research. At Truthdig, Peter held up the editorial side as managing editor, and with publisher Zuade Kaufman provided the indispensable leadership to the venture that has allowed us to win a considerable number of awards, including three Sigma Delta Chi awards from the Society of Professional Journalists and five Webby Awards. Larry Flynt, who delivers an impassioned and informed defense of privacy every time he speaks in my class, deserves the credit for suggesting to me that a book was needed on this subject. My original concern about the threat to privacy in the Internet Age began with a writing assignment from Barry Golson when he was the editor of *Yahoo! Internet Life*.

None of the above are responsible for any of the failings of this book, which are mine alone. That certainly absolves the Annenberg School for Communication and Journalism, where Dean Geoff Cowan, Dean Earnest Wilson, and my department chairman, the aforementioned Dr. Larry Gross, have been enormously supportive of my teaching at the school for years, during which I published four books that must have brought them some grief from my critics. They have their own strong views, developed during the course of distinguished scholarly and public service careers, but they gave me my space to experiment freely with ideas, and that is what this book asks the government to grant all of us.

Notes

Preface

1. "Google CEO on Privacy: 'If You Have Something You Don't Want Anyone to Know, Maybe You Shouldn't Be Doing It'" (video), *Huffington Post*, March 18, 2010.

Chapter 1: The TED Moment: His Head on a Robot

1. Amanda Wills, "How TED Got Edward Snowden and the NSA Deputy Director Onstage," *Mashable*, March 20, 2014, http://mashable.com/2014/03/20/how-ted-got-snowden-nsa/.

2. Spencer Ackerman, "US Tech Giants Knew of NSA Data Collection, Agency's Top Lawyer Insists," *Guardian*, March 19, 2014, http://www.theguardian.com/world/2014/mar/19/us-tech-giants-knew-nsa-data-collection-rajesh-de.

3. Quoted in Helen Waters, "The NSA Responds to Edward Snowden's Interview at TED," *TED* (blog), March 20, 2014, http://blog.ted.com/2014/03/20/the-nsa-responds-to-edward-snowdens-interview-at-ted/.

4. "Larry Page: Where's Google Going Next?" *TED* (blog), March 1, 2014, http://www.ted.com/talks/larry_page_where_s_google_going_next/transcript.

5. Jason Leopold, "Exclusive: Emails Reveal Close Google Relationship with NSA," *Al Jazeera America*, May 6, 2014.

6. Ibid.

7. Ibid.

8. "Defense Industrial Base Sector," official website of the Department of Homeland Security, June 12, 2014, http://www.dhs.gov/defense-industrial-base-sector.

9. "Science and Engineering Indicators 2012," National Science Foundation, January 1, 2012, http://www.nsf.gov/statistics/seind12/c5/c5s1.htm.

10. James C. Hagerty, "Text of the Address by President Eisenhower, Broadcast and Televised from His Office in the White House, Tuesday Evening, January 17, 1961," http://www.eisenhower.archives.gov/research/online_documents/farewell_address/1961_01_17_Press_Release.pdf.

11. Ron Bell, "Yahoo Files Suit Demanding Greater Accountability from the U.S. Government," *Yahoo Global Public Policy* (blog), September 9, 2013, http://yahoopolicy.tumblr.com/post/60753842342/yahoo-files-suit-demanding-greater-accountability-from.

12. Richard Salgado, "Shedding Some Light on Foreign Intelligence Surveillance Act (FISA) Requests" (blog), *Official Google Blog*, February 3, 2014, http://googleblog.blogspot.com/2014/02/shedding-some-light-on-foreign.html.

13. Jared Cohen and Eric Schmidt, "Introduction," *The New Digital Age: Reshaping the Future of People, Nations and Business* (New York: Alfred A. Knopf, 2013), p. 9.

14. Gregory McNeal, "It's Not a Surprise That Gmail Users Have No Reasonable Expectation of Privacy," *Forbes*, August 20, 2013.

15. David E. Sanger and Steve Lohr, "Call for Limits on Web Data of Customers," *New York Times*, May 1, 2014.

16. Quoted in ibid.

17. BackRub was a search engine that counted and qualified each backlink on the Web to estimate sites' relevance. BackRub was renamed Google in 1996.

18. "An Open Letter to Washington," *Reform Government Surveillance,*

December 19, 2013, https://www.reformgovernmentsurveillance
.com.

19. Leopold, "Exclusive: Emails Reveal Close Google Relationship
with NSA."

Chapter 2: Cyber Sound Bites

1. "Washington's Farewell Address 1796," Yale Law School Avalon
Project.
2. Thomas Andrews Drake, "Enemy of the State," unpublished proposal, 2012.
3. Jane Mayer, "The Secret Sharer," *New Yorker*, May 23, 2011.
4. Thomas Andrews Drake, email to Robert Scheer, "Following Up from
GAP Whistleblower Tour Stop," August 7, 2014.
5. Ibid.
6. Quoted in Amy Goodman and Juan Gonzalez, "National Security
Agency Whistleblower William Binney on Growing State Surveillance," *Democracy Now!*, April 20, 2012, http://www.democracynow
.org/2012/4/20/exclusive_national_security_agency_whistleblower
_william.
7. "Obama's Speech at Woodrow Wilson Center," Council on Foreign
Relations, August 1, 2007, http://www.cfr.org/elections/obamas
-speech-woodrow-wilson-center/p13974.
8. Barton Gellman and Greg Miller, "'Black Budget' Summary Details
U.S. Spy Network's Successes, Failures and Objectives," *Washington
Post*, August 29, 2013.
9. This total was not adjusted to account for inflation.
10. Gellman and Miller, "'Black Budget' Summary Details U.S. Spy
Network's Successes, Failures and Objectives."
11. Ibid.
12. Ibid.
13. "Transcript of President Obama's Speech on NSA Reforms," *NPR:
It's All Politics* (podcast), January 17, 2014.
14. Mark Mazzetti, "Burglars Who Took on FBI Abandon Shadows,"
New York Times, January 7, 2014.
15. Matthew M. Aid and William Burr, eds., "'Disreputable If Not
Outright Illegal': The National Security Agency Versus Martin Luther King, Muhammad Ali, Art Buchwald, Frank Church, *et al.*,"
National Security Archive, September 25, 2013.

16. Ibid.
17. Office of the Director of National Intelligence, "2013 Report on Security Clearance Determinations," April 17, 2014, p. 4.
18. "50 U.S. Code § 1861—Access to Certain Business Records for Foreign Intelligence and International Terrorism Investigations," n.d., Cornell University Law School Legal Information Institute, http://www.law.cornell.edu/uscode/text/50/1861.
19. "Remarks by the President on Review of Signals Intelligence," The White House, January 17, 2014, http://www.whitehouse.gov/the-press-office/2014/01/17/remarks-president-review-signals-intelligence.
20. Privacy and Civil Liberties Oversight Board, "Report on the Telephone Records Program Conducted Under Section 215 of the USA PATRIOT Act and on the Operations of the Foreign Intelligence Surveillance Court," by David Medine, Rachel Brand, Elisebeth Collins Cook, James Dempsey, and Patricia Wald (Washington, DC: January 23, 2014), https://www.eff.org/files/2014/01/23/final_report_1-23-14.pdf.
21. Ibid., p. 154.
22. Ibid.
23. US National Commission on Terrorist Attacks upon the United States, *9/11 Commission Report: The Official Report of the 9/11 Commission and Related Publications*, by Thomas H. Kean and Lee Hamilton, Y 3.2:T 27/2/FINAL (Washington, DC: Government Printing Office, 2004), p. 266.
24. Amita Sharma, "Questions Linger over San Diego 9/11 Hijackers' Ties to Saudi Government," KPBS, September 7, 2011.
25. Sharma, "Questions Linger over San Diego 9/11 Hijackers' Ties to Saudi Government."
26. US National Commission on Terrorist Attacks upon the United States, p. 222.
27. Ibid., p. 266.
28. "Director's Statement on the Release of the 9/11 IG Report Executive Summary," Central Intelligence Agency, August 21, 2007, https://www.cia.gov/news-information/press-releases-statements/press-release-archive-2007/911-ig-report-summary.html.
29. Ibid.
30. "CIA Criticises Ex-chief over 9/11," *BBC News*, August 22, 2007, http://news.bbc.co.uk/2/hi/americas/6957839.stm.

31. Jason Leopold, "Revealed: NSA Pushed 9/11 as Key 'Sound Bite' to Justify Surveillance," *Al Jazeera America,* October 30, 2013, http://america.aljazeera.com/articles/2013/10/30/revealed-nsa -pushed911askeysoundbitetojustifysurveillance.html.
32. Ibid.
33. Adam Serwer, "Support NSA Surveillance? That Might Depend on Who's President," MSNBC, June 10, 2013, http://www.msnbc .com/msnbc/support-nsa-surveillance.
34. Editorial board, "President Obama's Dragnet," *New York Times,* June 6, 2013.
35. "Author of Patriot Act: FBI'S FISA Order Is Abuse of Patriot Act," June 6, 2013, http://sensenbrenner.house.gov/news/documentsin-gle.aspx?DocumentID=337001.
36. Dan Roberts, "The USA Freedom Act: A Look at the Key Points of the Draft Bill," *Guardian,* October 10, 2013, http://www .theguardian.com/world/2013/oct/10/the-usa-freedom-act-a-look -at-the-key-points-of-the-draft-bill.
37. Select Committee on Intelligence of the United States Senate, Current and Projected National Security Threats to the United States: Hearing Before the Select Committee on Intelligence of the United States (Washington, DC: Government Printing Office, 2013).
38. Ibid.
39. Office of the Director of National Intelligence, "Director James R. Clapper Interview with Andrea Mitchell, NBC News Chief Foreign Affairs Correspondent," June 8, 2013.
40. Ibid.
41. Lee Tien in discussion with the author, June 16, 2014.
42. David E. Sanger and Steve Lohr, "Call for Limits on Web Data of Customers," *New York Times,* May 1, 2014.
43. John Podesta, "Big Data: Seizing Opportunities, Preserving Values," May 2014, p. 36.
44. David Cole, "We Kill People Based on Metadata," *New York Review of Books* (blog), May 10, 2014, http://www.nybooks.com/blogs /nyrblog/2014/may/10/we-kill-people-based-on-metadata/.
45. Steve Lohr and David Sanger, "Call for Limits on Web Data of Customers," *New York Times,* May 1, 2014, http://www.nytimes .com/2014/05/02/us/white-house-report-calls-for-transparency -in-online-data-collection.html?_r=0.

Chapter 3: Mad Men Wired

1. Scott Howe, "Acxiom Prepares New Audience Operating System Amid Wobbly Earnings," *Ad Exchanger*, August 1, 2013, http://www.adexchanger.com/analytics/acxiom-prepares-new-audience-operating-system-amid-wobbly-earnings/.

2. Acquire Media, "Acxiom to Acquire LiveRamp," Acxiom, May 14, 2014 (NASDAQ:ACXM), http://investors.acxiom.com/releasedetail.cfm?releaseid=848013.

3. Quoted in Susan Stellin, "Security Check Now Starts Long Before You Fly," *New York Times*, October 10, 2013, http://www.nytimes.com/2013/10/22/business/security-check-now-starts-long-before-you-fly.html?pagewanted=all&_r=0.

4. Author's interview with Aleecia M. McDonald, Stanford University Law School, June 19, 2014.

5. President's Council of Advisers on Science and Technology, "Big Data & Privacy: A Technological Perspective" (Washington, DC: Executive Office of the President, 2014).

6. "Before the Federal Trade Commission, Washington D.C., Complaint, Request for Investigation, Injunction, and Other Relief in the Matter of Facebook Inc.," *Epic*, December 17, 2009, http://epic.org/privacy/inrefacebook/EPIC-FacebookComplaint.pdf.

7. Jaron Lanier, *Who Owns the Future?* (New York: Simon & Schuster, 2013).

8. President's Council of Advisers on Science and Technology, "Big Data & Privacy: A Technological Perspective."

9. Julia Angwin, "Meet the Online Tracking Device That Is Virtually Impossible to Block," *ProPublica*, July 21, 2014, http://www.propublica.org/article/meet-the-online-tracking-device-that-is-virtually-impossible-to-block.

10. Aleecia M. McDonald, email to Robert Scheer, "Re: That Scheer Book," October 3, 2014.

11. David Lazarus, "Ownership of Personal Data Still Appears Up for Grabs," *Los Angeles Times*, May 5, 2014, http://www.latimes.com/business/la-fi-lazarus-20140506-column.html.

12. Samuel Gibbs, "Eric Schmidt: Europe Struck Wrong Balance on Right to Be Forgotten," *Guardian*, May 15, 2014, http://www.theguardian.com/technology/2014/may/15/google-eric-schmidt-europe-ruling-right-to-be-forgotten.

13. "Facebook to Acquire Whatsapp," Facebook, February 19, 2014, http://newsroom.fb.com/news/2014/02/facebook-to-acquire-whatsapp/.
14. Jessica Rich, letter to Erin Egan and Anne Hogue, April 10, 2014, Federal Trade Commission, http://www.ftc.gov/system/files/documents/public_statements/297701/140410facebookwhatappltr.pdf.
15. Christian de Looper, "What's App Costing Facebook Extra $3B but Social Network Doesn't Bat an Eye," *Tech Times*, October 6, 2014, http://www.techtimes.com/articles/17315/20141006/whatsapp-costing-facebook-extra-3b-social-network-doesnt-bat-eye.htm.
16. "WhatsApp: Legal Info," *WhatsApp*, July 7, 2012, http://www.whatsapp.com/legal/.
17. Ibid.
18. "Facebook's CEO Discusses Q4 2013 Results-Earnings Call Transcript," *Seekingalpha.com*, January 29, 2014, http://seekingalpha.com/article/1978461-facebooks-ceo-discusses-q4–2013-results-earnings-call-transcript?page=1.
19. Cotton Delo, "Facebook Ad Juggernaut Rolls on Amid Mega-Deals for WhatsApp, Oculus VR," *Advertising Age*, April 23, 2014.
20. Ibid.
21. Kristen Purcell, Joanna Brenner, and Lee Rainie, "Search Engine Use 2012," Pew Research Center's Internet & American Life Project, March 9, 2012, http://www.pewinternet.org/2012/03/09/search-engine-use-2012/.
22. Shane Wiley, "In Support of a Personalized User Experience" (blog), *Yahoo! Policy Blog*, October 26, 2012, http://www.ypolicyblog.com/policyblog/category/privacy/.
23. David Streitfeld, "European Court Lets Users Erase Records on Web," *New York Times*, May 13, 2014, http://www.nytimes.com/2014/05/14/technology/google-should-erase-web-links-to-some-personal-data-europes-highest-court-says.html.
24. Ibid.
25. Ibid.
26. Author's interview with Paul Schwartz, UC Berkeley, Boalt Hall, July 7, 2014.

Chapter 4: Privacy Is Freedom

1. Marshall Kirkpatrick, "Facebook's Zuckerberg Says the Age of Privacy Is Over," *ReadWrite*, January 9, 2010, http://readwrite.com/2010/01/09/facebooks_zuckerberg_says_the_age_of_privacy_is_ov.

2. Michael Zimmer, "Mark Zuckerberg's Theory of Privacy," *Washington Post*, February 3, 2014, http://www.washingtonpost.com/lifestyle /style/mark-zuckerbergs-theory-of-privacy/2014/02/03/2c1d780a -8cea-11e3–95dd-36ff657a4dae_story.html.

3. Ibid.

4. Polly Sprenger, "Sun on Privacy: 'Get Over It,'" *Wired*, January 26, 1999.

5. "Google CEO on Privacy: 'If You Have Something You Don't Want Anyone to Know, Maybe You Shouldn't Be Doing It'" (video), *Huffington Post*, March 18, 2010.

6. Claire Cain Miller, "Revelations of N.S.A. Spying Cost U.S. Tech Companies," *New York Times*, March 21, 2014, http://www.nytimes .com/2014/03/22/business/fallout-from-snowden-hurting-bottom -line-of-tech-companies.html.

7. Mark Zuckerberg, "Mark Zuckerberg (Official Page)—March 13, 2014 Post," Facebook, March 13, 2014, https://www.facebook.com /zuck/posts/10101301165605491.

8. Ibid.

9. Robinson Meyer, "Everything We Know About Facebook's Secret Mood Manipulation Experiment," *The Atlantic*, June 28, 2014.

10. Adam D. I. Kramer, Jamie E. Guillory, and Jeffrey T. Hancock, "Experimental Evidence of Massive-Scale Emotional Contagion Through Social Networks," *Proceedings of the National Academy of Sciences* 111 (June 17, 2014): 87–89, http://www.pnas.org/.

11. Vindu Goel, "Facebook Tinkers with Users' Emotions in News Feed Experiment, Stirring Outcry," *New York Times*, June 30, 2014, http:// www.nytimes.com/2014/06/30/technology/facebook-tinkers-with -users-emotions-in-news-feed-experiment-stirring-outcry.html?_r=0.

12. Adam D. I. Kramer, https://www.facebook.com/akramer/posts /10152987150867796.

13. Quoted in John Carberry, "Media Statement on Cornell University's Role in Facebook 'Emotional Contagion' Research," Cornell University Media Relations Office, June 30, 2014, http://mediarelations .cornell.edu/2014/06/30/media-statement-on-cornell-universitys -role-in-facebook-emotional-contagion-research/.

14. Goel, "Facebook Tinkers with Users' Emotions in News Feed Experiment, Stirring Outcry."

15. Tarleton Gillespie, "Facebook's Algorithm—Why Our Assumptions Are Wrong, and Our Concerns Are Right," *Culture Digitally*, July 4,

2014, http://culturedigitally.org/2014/07/facebooks-algorithm-why -our-assumptions-are-wrong-and-our-concerns-are-right.

16. Ibid.

17. Ibid.

18. Ibid.

19. R. Jai Krishna, "Sandberg: Facebook Study Was 'Poorly Communicated,'" *Wall Street Journal*, July 2, 2014, http://blogs.wsj.com /digits/2014/07/02/facebooks-sandberg-apologizes-for-news-feed -experiment/.

20. Jaron Lanier, "Should Facebook Manipulate Users?," *New York Times*, June 30, 2014, http://www.nytimes.com/2014/07/01/opinion/jaron -lanier-on-lack-of-transparency-in-facebook-study.html.

21. Gillespie, "Facebook's Algorithm—Why Our Assumptions Are Wrong, and Our Concerns Are Right."

22. "Program History & Overview," The Minerva Initiative, August 12, 2014, http://minerva.dtic.mil/overview.html.

23. Cornell University, Department of Communication, "Department Faculty and Academic Staff," 2014, https://communication.cals .cornell.edu/people/faculty-and-academic-staff.

24. Nafeez Ahmed, "Pentagon Preparing for Mass Civil Breakdown," *Guardian*, July 4, 2014, http://www.theguardian.com/environment /earth-insight/2014/jun/12/pentagon-mass-civil-breakdown.

25. Ibid.

26. Ibid.

27. "Facebook Case over Search Warrants for User Information," *New York Times*, June 26, 2014, http://www.nytimes.com/interactive/2014/06 /26/technology/facebook-search-warrants-case-documents.html.

28. "In Re 381 Search Warrants Directed to Facebook, Inc. and Dated July 23, 2013," New York State Supreme Court Appellate Division— First Department, July 23, 2013, https://www.eff.org/files/2014 /06/26/fbopening_brief_in_re_381_search_warrants.pdf.

29. "Facebook's Brief Seeking Review of the Case on Searches," Document Cloud-NYT News, *New York Times*, July 23, 2013, https:// www.documentcloud.org/documents/1209712-facebooks-brief -seeking-review-of-the-case-on.html.

30. "Supreme Court of the United States—Riley vs. California Opinions," Supreme Court, June 25, 2014, http://www.supremecourt.gov /opinions/13pdf/13–132_8l9c.pdf.

31. Ibid.

32. "In Re 381 Search Warrants Directed to Facebook, Inc. and Dated July 23, 2013."

33. "Google to Give Governments Street View Data," *New York Times*, June 3, 2010, http://www.nytimes.com/2010/06/04/business/global /04google.html.

34. David Streitfeld, "Supreme Court Rejects Google's Street View Appeal" (blog), *New York Times*, June 30, 2014, http://bits.blogs .nytimes.com/2014/06/30/supreme-court-rejects-googles-street -view-appeal/?assetType=nyt_now.

35. Ibid.

36. Mark Walsh, "A "View" from the Court: Some Morning Joe Before Digital Day" (blog), *SCOTUSblog*, June 25, 2014.

Chapter 5: The Military-Intelligence Complex

1. John Markoff, "New Force Behind Agency of Wonder," *New York Times*, April 12, 2010, http://www.nytimes.com/2010/04/13/science /13prof.html?pagewanted=all&_r=0.

2. Liz Gannes, "DARPA's Regina Dugan Will Join Google," *All Things D*, March 12, 2012, http://allthingsd.com/20120312/darpas-regina -dugan-will-join-google/#lizg-ethics.

3. "Google ATAP—About," Google Plus, https://plus.google.com /+GoogleATAP/about.

4. "Regina Dugan and Dennis Woodside: Full D11 Session," *Wall Street Journal* (video, 00:14:16), May 29, 2013, http://www.wsj .com/video/regina-dugan-and-dennis-woodside-full-d11-session /A0EF86EC-0520-4465-B915-FDC7B366778A.html.

5. "DARPA Reaches Beyond Technological Frontiers for Warfight- ers," Defense Advanced Research Projects Agency, April 25, 2013, http://www.defense.gov/news/newsarticle.aspx?id=119879.

6. "Total Information Awareness System," Internet Archive Wayback Machine: DARPA, n.d., http://web.archive.org/web/20021003053 651/http://www.darpa.mil/iao/tiasystems.htm.

7. Jeffrey Rosen, "Total Information Awareness," *New York Times*, De- cember 15, 2002, http://www.nytimes.com/2002/12/15/magazine /15TOTA.html?pagewanted=print.

8. "Civil Liberties Union Asks Court to Quash Iran-Contra Indict- ment," *New York Times*, July 21, 1988, http://www.nytimes.com/1988 /07/21/us/civil-liberties-union-asks-court-to-quash-iran-contra -indictment.html.

9. Spenser Reiss, "Poindexter Confidential," *Wired*, May 2004, http://archive.wired.com/wired/archive/12.05/poindexter.html.

10. William Safire, "You Are a Suspect," *New York Times*, November 4, 2002, http://www.nytimes.com/2002/11/14/opinion/14SAFI.html.

11. William Safire, "Don't Bank on It," *New York Times*, April 16, 1998. http://www.nytimes.com/1998/04/16/opinion/essay-don-t-bank-on-it.html.

12. Safire, "You Are a Suspect."

13. "Terrorism Information Awareness" (TIA) Program," formerly known as "Total Information Awareness," Information Warfare Site, http://www.iwar.org.uk/news-archive/tia/total-information-awareness.htm.

14. Ryan Singel, "Pentagon Defends Data Search Plan," *Wired*, May 21, 2003, http://archive.wired.com/politics/security/news/2003/05/58936?currentPage=all.

15. Hendrik Hertzberg, "Too Much Information," *New Yorker*, December 9, 2002, http://www.newyorker.com/magazine/2002/12/09/too-much-information.

16. "Booz Allen at a Glance," Booz Allen Hamilton, 2014, http://investors.boozallen.com/glance.cfm.

17. "In-Q-Tel, Inc.," Hoovers Inc., 2014, http://www.hoovers.com/company-information/cs/company-profile.In-Q-Tel_Inc.23e1db89928dd9e6.html.

18. "The IQT Mission," In-Q-Tel, 2014, https://www.iqt.org.

19. Terence O'Hara, "In-Q-Tel, CIA's Venture Arm, Invests in Secrets," *Washington Post*, August 15, 2005, http://www.washingtonpost.com/wp-dyn/content/article/2005/08/14/AR2005081401108.html.

20. Noah Shachtman, "Exclusive: Google, CIA Invest in 'Future' of WebMonitoring." *Wired*, July 28, 2010, http://www.wired.com/2010/07/exclusive-google-cia/.

21. O'Hara, "In-Q-Tel, CIA's Venture Arm, Invests in Secrets."

22. Tim Shorrock, "The Corporate Takeover of U.S. Intelligence," *Salon*, June 1, 2007, http://www.salon.com/2007/06/01/intel_contractors/.

23. "Palantir: Home," Palantir, 2014, https://www.palantir.com.

24. "Beware of Data Miners Offering Protection," ACLU, December 1, 2011, https://www.aclu.org/blog/technology-and-liberty/beware-data-miners-offering-protection%20%20.

25. "Philanthropy Engineering," Palantir, 2013, https://www.palantir.com/philanthropy-engineering/.

26. Reed Albergotti, "Big Data, Big Dollars: Palantir Valued at $9 Billion," *Wall Street Journal*, December 5, 2013, http://online.wsj.com/news /articles/SB10001424052702303497804579240501078423362.

27. Andy Greenberg and Ryan Mac, "How a 'Deviant' Philosopher Built Palantir, a CIA-Funded Data-Mining Juggernaut," *Forbes*, September 2, 2013, http://www.forbes.com/sites/andygreenberg /2013/08/14/agent-of-intelligence-how-a-deviant-philosopher -built-palantir-a-cia-funded-data-mining-juggernaut/.

28. Shane Harris, *The Watchers* (New York: Penguin Books, 2010).

29. Shane Harris, "Killer App," *Washingtonian*, January 31, 2012, http:// www.washingtonian.com/articles/people/killer-app/indexp2.php.

30. "Henry M. Jackson (United States Senator)," *Encyclopedia Britannica*, January 31, 2014, http://www.britannica.com/EBchecked/topic /1536879/Henry-M-Jackson.

31. David Corn, "And the Most Outrageous Neocon Iraq War Anni- versary Remark Is . . . ," *Mother Jones*, March 20, 2013, http://www .motherjones.com/mojo/2013/03/iraq-war-richard-perle-npr.

32. Harris, "Killer App."

33. Ibid.

34. Shane Harris, "Palantir Technologies Spots Patterns to Solve Crimes and Track Terrorists," *Wired UK*, July 31, 2012. http://www.wired .co.uk/magazine/archive/2012/09/features/joining-the-dots /page/2.

35. Greenberg and Mac, "How a 'Deviant' Philosopher Built Palantir, a CIA-Funded Data-Mining Juggernaut."

36. Dafna Linzer, "Tenet Says He Was Made a Scapegoat over Iraq War," *Washington Post*, April 27, 2007, http://www.washingtonpost .com/wp-dyn/content/article/2007/04/26/AR2007042602247.html.

37. Dennis Jett, "Why It Isn't More Apparent," in Jett's *Why American Foreign Policy Fails: Unsafe at Home and Despised Abroad* (Basingstoke, UK: Palgrave MacMillan, 2008).

38. Tim Shorrock, "George Tenet Cashes In on Iraq," *Salon*, May 7, 2007, http://www.salon.com/2007/05/07/tenet_money/.

39. Ibid.

40. Ibid.

41. "EnCase: Cybersecurity, E-Discovery, Digital Forensics," World Leader in Digital Investigations, n.d., https://www.guidance software.com.

42. Ibid.

43. "Identity Services," MorphoTrustUSA, n.d., http://www.morpho
    trust.com/IdentityServices.aspx.
44. "Identity Services: Authorized Channeler," MorphoTrustUSA, n.d.,
    http://www.morphotrust.com/IdentityServices/EnrollmentServices
    /AuthorizedChanneler.aspx.
45. Shorrock, "George Tenet Cashes In on Iraq."
46. "George Tenet: Executive Profile & Biography," *Businessweek*, Au-
    gust 21, 2014, http://investing.businessweek.com/research/stocks
    /people/person.asp?personId=25237073&ticker=GUID.
47. Greenberg and Mac, "How a 'Deviant' Philosopher Built Palantir, a
    CIA-Funded Data-Mining Juggernaut."
48. Ibid.
49. "Audit Logging," Palantir, March 2013, https://www.palantir.com/
    wp-assets/wp-content/uploads/2013/03/PCL_AuditLogging.pdf.
50. Peter Ludlow, "The Real War on Reality," *New York Times*, June 14,
    2013, http://opinionator.blogs.nytimes.com/2013/06/14/the-real
    -war-on-reality.
51. From the homepage of Public Citizen's US Chamber Watch website,
    http://www.fixtheuschamber.org/about-chamber-watch-0.
52. Ibid.
53. Eric Lipton and Charlie Savage, "Hackers Reveal Offers to Spy on
    Corporate Rivals," *New York Times*, February 11, 2011, http://www
    .nytimes.com/2011/02/12/us/politics/12hackers.html?
54. Ibid.
55. Arun Gupta, "How Barrett Brown Shone Light on the Murky
    World of Security Contractors," *Guardian*, June 24, 2013, http://
    www.theguardian.com/commentisfree/2013/jun/24/surveillance
    -us-national-security.
56. Hanni Fakhoury and Jennifer Lynch, "Prosecution of Barrett Brown
    Still Threatens Journalistic Freedom in U.S.," Electronic Frontier
    Foundation, March 12, 2014.
57. Stephen Hsieh, "DOJ Drops Most of the Charges Against a Jour-
    nalist Indicted for Sharing a Link," *The Nation*, March 5, 2014,
    http://www.thenation.com/blog/178711/doj-drops-most-charges
    -against-journalist-indicted-sharing-link#.
58. Christian Stork, "What Was Hastings Working On?" *WhoWhatWhy*,
    August 7, 2013, http://whowhatwhy.com/2013/08/07/connections
    -between-michael-hastings-edward-snowden-and-barrett-brown
    -the-war-with-the-security-state/-sthash.EJR0Awpu.dpuf.

59. Ibid.

60. Ibid.

61. Lee Fang, "How Spy Agency Contractors Have Already Abused Their Power," *The Nation*, June 11, 2013, http://www.thenation.com/blog/174741/how-spy-agency-contractors-have-already-abused-their-power#.

62. Quoted in Harris, "Palantir Technologies Spots Patterns to Solve Crimes and Track Terrorists."

63. "From Berico Co-Founders: Guy Filippelli (CEO) and Nick Hallam (COOC)," Berico Technologies statement to the press, February 11, 2011, http://thinkprogress.org/wp-content/uploads/2011/02/Berico-Technologies-Statement.pdf.

64. Quoted in Andy Greenberg, "Palantir Apologizes for WikiLeaks Attack Proposal, Cuts Ties with HBGary," *Forbes*, February 11, 2011, http://www.forbes.com/sites/andygreenberg/2011/02/11/palantir-apologizes-for-wikileaks-attack-proposal-cuts-ties-with-hbgary/.

65. Glenn Greenwald, "The Leaked Campaign to Attack WikiLeaks and Its Supporters," *Salon*, February 11, 2011, http://www.salon.com/2011/02/11/campaigns_4/.

66. Charles Arthur, "WikiLeaks Claims Court Victory Against Visa," *Guardian*, July 12, 2012, http://www.theguardian.com/media/2012/jul/12/wikileaks-court-victory-visa.

67. Ronald Bailey, "'Technology Is at the Center'" *Reason*, May 1, 2008, http://reason.com/archives/2008/05/01/technology-is-at-the-center.

68. "What We Believe," Palantir, 2014, https://www.palantir.com/what-we-believe/.

69. Ibid.

Chapter 6: A Whistleblower Shall Set Us Free

1. "US Knew British Government Would Destroy Newspaper's Data," Associated Press, July 11, 2014.

2. Ewen MacAskill and Alan Rusbridger, "Edward Snowden Interview—The Edited Transcript," *Guardian*, July 18, 2014, http://www.theguardian.com/world/2014/jul/18/-sp-edward-snowden-nsa-whistleblower-interview-transcript.

3. Luke Harding, "Shoot the Messenger," in Harding's *The Snowden Files: The Inside Story of the World's Most Wanted Man* (London: Vintage Books, 2014), p. 3635.

4. MacAskill and Rusbridger, "Edward Snowden Interview—The Edited Transcript."

5. Quoted in Jack Gillum, "US Given Heads Up About Newspaper Data Destruction," *The Big Story*, July 11, 2014.

6. Ibid.

7. Glenn Greenwald, "Newly Obtained Emails Contradict Administration Claims on Guardian Laptop Destruction—The Intercept," *The Intercept*, July 11, 2014.

8. Julian Borger, "NSA Files: Why the Guardian in London Destroyed Hard Drives of Leaked Files," *Guardian*, August 20, 2013, http://www.theguardian.com/world/2013/aug/20/nsa-snowden -files-drives-destroyed-london.

9. Alan Rusbridger, "The Snowden Leaks and the Public," *New York Review of Books*, November 21, 2013.

10. "Transcript: 'You're Being Watched': Edward Snowden Emerges as Source Behind Explosive Revelations of NSA Spying," *Democracy Now!*, June 10, 2013.

11. Editorial board, "What's the Point of a Summit," *New York Times*, August 6, 2013, http://www.nytimes.com/2013/08/07/opinion /whats-the-point-of-a-summit.html.

12. Quoted in Ken Auletta, "Freedom of Information," *New Yorker*, October 7, 2013, http://www.newyorker.com/magazine/2013/10/07 /freedom-of-information?currentPage=all.

13. Eric Lichtblau and James Risen, "Bush Lets U.S. Spy on Callers Without Courts," *New York Times*, December 16, 2005, http://www .nytimes.com/2005/12/16/politics/16program.html?pagewanted =all.

14. Eric Lichtblau and Scott Shane, "Files Say Agency Initiated Growth of Spying Effort," *New York Times*, January 4, 2006, http://www .nytimes.com/2006/01/04/politics/04nsa.html.

15. John Markoff and Scott Shane, "Documents Show Link Between AT&T and Agency in Eavesdropping Case," *New York Times*, April 13, 2006. http://www.nytimes.com/2006/04/13/us /nationalspecial3/13nsa.html?pagewanted=print.

16. Lichtblau and Risen, "Bush Lets U.S. Spy on Callers Without Courts."

17. Quoted in Amy Goodman and Juan Gonzalez, "NSA Whistleblowers: 'All U.S. Citizens' Targeted by Surveillance Program, Not Just Verizon Customers," *Democracy Now!*, June 6, 2013,

http://www.democracynow.org/2013/6/6/nsa_whistleblowers _all_us_citizens_targeted.

18. Josh Gerstein, "Ex-NSA Official Thomas Drake Takes Plea Deal," *Politico*, June 9, 2011 (accessed October 5, 2014), http://www.politico.com/news/stories/0611/56665.html.

19. Ellen Nakashima, "Judge: Government's Treatment of Alleged Leaker Thomas Drake Was 'Unconscionable,'" *Washington Post*, July 29, 2011, http://www.washingtonpost.com/blogs/checkpoint -washington/post/judge-governments-treatment-of-alleged -leaker-thomas-drake-was-/2011/07/29/gIQAPcVThI_blog .html.

20. Leonard Downie and Sarah Rafsky, "The Obama Administration and the Press," Committee to Protect Journalists, October 10, 2013, http://cpj.org/reports/2013/10/obama-and-the-press-us-leaks -surveillance-post-911.php.

21. Ibid.

22. Ibid.

23. Mike Allen and Jim Vandehei, "Obama, the Puppet Master," *Politico*, February 18, 2013.

24. Downie and Rafsky, "The Obama Administration and the Press."

25. Quoted in Juliet Eilperin, "How Obama's Anti-Leak Policy Has Chilled the Free Press," *Washington Post*, October 11, 2013.

26. Kimberly Dozier, "CIA Papers Show Panetta Spoke on Bin Laden Raid," Associated Press, December 10, 2013, http://bigstory.ap .org/article/cia-papers-show-panetta-spilled-bin-laden-secrets.

27. John Kiriakou, "I Got 30 Months in Prison. Why Does Leon Panetta Get a Pass?" *Los Angeles Times*, May 9, 2014, http://articles .latimes.com/2014/mar/09/opinion/la-oe-kiriakou-panetta -whistleblower-20140309.

28. Inspector General, United States Department of Defense, "Congressionally Requested Action on Released Department of Defense Information to the Media," Report No. DODIG-2013–092 (Washington, DC: Government Printing Office, 2013).

29. Ibid.

30. Kiriakou, "I Got 30 Months in Prison. Why Does Leon Panetta Get a Pass?"

31. United States Department of Justice, Office of Public Affairs, "with Disclosing Covert Officer's Identity and Other Classified Information to Journalists and Lying to CIA'S Publications Review Board,"

January 12, 2012, http://www.justice.gov/opa/pr/2012/January/12 -ag-083.html.

32. Scott Shane, "Ex-Officer Is First from C.I.A. to Face Prison for a Leak," *New York Times,* January 5, 2013, http://www.nytimes. com/2013/01/06/us/former-cia-officer-is-the-first-to-face-prison -for-a-classified-leak.html?pagewanted=all.

33. Quoted in ibid.

34. Downie and Rafsky, "The Obama Administration and the Press."

35. Amy Goodman, Aaron Mate, Jeremy Scahill, and Alexa Sinha, "Transcript: Mass U.S. Surveillance Targeting Journalists and Lawyers Seen as Threat to American Democracy," *Democracy Now!,* July 29, 2014, http://www.democracynow.org/2014/7/29/mass_us _surveillance_targeting_journalists_and.

36. Ibid.

37. Ibid.

38. Ibid.

39. MacAskill and Rusbridger, "Edward Snowden Interview—The Edited Transcript," *Guardian,* July 18, 2014, http://www.theguardian .com/world/2014/jul/18/-sp-edward-snowden-nsa-whistleblower -interview-transcript.

40. Ibid.

41. Ibid.

Chapter 7: Foreign Policy: A Tissue of Lies

1. Patrick Cockburn, "Isis Consolidates," *London Review of Books,* August 21, 2014.

2. Daniel Ellsberg, *Secrets: A Memoir of Vietnam and the Pentagon Papers* (New York: Penguin Books, 2003).

3. Author's interview with Daniel Ellsberg, Ellsberg residence, California, July 30, 2014.

4. Office of the Director of National Intelligence, *2013 Report on Security Clearance Determinations* (Washington, DC: Government Printing Office, 2014), p.4; http://www.dni.gov/files/documents/201320 Report%20on%20Security%20Clearance%20Determinations.pdf.

5. Downie and Rafsky, "The Obama Administration and the Press."

6. Daniel Ellsberg, unpublished manuscript, 2014.

7. Scott Shane, "Leibowitz Received a 20-Month Sentence," *New York Times,* September 5, 2011, http://www.nytimes.com/2011/09/06 /us/06leak.html?pagewanted=all.

8. Patrick Caldwell, "Watch: Hillary Clinton Blasts Edward Snowden for Fleeing to Russia and China," *Mother Jones*, April 25, 2014, http://www.motherjones.com/politics/2014/04/hillary-clinton-snowden-nsa-russia-china.

9. Trevor Timm, "Fact-Checking Hillary Clinton's Comments About Edward Snowden and the NSA," Freedom of the Press Foundation Blog , April 28, 2014; https://freedom.press/blog/2014/04/fact-checking-hillary-clintons-comments-about-edwardsnowden-and-nsa.

10. Ellsberg, *Secrets: A Memoir of Vietnam and the Pentagon Papers.*

11. Ibid.

12. Caldwell, "Watch: Hillary Clinton Blasts Edward Snowden for Fleeing to Russia and China."

13. Ibid.

14. Quoted in David Sanger, "New N.S.A. Chief Calls Damage from Snowden Leaks Manageable," *New York Times*, June 29, 2014, http://www.nytimes.com/2014/06/30/us/sky-isnt-falling-after-snowden-nsa-chief-says.html.

15. The results of this joint survey are available at "Poll Results: Snowden," *YouGov*, March 28, 2014, https://today.yougov.com/news/2014/03/28/poll-results-snowden/.

16. "Report of the Office of the United Nations High Commissioner for Human Rights: Right to Privacy in the Digital Age," Office of the United Nations High Commissioner for Human Rights, June 30, 2014, http://www.ohchr.org/EN/HRBodies/HRC/RegularSessions/Session27/Documents/A.HRC.27.37_en.pdf.

17. Quoted in "UN's Pillay Suggests Snowden Should Not Face Trial," Reuter's, July 16, 2014, http://in.reuters.com/article/2014/07/16/usa-security-un-idINL6N0PR1S920140716.

18. Ibid.

19. Chris Huhne, "Prism and Tempora: The Cabinet Was Told Nothing of the Surveillance State's Excesses," *Guardian*, October 6, 2013, http://www.theguardian.com/commentisfree/2013/oct/06/prism-tempora-cabinet-surveillance-state.

20. Jim Sensenbrenner, "NSA Abused Trust, Must Be Reined In," *Milwaukee Journal Sentinel*, November 2, 2013, http://www.jsonline.com/news/opinion/nsa-abused-trust-must-be-reined-in-b99131601z1-230292131.html.

21. Seymour Hersh, "Huge C.I.A. Operation Reported in U.S. Against Antiwar Forces, Other Dissidents in Nixon Years," *New York Times*

(1923–Current File), December 22, 1974, http://search.proquest
.com/docview/120166079?accountid=14749.

22. "94th Congress, First Session, Senate Resolution 21," United States
Senate, January 7, 1975, https://www.senate.gov/artandhistory/history
/common/investigations/pdf/ChurchCommittee_SRes21.pdf.

23. Ibid.

24. "Senate Select Committee to Study Governmental Operations
with Respect to Intelligence Activities," Senate History, https://
www.senate.gov/artandhistory/history/common/investigations/
ChurchCommittee.htm.

25. "Feinstein Statement at Intelligence Committee Hearing on Worldwide Threats," Dianne Feinstein, United States Senator of California,
January 29, 2014, http://www.feinstein.senate.gov/public/index
.cfm/2014/1/feinstein-statement-at-intelligence-committee-hearing
-on-worldwide-threats.

26. Ibid.

27. Tim Cavanaugh, "What Do They Know About You? An Interview
with NSA Analyst William Binney," *Daily Caller*, June 10, 2013,
http://dailycaller.com/2013/06/10/what-do-they-know-about
-you-an-interview-with-nsa-analyst-william-binney/3/.

Chapter 8: How the Digital Cookie Crumbles

1. Robert Scheer, "Nowhere to Hide," *Yahoo! Internet Life*, October 1,
2000.

2. Eric Schmidt and Jared Cohen, "The Dark Side of the Digital Revolution," *Wall Street Journal*, April 19, 2013, http://online.wsj.com
/news/articles/SB10001424127887324030704578424465047928521.

3. Samuel Warren and Louis Brandeis, "The Right to Privacy," *Harvard
Law Review* 4, no. 5 (1890).

4. "Olmstead v. United States: The Constitutional Challenges of Prohibition Enforcement," Federal Judicial Center, 1928, http://www.fjc
.gov/history/home.nsf/page/tu_olmstead_doc_15.html.

5. Kristin McGrath, "Status Update: Facebook Logs 500 Million
Members," *USA Today*, July 21, 2010, http://usatoday30.usatoday
.com/tech/news/2010–07–21-facebook-hits-500-million-users_N
.htm.

6. "How Tweet It Is! Library Acquires Entire Twitter Archive" (blog), Library of Congress, April 14, 2010, http://blogs.loc.gov/loc/2010/04
/how-tweet-it-is-library-acquires-entire-twitter-archive/.

7. Jeffrey Rosen, "The Web Means the End of Forgetting," *New York Times*, July 21, 2010, http://www.nytimes.com/2010/07/25 /magazine/25privacy-t2.html.

8. James Risen and Eric Lichtblau, "Revelations Give Look at Spy Agency's Wider Reach," *New York Times*, June 8, 2013.

9. Michael Shear, "Making Legislative History, with Nod from Obama and Stroke of an Autopen," *New York Times*, May 28, 2011, http:// www.nytimes.com/2011/05/28/us/politics/28sign.html.

10. "Illusion of Justice: Human Rights Abuses in US Terrorism Prosecutions," Human Rights Watch, July 21, 2014, http://www.hrw.org /node/126101.

11. Quoted in Adam Goldman, "Human Rights Report Takes at U.S. Terrorism Prosecutions, Criticizes FBI Tactics," *Washington Post*, July 21, 2014, http://www.washingtonpost.com/world/national -security/human-rights-report-takes-at-us-terror-prosecutions -criticizes-fbi-tactics/2014/07/21/018376ce-0e88-11e4-8341 -b8072b1e7348_story.html (site discontinued).

12. Leonard Downie and Sarah Rafsky, "The Obama Administration and the Press," *Committee to Protect Journalists*, October 10, 2013, http://cpj.org/reports/2013/10/obama-and-the-press-us-leaks -surveillance-post-911.php.

13. Ibid.

14. Ibid.

15. Quoted in Maureen Dowd, "Where's the Justice at Justice?," *New York Times*, August 16, 2014, http://www.nytimes.com/2014/08/17 /opinion/sunday/maureen-dowd-wheres-the-justice-atjustice.html.

16. Ibid.

17. Barack Obama, "Transparency and Open Government," White House, n.d., http://www.whitehouse.gov/the_press_office/Trans parencyandOpenGovernment.

18. Charlie Savage, "Reagan-Era Order on Surveillance Violates Rights, Says Departing Aide," *New York Times*, August 13, 2014, http:// www.nytimes.com/2014/08/14/us/politics/reagan-era-order-on -surveillance-violates-rights-says-departing-aide.html?_r=0.

19. Ibid.

20. Frank Konkel, "Daring Deal," *Government Executive*, July 9, 2014, http://www.govexec.com/magazine/features/2014/07/daring-deal /88207/.

21. Lee Ferran, "Edward Snowden and NSA Official Reveal Oddly Similar Christmas Wishes," *ABC News*, December 24, 2013, http://abcnews.go.com/blogs/headlines/2013/12/edward-snowden-and-nsa-official-reveal-oddly-similar-christmas-wishes/.

22. Thomas Jefferson, "Preamble to a Bill for the More General Diffusion of Knowledge," *The Founders' Constitution*, Volume 1, Chapter 18, Document 11 (Fall 1778), http://press-pubs.uchicago.edu/founders/documents/v1ch18s11.html.

23. Thomas Jefferson, "Letter CXXVII—To Mr. Leiper, June 12, 1815," in *Memoir, Correspondence, and Miscellanies, from the Papers of Thomas Jefferson*, Volume 4 (1815), http://www.gutenberg.org/files/16784/16784-h/16784-h.htm#link2H_4_0127.

24. Adi Ignatius and Sheryl Sandberg, "Now Is Our Time," *Harvard Business Review*, April 2013, http://hbr.org/2013/04/now-is-our-time/ar/1.

Epilogue

1. Stanford University, Office of University Communications, "Stanford Facts 2014," p. 28, http://facts.stanford.edu/pdf/StanfordFacts_2014.pdf.

2. Michael McDonald, "Colleges Raise Record $33.8 Billion Exceeding U.S. Peak in 2009," *Bloomberg*, February 12, 2014, http://www.bloomberg.com/news/2014-02-12/college-donations-rise-to-record-as-stocks-gain-fueled-giving.html.

3. Ryan Flinn, "Stanford President Adds to Technology Fortune with Atheros Deal," *Bloomberg*, January 5, 2011, http://www.bloomberg.com/news/2011-01-06/stanford-s-president-hennessy-adds-to-technology-fortune-with-atheros-deal.html.

4. Charles Arthur, "Google to Pay Record $22.5m Fine to FTC over Safari Tracking," *Guardian*, August 9, 2012, http://www.theguardian.com/technology/2012/aug/09/google-record-fine-ftc-safari.

5. "Steve Jackson Games v. Secret Service Case Archive," Electronic Frontier Foundation, n.d., https://www.eff.org/cases/steve-jackson-games-v-secret-service-case-archive.

6. "Bernstein v. US Department of Justice," Electronic Frontier Foundation, n.d., https://www.eff.org/cases/bernstein-v-us-dept-justice.

7. "SecureDrop," Freedom of the Press Foundation, n.d., https://pressfreedomfoundation.org/securedrop.

8. This directory can be found at https://pressfreedomfoundation.org /securedrop/directory.

9. "Encryption Works: How to Protect Your Privacy in the Age of NSA Surveillance," Freedom of the Press Foundation, July 2, 2013, https://pressfreedomfoundation.org/encryption-works.

10. "About The Intercept," *The Intercept*, n.d., https://firstlook.org /theintercept/about/.

11. Author's interview with Micah Lee, Berkeley, CA, June 22, 2014.

12. Anu Bradford, "The Brussels Effect," *Northwestern University Law Review* 107, no. 1 (2012): 22.

13. Alexei Oreskovic, "Google Takes Steps to Comply with EU's 'Right to Be Forgotten' Ruling," Reuter's, May 30, 2014, http:// www.reuters.com/article/2014/05/30/us-google-eu-idUSKBN 0EA04O20140530.

14. Danny Hakim, "Google Is Target of European Backlash on U.S. Tech Dominance," *New York Times*, September 8, 2014, http://www .nytimes.com/2014/09/09/technology/google-is-target-of-european -backlash-on-us-tech-dominance.html.

15. Mathias Döpfner, "You Don't Have to Be a Conspiracy Theorist to Find Google Alarming," *Guardian*, April 18, 2014, http:// www.theguardian.com/commentisfree/2014/apr/18/google -alarming-no-conspiracy-theorist.

16. Ari Levy, "Alibaba IPO Propels China Web Market Across the Globe," CNBC, September 11, 2014, http://www.cnbc.com/id /101976709.

17. Charlie Savage and Vindu Goel, "Government's Threat of Daily Fine for Yahoo Shows Aggressive Push for Data," *New York Times*, September 11, 2014, http://www.nytimes.com/2014/09/12/technology /documents-unsealed-in-yahoos-case-against-us-data-requests.html.

18. Ronald Bell, "Shedding Light on the Foreign Intelligence Surveillance Court (FISC): Court Findings from Our 2007–2008 Case," Yahoo Global Public Policy Blog, September 11, 2014, http:// yahoopolicy.tumblr.com/post/97238899258/shedding-light -on-the-foreign-intelligence-surveillance.

19. Savage and Goel, "Government's Threat of Daily Fine for Yahoo Shows Aggressive Push for Data."

20. Glenn Greenwald, Laura Poitras, Spencer Ackerman, and Dominic Rushe, "Microsoft Handed the NSA Access to Encrypted Mes-

sages," *Guardian*, July 11, 2013, http://www.theguardian.com/world
/2013/jul/11/microsoft-nsa-collaboration-user-data.

21. Brian X. Chen and Steve Lohr, "With Apple Pay and Smartwatch,
a Privacy Challenge," *New York Times*, September 10, 2014, http://
www.nytimes.com/2014/09/11/technology/with-new-apple
-products-a-privacy-challenge.html.

22. Ibid.

23. Ibid.

24. Dustin Voltz, "NSA Reform Will Likely Have to Wait Until After
the Election," *National Journal*, September 8, 2014, http://www
.nationaljournal.com/tech/nsa-reform-will-likely-have-to-wait
until-after-the-election-20140907.

25. Craig Timberg, "U.S. Threatened Massive Fine to Force Yahoo to
Release Data," *Washington Post*, September 11, 2014, http://www
.washingtonpost.com/business/technology/us-threatened-massive
-fine-to-force-yahoo-to-release-data/2014/09/11/38a7f69e-39e8
-11e4-9c9f-ebb47272e40e_story.html.

26. Ibid.

27. Erika Solomon and Borzou Daragahi, "Isis Militants Say UK Aid
Worker Beheaded," *Financial Times*, September 14, 2014, http://
www.ft.com/intl/cms/s/0/f1c7eac2-3bb8-11e4-84b4-00144
feabdc0.html#axzz3DJ399Esp.

28. "Backgrounders—Islamic State in Iraq and Syria," Council on Foreign Relations, August 8, 2014, http://www.cfr.org/iraq/islamic
-state-iraq-syria/p14811.

29. "Transcript of Obama's Remarks on the Fight Against ISIS," *New
York Times*, September 10, 2014, http://www.nytimes.com/2014/09
/11/world/middleeast/obamas-remarks-on-the-fight-against-isis
.html.

30. Quoted in Missy Ryan, "Islamic State Threat 'Beyond Anything
We've Seen': Pentagon," Reuter's, August 21, 2014, http://www
.reuters.com/article/2014/08/21/us-usa-islamicstate-idUSKBN
0GL24V20140821.

31. Adam Gopnik, "Does It Help to Know History?" *New Yorker*, August 28, 2014, http://www.newyorker.com/news/daily-comment
/help-know-history.

Index

ROBERT SCHEER is editor-in-chief of the Webby Award-winning online magazine Truthdig, professor at the University of Southern California's Annenberg School for Communication and Journalism, and co-host of *Left, Right & Center*, a weekly syndicated radio show broadcast from NPR's west coast affiliate, KCRW. In the 1960s, he was editor of *Ramparts* magazine and later was national correspondent and columnist for the *Los Angeles Times*. Scheer is the author of nine books, including *The Great American Stickup*. He lives in Los Angeles.

NATION
BOOKS

The Nation Institute

Founded in 2000, **Nation Books** has become a leading voice in American independent publishing. The inspiration for the imprint came from the *Nation* magazine, the oldest independent and continuously published weekly magazine of politics and culture in the United States.

The imprint's mission is to produce authoritative books that break new ground and shed light on current social and political issues. We publish established authors who are leaders in their area of expertise, and endeavor to cultivate a new generation of emerging and talented writers. With each of our books we aim to positively affect cultural and political discourse.

Nation Books is a project of The Nation Institute, a nonprofit media center dedicated to strengthening the independent press and advancing social justice and civil rights. The Nation Institute is home to a dynamic range of programs: the award-winning Investigative Fund, which supports groundbreaking investigative journalism; the widely read and syndicated website TomDispatch; the Victor S. Navasky Internship Program in conjunction with the *Nation* magazine; and Journalism Fellowships that support up to 25 high-profile reporters every year.

For more information on Nation Books, The Nation Institute, and the *Nation* magazine, please visit:

www.nationbooks.org

www.nationinstitute.org

www.thenation.com

www.facebook.com/nationbooks.ny

Twitter: @nationbooks